D0898017

WOMEN AND CATHOLIC PRIESTHOOD: AN EXPANDED VISION
Proceedings of the Detroit Ordination Conference

edited by
ANNE MARIE GARDINER, S.S.N.D.

PAULIST PRESS
New York/Paramus/Toronto

Library of Congress
Catalog Card Number: 76-12653

ISBN: 0-8091-1955-2

Published by Paulist Press
Editorial Office: 1865 Broadway, N.Y., N.Y. 10023
Business Office: 400 Sette Drive, Paramus, N.J. 07652

Printed and bound in the
United States of America

Contents

PART 3

LITURGICAL PRAYER

PART 4

A LOOK AT THE ASSEMBLY

APPENDICES

PART 1

WE CLAIM OURSELVES AS CHURCH

I

Who Are These Women?

Nadine Foley, O.P.

NADINE FOLEY, O.P., a member of the General Council of the Adrian Dominican Congregation since 1971, holds a Ph.D. in Philosophy from the Catholic University of America and an S.T.M. in Scripture from Union Theological Seminary. Having taught in both secondary schools and colleges, she most recently served as a campus minister at the University of New Mexico, the University of Houston, and Drake University. Nadine holds membership in the Society of Biblical Literature, the Catholic Theological Society of America, and the Ecclesial Role of Women Committee of the Leadership Conference of Women Religious.

Who *are* these women? The quizzical expression of the prelate who asked the question was genuine in its perplexity. He asked it in an evidently sincere effort to understand. In some ways this question became and continues to be a succinct formulation of the situation, not only of the task force members about whom it was asked, nor of the more than twelve hundred others, women predominantly, who joined them in Southfield, Michigan, on Thanksgiving weekend 1975, but of women generally in the Roman Catholic Church. Who *are* they? That is the question. In the light of it Sister Margaret Farley's plaintive ending to "The Moral Imperatives for the Ordination of Women" is counterpoint, "Have we been so long with you and you have not known us?"

The questions are more than symbolic. In an era of renewed biblical faith, which is also a time of growing awareness of personal worth and valuation of human potential, a woman has reason to ask, "Who am I in the Church?" Women of Christian Faith today know that the Gospel of Jesus Christ is a message of openness and inclusiveness, that it counters the narrow stricture of the Hellenistic, Roman

3

and Semitic cultures which formed the milieu of Jesus's time, that it has compelled with missionary zeal persons acculturated in every place and time, that it resonates in its liberating truth with the contemporary experience of women. Women of faith today know too that their commitment to Jesus Christ and his Gospel involves them in the continuation of his mission; it involves them in ministry. They perceive themselves to be called to a fullness of ministerial activity in response to the multiple, challenging needs of the contemporary world. They stand ready for full Christian ministry.

Yet official Church statements, teachings, policies, and programs stand in apparent conflict both with the Gospels and with the emergent self-awareness of women. In the context of Vatican Council II's description of the apostolate of the laity, there is allusion to "women also" (cf. Decree on the Apostolate of the Laity, 8-9). Women, it seems, are not understood to be members of the laity. The Apostolic Letter *Ministeria Quaedam* begins with reference to the desire that "all the faithful" participate fully in liturgical celebration, and affirms that such is their right and duty as "Christian people," "because of their baptism" (14). Later this document states, "In accordance with the venerable tradition of the church, installation in the ministries of lector and acolyte is reserved to men." By inference, women are thereby excluded from "all the faithful," from "Christian people," from those who have rights and duties by reason of their baptism. Liturgical decrees had earlier designated their place as appropriately "outside the sanctuary." Women are barred from programs of preparation for the permanent diaconate. Even now with new revisions in canon law provision is made for diocesan administrative councils in which the layman may be a judge, but not a laywoman. Similarly, new procedural norms for the American Church will allow a layman to join two priests as judges in the marriage tribunal, but a laywoman may not so serve.

The conflict between official Church pronouncements and the spirit of the Gospel with its message of freedom of persons through the redemptive activity of Jesus Christ is not merely theoretical. It is experienced uniquely today by women fully aware of the authentic personhood and the ministerial potential of their womanhood. As laywomen, single and married, as women religious, they have served the mission of the Gospel faithfully in times past and present. They experience no limit to their personal commitment to ministry in the Church, nor do they see any boundaries to the possibilities for Christian service in the public sector of a world whose needs cry out for the saving ministry of Jesus Christ. They are invited by the Church to engage in evangelization, but evangelization in a restricted modality. Their caring service leads to the threshold of sacramental ministry, in their teaching, counseling, pastoral and social service roles. Their sensitive attention to the building of interpersonal relationships in a variety of apostolic endeavors is the prerequisite fundament of sacrament, if sacrament is to be other than *ex opere operato* (sacramental signs are efficacious in themselves) formalism. Women today know the *possibility* of sacramental ministry, both from the sense of *who they are* as persons and from their involvement in an expanded ministerial experience which presents continually new demands from people to whom they would respond. They are led to ask "why not?" And they bring their questioning into the mainstream of contemporary Roman Catholic theological and pastoral reflection out of a sense of responsibility for the credibility and effectiveness of the Church today. Such an event as the conference "Women in Future Priesthood Now—A Call for Action" is one result.

Mary Lynch was by some standards an unlikely progenitor of this event. Mary is quiet, soft spoken, no claimer of the limelight. But she is persistent. She has her own vision. And she asks questions. To thirty-one of her acquaintances, whom she called together at the Catholic Theological Union in Chicago on December 14, 1974, she put one of them: Is it time, in the International Women's Year, to raise the issue of the ordination of women in the Roman Catholic Church? There was little hesitation in the thirty-one. Indeed it was time and indeed the question should be raised. They gave their answer concrete form. There should be a conference of national scope, a conference in which not just talking would be done, but one which would consider actions to be carried out. It should have a name and they provided it. It would have objectives. They wrote them. People were needed to bring the conference into being. There were eleven volunteers. These formed the core of the task force which convened for the first of many meetings on January 18, 1975. Others later joined their ranks to bring the complement to twenty-one (cf. the second entry in part 4).

Undoubtedly each who came to the initial task force meeting looked at the women assembled around the table and inwardly asked her own version of the question, "who *are* these women?" There were no "household names" among them even from such a restricted household as that of the faith. But in another sense they knew who they were in terms of a shared consciousness, and a determined willingness to tackle the impossible task. None present had ever been involved in organizing a conference of national scope. No one was sure who, or how many, would attend a conference on the ordination of women. There was no clearly identifiable source of support, moral or financial. It was a strange mandate which the task force had accepted. Yet the enterprise was undertaken with enthusiasm and in good faith.

Initial dialogue among the task force members resulted in one element of consensus which remained consistent throughout the months of preparation. The conference would take place *within* the Church. There would be nothing extralegal or irregular in its planned program, including its liturgical celebrations. There was an excitement about the possibilities of a conference that would be an expression of the Church as people of God. In this spirit the first major mailing was a letter to all the American bishops in January, 1975. Subsequent mailings went to the major superiors of women and of men, as well as to other organizations and influential leaders within the Church.

There were several types of responses to these beginning overtures. First, a base of support emerged. A few bishops, a few major superiors of men, more major superiors of women, a number of individuals, lay, religious and clerical, returned financial contributions and/or statements of support. Second, a considerable number of negative responses were returned objecting to the declared purposes of the conference. The most frequent objections registered were that the theological work on the issue had not been done; that the conference was closed in the sense that it would present only one side of the question; that words like "action" and "strategy" implied irresponsible aggression; that Pope Paul's statement on the ordination of women was being ignored. While not communicated explicitly through the written word, there was another type of response, which can be described as a discrediting of the task force members themselves. They soon learned that it is not enough to be "the people of God." They were suspect in the hierarchical Church because they had no official accreditation. In effect they learned from experience how really unempowered a concerned laity in the Church really is, and even more so when that laity is composed predominantly of women. (The word *laity* is used here in the sense employed in *Lumen Gentium* (43) which stratifies the Church as composed of bishops, clergy and laity. All women of the Church in this categorization fall within the ranks of the laity.) This they came to know through repeated invitations to Church leaders to be present at the conference. But the members of the Church live in the tension of its self-understanding as hierarchical and as people of God. Authentication came.

It came from literally hundreds who responded to the invitation to attend a conference on the ordination of women. To the approximately seventeen hundred application forms, five hundred of which were returned for lack of space, must be added the steady stream of support statements signed by groups of women and men which came as the conference was about to begin and again after its conclusion.

The conference on the ordination of women was in the end an experience of *being Church* as a "people of God" which the organizers had hoped it would be. It was above all a profoundly moving experience for those who attended. These proceedings cannot convey the quality of the event in that respect. What they can do primarily is acquaint the reader with the exceptional competence which the speakers, respondents, liturgists and facilitators brought to the conference.

In opening the question of the ordination of women for public discussion many issues emerge. What is the Church? What are the implications of baptism? Who are members of the Church? Who has responsibility for ministry? How is call to ministry to be ascertained? Are the present structures for sacramental ministry within priesthood adequate for the needs of people today? Because these are the questions, the issue is not one of "women's concerns." It is an issue of *Church*. At its roots it calls for an ecclesiology rooted in a reconsidered anthropology, where the question "who are these women?" will have an answer founded in the redemptive message of Jesus Christ.

The question at the beginning is still the question at the end, but the event of "Women in Future Priesthood Now—A Call for Action" has made a difference. It allowed women to experience the possibilities of influence within themselves, to know solidarity with one another and to take courage and initiative from a shared vision. If it is true that communities are bonded through common purposes, that new initiatives in leadership flourish when there are shared values, then the conference was only a beginning. These women know who they are. And others will come to know. Such is the faith and the hope and the love that the Gospel inspires.

2

Informing the Church:
"Good News" as News

Patricia Hughes

PATRICIA HUGHES is a candidate for the Master of Divinity degree at the Jesuit School of Theology in Chicago. She has published in LITURGY and AMERICA and served as Executive Committee member and Publicity Coordinator for the Ordination Conference.

From the outside looking in, they called it a "media strategy." The task force members responsible for it thought of it as a form of ministry. On December 14, 1974, when the Ordination Conference was christened, three goals for it were expressed.

(1)   This conference will convene persons committed to making the talents of women fully available for ministerial service in the Roman Catholic Church.

(2)   It will inform the Church about women preparing for a new expression of full priesthood.

(3)   The participants will examine the present status of the ordination issue and will develop strategies for effective action.

The publicity committee for the conference regarded its work as an essential component of an educational process. The variety of channels which ultimately established the visibility and significance of the Ordination Conference, and more importantly, the issue about which it was being held, reflects the concept of Church held by the conference planners. Because the question of the ordination of women was a *Church* question, men should hear of it as well as women; the

8

members of the hierarchy should be kept informed, as well as laity, religious, and clergy; all of the members of the Church could be involved in the question and the response. The very raising of the issue was, in fact, a statement about the Church, so ecumenical groups might well be made aware of it, as might the women and men who express no affiliation with an organized religious body.

The ordination issue is theologically and sociologically complex. Every effort was made to communicate the goals and procedures of the conference in a consistently responsible manner. The news network that was organized and then expanded to include both the print and electronic media had fact sheets and press releases and an extensive press briefing immediately before the conference. A resource library of Church documentation was accessible to the Detroit Press Corps. A gifted, professional press staff facilitated journalistic requirements, from press conference with speakers and respondents, to interviews with women who were in ministry and sensed a call to ordination, to filming and photographing and general interpretation.

They called it a "media strategy," and they said it worked. Analysts of the success of the Ordination Conference had access to data which gave some indication of just how widespread was the news coverage received by the Detroit gathering. A correspondent from the *Westmont World* wrote a first-person report for the subscribers to that diocesan weekly published for Helena, Montana. Delegates to the Fifth General Assembly of the World Council of Churches meeting in Nairobi, Kenya read about the conference in the *International Herald Tribune* which carried a by-line from the *Washington Post* wire.

Anyone who missed seeing a report of the conference on either the CBS or NBC network news on Saturday, November 29th, might have heard a broadcast that weekend on National Public Radio. *The Wanderer* and *National Catholic Reporter* provided detailed accounts and analysis of the conference, both enjoying the advantages resulting from a weekly deadline. Periodical articles with "Women in Future Priesthood Now" as source are just beginning to appear. *Saint Anthony Messenger* would cover it, as would *America. Emmanuel*, a priests' journal, took special interest in the conference, as did *Worship* and *The Woman's Pulpit*.

It would be impossible to estimate the number of people who either read, or saw, or heard a report on the Ordination Conference. There were more than seventy-five credentialled members of the press in attendance at Detroit, and countless other participants wrote of the event for less defined constituencies.

Dissemination of the message of the conference continues: these proceedings, NCR cassette recordings of the major addresses, and a documentary film, "Some Day is Not Soon Enough: Women and the Roman Catholic Priesthood," produced by Mtume Consultants of Bayville, New York.

Jesus told his disciples that the truth would set them free (John 8:32). The Ordination Conference was an attempt to explore the truth of the experience of the Church of our day, and the publicity which the conference received will insure the testing of that truth.

PART 2
ONE PART OF THE DIALOGUE

3
The Proper Place for Women in the Church

Elizabeth R. Carroll, R.S.M.

SISTER ELIZABETH CARROLL, R.S.M. has long been fa-miliar to the work of renewal of the Church and congregations of women religious. Having her M.A. from the University of Toronto and her Ph.D. from Catholic University, her academic career included teaching at Marquette University, Catholic University, as well as serving as Dean and President of Carlow College. Her involvement with the Pittsburgh Sisters of Mercy is equally extensive, as she served as President and Executive Board Member of the Federation. Sister Elizabeth Carroll was also president of the Conference of Major Superiors of Women. 1967-73, and president of the Leadership Conference of Women Religious, 1970-72. Her articles have appeared in REVIEW FOR RELIGIOUS, AMERICA, THE WAY, SPIRITUAL LIFE, RELIGIOUS LIFE IN THE SEVENTIES, among others. Her research in EXPERIENCE OF WOMEN RELI-GIOUS IN THE MINISTRY OF THE CHURCH was pub-lished by the National Federation of Priests' Councils. Current-ly, Sister Carroll serves as staff associate at the Center of Concern, a value-oriented, public-interest group, based in Wash-ington, D.C., focussing on global issues of human dignity and de-velopment.

We meet in many moods—angry or expectant, skeptical or im-patient, fearful or exultant. But we meet as people of faith. We have confidence in that God who promised, "I will pour out my spirit on all humankind, your sons and daughters shall prophesy" (Joel 3:1). Under the influence of this Spirit who is the Spirit of Jesus, we proclaim that it is Jesus who is Lord, continually taking form in woman and man to build the Church, an ever new Church. We believe in this Church and in ministry and in the value of sacramental orders. We respond to the Spirit who calls us to be a speaking, listening, reflecting, responding Church. We are not the whole Church nor do we claim to speak for the whole Church. Some may even dispute our right to meet as a Church at all, for we have not been called together by any official of our hierarchy. We would have welcomed such an invitation, but none has been forthcoming. Therefore, we speak our part of the dialogue publicly, unofficially, but nonetheless as Church. We ask the question, as the Psalmist did, "Who has the right to go up the Lord's hill? Who is allowed to enter the holy temple?" (Ps. 24).

In our gratitude for being Church let us pledge ourselves and our time so that the Church may be found, as the Second Vatican Council prayed, "increasingly faithful to the gospel of Christ." To that end we will do everything we can to deepen our faith, to expand our love and to nourish hope—not only our own hope but that of persons throughout the world and for generations to come. Only thus will we be in a position to examine in a loving way the history, the teachings and the future structures of the Church in order to enter (in the words of Congar) upon a true and not a false reform. Our faith lives if it is open to surprises of the Spirit, if it acknowledges that God's ways are not always men's ways, and if it expresses itself in courage.

Women's "Place"

My theme is the proper place for women in the Church. In one sense this theme has been long on the human agenda, and readily disposed of: woman is to be silent in Church, with head covered, passive, not in need of nor capable of theological education, obedient, responsible for men's sexual virtue, helpful in the practical and unimportant tasks of church socials and teaching small children.

Women for the most part accepted this role description unquestioningly. I remember that in the early 60s when I learned that the Preparatory Commission of the Second Vatican Council was seeking recommendations, I had nothing to say. Our own self-consciousness about a proper place for women in the Church is of very recent history. The Council helped immeasurably, if accidentally, by force of the very logic of its central themes: the Church as people of God and the dignity of personhood. The prohibition against discrimination because of sex found expression, and the encouragement of the activity of women in society could not long prevent their seeking a more active role in the Church.

Women religious profited from the commissions given them in the post-Conciliar decrees of Pope Paul to establish control over their own life style, to study deeply their own meaning for the Church and the world, and to learn the values of mutual support and coalition building. In the Synod of 1971 a few brave bishops sought to identify the proper place for women in the Church, and a Pontifical Commission on the Status of Women in Church and Society was established. Pope Paul gave great hope by recognizing International Women's Year as a "sign of the times" and a "breath of the Spirit." Nonetheless action within the Church and the response of the curia, the bishops, and male theologians have been, with notable exceptions, cautious and guarded.

The document on the reform of minor orders in 1972 went too far, however, in excluding women as a result of "sacred tradition" from the new lay offices of lector and acolyte. National hierarchies responded quickly that women were not thereby to be prohibited from all liturgical service, but only from official installation into these offices. The national picture in the United States is quite varied and tense. In some areas women are refused any active participation in the Church. In other areas they have undertaken, with official encouragement, the praxis of ministry on a very broad scale. They serve as ministers of the Eucharist both in churches and in visitations to the sick. They design and participate actively in liturgies as acolytes, readers, leaders of song, commentators. They teach adults in formal and informal theological classes, lead discussions on moral and spiritual values, preach retreats, counsel and act as spiritual directors, teach and serve on formation teams in seminaries. Numbers of women are pursuing the highest theological degrees in secular universities, in Protestant theological schools, and now finally, as they become open, in Catholic seminaries and pontifical faculties.

As a result of such experience women gained insight into what a renewed ministry in the Church might be and at the same time experienced frustration and sensed danger as they saw their work separated from the often formal conferral of sacrament and the official communication of doctrine in Gospel and homily. Women and a few male theologians have undertaken to study seriously the proper place of women in the Church.

Some women were beginning to feel, or to become free enough

to admit the feeling, that the Holy Spirit was calling them to orders, to ordination to the priesthood. Not, they hastened to add, to the priesthood as presently practiced, but to the priesthood deserved by the Church of Christ. Let us articulate to one another what our study has thus far uncovered, what our praxis of ministry is revealing, and how we may help the Church to test the validity of women's call to orders.

Another Look at Genesis

The first chapter of Genesis contains a classic challenge to women and men, to society and to the Church. Woman equally with man is Adam-humankind, made by God to be the image and likeness of God. Woman like man is person, a kind of sacred autonomy, gifted with life, freedom, creativity, intellect, capacity for interpersonal relationships, affectivity, dominion. These are prerogatives readily ascribed to God and potentially to be developed in humankind as image of God. The object of institutions—society and Church—is to facilitate the growth of women and men in these basically human—because divine—potentials.

According to Genesis I, the proper place for women in the Church is in every sphere in which she can promote life, exercise freedom of choice and expression, be creative aesthetically and intellectually as well as physiologically, grow in knowledge and understanding, study, exert private and public influence, love, and help to develop and control the forces of nature to produce a humanizing environment.

Over the long reaches of human history women have not been thus defined as persons. They have been defined rather by those characteristics which differentiate them from men, which subordinate them to men. The life of the female at birth has been undervalued in many societies; her freedom almost always restricted; her creativity limited to the physiological and domestic; her intellect scorned and stunted; her interpersonal relationships privatized; and her affectivity valued and exploited.

Women in Gospel Proclamations

Into this history of the repudiation of God's vision by men, Jesus erupted, to bring (as St. Paul saw it) to all human beings the power to live on another plane, a plane where "there are no more distinctions between Jew and Greek, slave and free, male and female, but all of

you are one in Christ Jesus" (Gal. 3:27-28). The evangelists later portrayed Jesus in the Gospels as defying social categories and taboos to
accept women as persons, capable of intelligent discourse, journeying
with him on the way from Galilee to Jerusalem, remaining faithful
beyond most of his male disciples, being entrusted with the most fundamental proclamation of his good news—his resurrection from the
dead. *Acts* told of women being present in the company which received the Pentecostal effusion of the Holy Spirit, of women as
prophesiers, of women welcoming Christian communities to their
homes or churches. There is nothing in the Gospels or *Acts,* nor in the
central doctrine of Paul, to warrant the exclusion of women from as
active a ministry in the Church as men exercise.

From this tradition it would seem that the proper place of women
in the Church is everywhere, in the service functions with which Jesus
identified, in discipleship as with Martha and Mary, in the proclamation of the Word as with the Samaritan woman, in witness as with the
women at the cross and in the first appearances of the risen Lord, in
reception of the Spirit with the male disciples at Pentecost, in prophe-
sying and bearing authority in the early Christian communities.

Variety of Traditions

What seems to have happened to this development is that the antifeminism deeply ingrained in the Jewish and Greek traditions became dominant over the example of Jesus and the convictions of Paul
and the evangelists. Passages in Paul's letters and in the Pastorals are
in immediate contradiction to other elements therein and to the Gospel tradition of Jesus. Biblical exegetes have either emphasized the
passages hostile to women's ministry and neglected the others, or
have pictured Paul as totally ambiguous towards women, or have performed involved exegetical feats to reconcile the differences, or have
come to admit that certain antifeminine texts are interpolations, and
that the Pastoral letters, Ephesians and possibly Colossians, are not
from Paul's hand. For our purpose the important fact to be recognized is that some forty years after the death of Jesus a strong strain
of antifeminism appeared among the followers of Christ seeking to
eliminate the influence of women within the Christian assemblies. In
this light the positive evidence in the Gospels of Jesus's attitude toward women and in the Pauline letters and *Acts* of their influence in
the early Church provides a strong witness to biblical inspiration. At
any rate we cannot speak of one unbroken tradition in the Church:

we must speak of two traditions—that of Jesus and the earliest Church; that which countered this tradition and became influential at the time the ordering of Church offices was undertaken.

Blueprint or Development

In recent years Catholic biblical and historical scholarship has provided important new insights into the composition of the New Testament and the organization of the Church. These readings leave us unsure about who were present at the Last Supper; nor do we have the *ipsissima verba* of Jesus there, but rather liturgical formulas with which the evangelists were familiar transposed into their version of the Last Supper. The Gospels never present Jesus as referring to his followers as priests. Moreover, the founding of the Church (based on post-resurrectional recognition of the divinity of Christ), the establishment of its basic sacraments (symbolizing the earlier ministry of Jesus) occurred after the resurrection of Christ. The Eucharist depends for its efficacy upon the reality of Jesus's death and resurrection, and the witness to that reality of a believing community. Was it mere accident that the Spirit had the evangelists present women as predominantly faithful at the cross, and as the especially chosen witnesses of the resurrection?

A critical point of inquiry revolves around the mission of the Twelve. Assuredly Jesus chose them. He chose them, twelve and male, as the link between his new covenant and that of the Old Law: the Twelve represented the continuity of the Twelve Tribes of Israel. As such they had to be twelve (witness the election of Matthias) and they had to be male, because the Covenant of God with the Hebrew people was symbolized only through the male. Nonetheless, the Twelve are not the only apostles (witness Paul and others), nor do they exercise all final authority in the early Church (witness James at the so-called Council of Jerusalem), nor do they assume the headship of particular churches, where a larger role seems to belong to both James and Paul. The separate orders of episcopate (sometimes collegial), the diaconate, and finally the priesthood were organized by the Church as established on the authority of the Twelve to accommodate particular circumstances and needs of the Christian communities.

Of immediate relevance to our topic is the fact that the development of such orders occurred in the period (particularly the last third of the first century) when antifeminist parties seem to have been active in the Church. The overwhelmingly male culture provided thus an inadequate response to the initiative of Jesus. If such be the case, "sacred tradition" with regard to the exclusion of women from church ministry is not of divine origin, but only the prolongation of an inadequate response imposed on the Gospel message by the dominant culture.

Modern biblical research then, and much contemporary theology, seem to indicate that the proper place of woman in the Church is as a sharer in the total expression of ministry in whatever forms are or become institutionalized. Past cultures, because of the prevalence of antifeminine bias and lack of development of women, were perhaps unable to hear such a message. But our age is notable precisely for the vindication of women's potential in all fields of human endeavor. Hence, the denial of their proper place in ministry to women becomes an affront to that doctrine of personhood which our Church has emphasized, a failure to develop the recognition by Pope Paul VI of women as "disciples and co-workers" of Jesus, and of Mary as "the first and the most perfect of Christ's disciples."

Official Statements

Archbishop Bernardin speaking for the Administrative Committee of the National Conference of Catholic Bishops (cf. Appendix A for complete statement), recently has made known their stance on some of the questions we are raising. The first impression which the Archbishop's statement conveys is that these bishops have taken neither women's ordination nor their own teaching power very seriously. In stating that women are not to be ordained they rely upon a summary report of 1972 entitled *Theological Reflections on the Ordination of Women*, which states:

> "Theologians and canonists have been unanimous *until modern times* in considering this exclusion (of women) as absolute and of divine origin. *Until recent times* no theologian or canonist seemingly has judged this to be only of ecclesiastical law." (Emphasis added.)

Apparently contemporary biblical scholars, theologians and canonists can be as readily excluded from a hearing as women can be from ordination! Such exclusion is unrealistic especially when the bishops go on to admit that "arguments presented in times gone by on this subject may not be defensible today." What are the indefensible arguments? What arguments remain after the indefensible ones have been abandoned? If the only answer is tradition, the way things have always been done, but unsupported by adequate doctrine, a change in the tradition seems imperative. Slavery as the way it was done was accepted practice in the Church for centuries; it no longer is regarded as a Christian social structure. During the Council, the Canon of the Mass was presented as unchangeable tradition. Then Pope John changed it by adding the name of St. Joseph. Nonassociation with Protestants was the tradition bulwarked by anathemas until ecumenism prevailed. Tradition maintained a Latin liturgy. A return to it today is unthinkable.

By taking their stand totally on tradition the bishops also give the impression of supporting an inadequate ecclesiology. For, surely if *Gaudium et Spes* taught us anything it was that the Church is for the world, that the Church must so discern the design of God (and I call attention again to Gen. 1 and Gal. 3) as to assist the humanization of the world, the development of personhood in all women and men, the equality of these with each other. Nonetheless, Archbishop Bernardin's stance for tradition relates uniquely to the ordination of women to the priesthood and not in an absolute fashion, but "*unless and until* a contrary theological movement takes place." My position is that a contrary theological movement has taken place but is being ignored.

The statement indicates that the ordination of women to the priesthood is not a justice issue. The claim is not, as this rejoinder makes it, that every woman has a God-given right to priesthood. The claim is that any woman has the same right to have her call to ordination tested as any man has. Injustice enters when the denial of ordination rests upon a category: womanhood. Such a denial implies that there is something wrong or incomplete or deficient not in individual women but in the genus of womankind. This view contradicts the design of God made explicit in Gen. 1. It seems rather to rest upon "arguments presented in times gone by on this subject [which] may not be defensible today." If this is not the case, justice certainly requires that we hear the arguments. Otherwise, all the dark fears from primordial myth and inadequate knowledge that are incorporated in the patristic and medieval theological tradition about women are revived.

Ordination: for What?

The proper place for women in the Church is not participation in but questioning of that system of priestly relations which leaves many young ordained feeling as oppressed as women do. Is the priesthood as it is now experienced promotive of the values of personhood, love, cooperation, community building, service, faith and justice? Or is it one more locus for elitism, judgmentalism, fear, competition, power struggle, mistrust? Are the dominant forces of our male culture preventing or weakening the search for the deeply unifying doctrinal insights to be drawn from the message of Jesus? Administrative structures of secrecy, vindictiveness, reliance on fear are totalitarian, not Christian, ways of proceeding. It is unfortunately true that, though not all priests have power, yet priesthood is the one door to power in the Church. Women who desire ordination in order to participate in the power of the Church do neither the Church nor women any favor. Their proper place in the Church must be in the support of those not negligible forces working for the expansion of ecclesiastical structures which will honor openness, honesty and the best service of the people of God.

Archbishop Bernardin's statement provides a hope for such forces. He indicates that

". . . discussion of the possibility of ordaining women to the priesthood in the Roman Catholic Church . . . can contribute to a better understanding of ministry, priesthood and the role of women in the Church. . . ."

The bishops acknowledge the benefit of discussion—but apparently not at women's initiative (witness Detroit Ordination Conference November, 1975). They have not, to public knowledge, entered upon serious, continuing dialogue with women about women. The proper place for women in the Church will be in pressing for channels for such dialogue and for accountability within the channels which exist, such as the National Commission on the Status of Women in Church and Society. In areas where the conference has provided a hearing for women as well as men, such as the consultation on the Catechetical Directory and the Bicentennial Hearings, the bishops have aroused great good will.

Their recent Statement on Ordination carries seeds of a far-

reaching reform, if it is literally implemented, in the declaration that
the

> ". . . contributions [of women] are needed in the decision-mak-
> ing process at the parochial, diocesan, national and universal
> levels. . . ."

If nonordained women and men are to share intimately and responsi-
bly in all decision-making of the Church they may free the ordained
to be channels of the Gospel message of love and reconciliation and
unity not apart from, but with the rest of, the people of God. The
clericalism which has been entrenched in the Church since its adaptation to the structures of the Roman Empire has promoted a situation
where all too easily the Church is thought of as existing for the
clergy, for the hierarchy. Imagine the purification possible in priesthood if it could be disengaged from power! The most often repeated
warning of Jesus to his disciples was that they not be the first nor
aspire to be the greatest, but that they humble themselves and serve.
Behavioral sciences and management techniques today are demon-
strating that a diffusion of power can be the most effective means for
action.

Who Decides? Who Defines?

The proper place for women in the Church is in helping to translate this acknowledged need for their services in decision-making into
actual structures. They may help by questions. For instance, had
Archbishop Bernardin or the Administrative Committee of the
NCCB considered including women in the process of devising a statement on the ordination of women? Can decision-making by women
be honestly advocated when present discipline links all jurisdiction to
orders? Are the bishops recommending that this discipline change,
that jurisdiction be separate from ordination? Or are women sadly to
discover that the bishops are using the word "decision-making" in
that reductionist mode which means token consultation with no real
effect upon the final decision?

Is not skepticism warranted unless and until actions indicate a
seriousness about the structuring of women's participation in decision-making bodies? Every congregation of the Roman Curia is totally male. The Pontifical Commission for the Revision of Law is totally
male. Even the latest norms for ecclesiastical trials of marriage cases
formally exclude women as judges. Bishops' Boards of Consultors

remain male. Only a few diocesan councils and a small percentage of parish councils which include women have decision-making power. But the word has been written: women are needed in decision-making in the Church. Can we establish that the proper place for women in the Church is not only at every level, but also at every point in the decision-making process? In fact-finding, producing creative alternatives, choice-making, implementing and evaluating? Can we pledge women able and willing to participate at every level and at every point?

In contemporary society women have shown themselves intelligent, able to acquire the same academic degrees in theology as men do, capable of positions of great public responsibility and trust, and particularly adept at pastoral ministry. If the Women's Movement is, as Pope Paul declared, "a call of the Spirit" why have so few bishops, so few theologians, in fact so few women conceived it as a matter of conscience to address it seriously with emotional as well as intellectual openness?

Some Concrete Proposals

What can women and men who wish to respond to this call of the Spirit do? (1) pray; (2) study; (3) proclaim; (4) serve; (5) challenge; (6) practice ministry effectively; (7) support; (8) promote recognition of women in other Christian churches and other religious traditions; (9) hope; and (10) love.

1. *Pray.* The prayer of faith counts upon the Spirit of God being at work in the Church and in human hearts to bring the message of Jesus to fruition in the changing conditions of world culture. Prayer opens hearts and minds to the influence of the Spirit. Let us pray!

2. *Study.* Become serious students of biblical, theological scholarship. Attend and support the attendance of other women at all levels of theological study from diocesan seminary to prestigious university and research centers. Study also the requirements of justice in our society, and ways in which the Gospel can be made effective.

3. *Proclaim.* Become skillful in communications—written and oral—practicing assertiveness at every level from your living group to the papal curia.

4. *Serve.* Make advances at every level to see that channels for decision-making are created, and then generously fill them. Serve as community organizers. Serve as publicists. Serve not in unilateral but in mutual assertiveness and submission.

5. *Challenge.* Challenge the system, the mind-sets. Resist inade-

quate solutions. Demand honest coordination of word and deed in ourselves and in others.

6. *Practice ministry effectively.* Seek openings for ministry. The broad range of ministry engaged in by women today is largely, though not entirely, a result of women's initiative. Keep expanding the opportunities, working for equitable treatment therein, and above all witnessing in them to the power God is willing to convey through this ministry.

7. *Support.* Support one another. Women religious have discovered in the past five years in particular the strength that derives from mutual support, from coalitions. Now extend that support system to lay women and to men who are willing to be enrolled in the campaign for justice to women.

8. *Promote women.* Promote the consciousness and struggles of Christian women in other churches, especially the Episcopalian but also the Eastern Catholic and the Orthodox. Support ordained women in public recognition of their office and talents. Challenge world religions to examine their traditions, as we are now examining the Christian tradition, to bring forth from their storehouses new messages to women about women which acknowledge their personhood, potential and dignity.

9. *Hope.* Fundamental social change of a blindness as deeply built into persons' subconscious and into tradition as are sex stereotypes will not be wrought in a day nor in an International Women's Year. Hope in the power of the Spirit to change hearts—our hearts to keep faithful and strong; others' hearts to be purified of sexism; all hearts to seek unity in imaging God, the creator of all Adams—male and female.

10. *Love.* If love is not enhanced in the struggle for ordination of women we may win the battle and lose the war. The war is the renewal of the Church in the Spirit of Jesus. That Spirit is undeniably love. Anger may exist within love; anger must not substitute itself for love. An embittered female clergy would be a worse abomination than the present situation. Hence, self-struggle is a predominant part of our contest—self-struggle not to eliminate anger but to temper it with the fire of love into a steel-like insistence upon justice. In such a self-struggle wherein the Spirit is permitted to dominate our personal response, we can be full of hope that the same Spirit will blow with a mighty wind through all the emptied husks of an antifeminist tradition and raise up a priesthood—male and female—capable of re-enspiriting this world. Then the proper place of women in the Church will be to serve and help all others to serve in love.

4

Women's Place:
A Biblical View

Carroll Stuhlmueller, C.P.

CARROLL STUHLMUELLER is a member of the Passionist Fathers, Chicago Province. Having completed seminary and pastoral training, he received his S.T.L. from Catholic University, 1952 and an S.S.L. and S.S.D. at the Pontifical Biblical Institute, Rome, 1954, 1968. After teaching Scripture at St. Meinrad Seminary, Catholic Theological Union, Chicago, and St. John's University, New York, his work included visiting professorships at Ecole Biblique et Archeologique, Jerusalem and Theological Schools in South Africa and the Orient, He has served since 1964 as Associate Editor of the OLD TESTAMENT READING GUIDE, and since 1973 of the CATHOLIC BIBLICAL QUARTERLY. His research and contributions to biblical scholarship are well known nationally and internationally.

Sister Elizabeth Carroll's perception of "The Proper Place for Women in the Church" is totally unlike the mighty and fearsome dreams of the prophet Daniel. Sister Elizabeth Carroll's vision is calm and incisive, more of an invitation to thought and study, than a whirlwind out of which emerge beasts of destruction, so terrifying to Daniel that the prophet became weak and ill (Dan. 8:18; 10:7-9). I suggest, however, that unless the Church seriously consider the content of Sister Carroll's paper, the apocalyptic visions of Daniel may burst upon us.

Reinterpretation

Her study springs from a carefully nuanced understanding of biblical data on the question of woman's role in church leadership and priesthood. The key issue, I propose, is a hermeneutical one: how does one interpret the Bible today? One *must* reinterpret, always in continuity with the past, of course, and always with responsibility

25

toward future generations. Continuity with the past offers security for the present moment; responsibility toward the future forces us to challenge the present that it may be a purer world for the unborn. Only by reinterpreting *now* can we avoid the fearful, abrupt transitions announced by Daniel.

When Sister Elizabeth Carroll quotes from Ps. 24, she uses *Today's English Version* which reads, "Who has the *right* to go up to the Lord's hill?" This rendition reinterprets the more neutral reading of the Hebrew: "Who *can* go up . . . *mi ya 'aleh behar-yahweh?"* Actually, in the Hebrew the question does not concern who is priest. Rather it is the priests' examination of conscience for the lay persons!

Yet, to reread the question with a new slant for our circumstances follows a good biblical style. For instance, the book of Joel, also cited by Sister Elizabeth Carroll, so applies Isaiah's vision of peace as to reverse its original meaning. In Joel, plowshares are to be beaten back into swords and pruning hooks to be turned back into spears (Is. 2:4; Joel 4:10). Another important text of Joel undergoes revision in the New Testament. Joel's vision that the spirit will be poured out upon all mankind centers upon the Jerusalem temple at Mount Zion and official Judaism (Joel 3:1-5). The New Testament sees it fulfilled in the Upper Room (not the temple) and with nonofficial Judaism, the first disciples of Jesus (not the official Sanhedrin) in chapter two of Acts.

The Bible, therefore, asks us to perceive the literal sense of the scriptures within the living circumstances of our own day. How to unfold the ideals and norms of scripture and Church tradition for priesthood and leadership today is the biblical task in which we are engaged.

The challenge of reinterpretation goes deep. Sister Elizabeth Carroll is insistent: that women as priests do not become "men priests," that is, doing the same thing men are doing in the same way! Priesthood must be reinterpreted within today's pastoral expectations. Usually, it is a prophet outside the organization who intuits new directions.

Again, the Bible assists us in this on-going task of reinterpretation. First, a careful study of leadership in biblical times concludes that forms not only of civil authority but also of religious government are *not* directly revealed by God. Biblical people absorbed them from the combined social and religious environment of their time, whether these be prophecy (1 Kgs. 18; 22), priesthood (Jdg. 17:5), royalty

(1 Sam. 8:5), judgeship (Jdg. 8:16), or a system of elders and scribes (Ex. 18). New Testament documents show how Jesus and the early Church fitted into the sociological patterns of *their* time. They did not reveal new forms of leadership but rather they saw new insights in the old forms.

In gathering disciples Jesus followed the style of the Pharisees and prophets; ritual acts of baptizing and of sacrificial meals were received from popular practices as we see them performed by John the Baptist and the Dead Sea Covenanters of Qumran. Yet, Jesus not only fitted into a succession of religious and social continuity, but he also challenged, purified and transformed what was being done, but again, from tradition. He revived the notion of the Kingdom of God (Zech. 14:16; Mark 1:15), thereby avoiding the political and national implications of the Kingdom of David. He ate with the poor and the outcasts (Mark 2:16; 6:34-44), and he foresaw (according to a few, orphan Old Testament passages) that gentiles from the east and the west would sit down with Abraham, Isaac and Jacob in the Kingdom of God (Matt. 8:11).

Prophet or Priest?

This prophetical stance of Jesus brings me back to Sister Elizabeth Carroll's prophetical challenge to Roman Catholic priesthood today. Here I make my most serious proposal in the form of a question. Is *now* the time for women to move from their *prophetical* position, in ministerial activity but outside the "priestly"—that is "hierarchical"—organization, *or* is it better for women to acquire more pastoral experience first?

In other words, where is the Church today? Where do women, in their ministerial action and in their call for future priesthood now, find their closest parallel:

(1) in the life of Jesus, who was not a member of the Jewish priesthood but a prophetical challenge to it?

(2) in the crucial, transitional, apocalyptic time of the Cross, Resurrection, and Pentecost—when women were present as witnesses?

(3) in the very early days, when the Church, as a part of the Jewish synagogue, possessed no priesthood and was constituted under prophets and disciples of Jesus—again with women acting as deacons and coworkers? (The Church at this time was undergoing radical transition—even away from the or-

ganizational style set up by Jesus. For instance, Paul became the thirteenth apostle, the office of the "seventy-two" faded away.)

(4) in the complete organization of the Pastoral epistles, necessary when the Church was definitely separated from the synagogue and could now for the first time call Jesus "priest" (as in the epistle to the Hebrews) and name its own religious rulers, again for the first time "priests?"

The Church must seriously identify which of these four stages is the one for today:

women, like Jesus, challenging priesthood from outside;

women, like the moment of the Resurrection and Pentecost, witnessing a new covenant;

women, as in Acts and in the great epistles of St. Paul, undertaking new pastoral roles;

women, as in the Pastoral epistles, thoroughly a part of the organization.

How Catholic Is Our Priesthood?

Another question persists regarding the intimate association of priesthood with sacramental action, especially the Eucharist, within the Roman Catholic Church. If the Roman Catholic Church continues to restrict priesthood to celibate, male Christians, then pastoral activity—like teaching, preaching, healing, counseling, reaffirming in the forgiveness of God's love, inspirational leadership at prayer—will become more and more noneucharistic, and therefore more and more in accord with Protestant styles of piety. While Protestant piety has produced most saintly people, the Roman Catholic Church must ask if she should abandon her traditional eucharistic, liturgical style of piety, in order to maintain that single tradition of male, celibate priesthood. When eucharistic piety declines, so does the charism of unity in the Church disintegrate.

Three challenges (among many) become more clearly focused in these reflections: (1) the hermeneutical question of reinterpreting or rereading the Bible to arrive at the inspired literal sense for today; (2) the application of a biblical norm that forms of leadership are not directly revealed by God but are accepted from society and then are further purified; and (3) the identification of where we are today in the light of the four stages of development in the New Testament: Jesus's words and actions, outside of Jewish priesthood; his resurrection to new life; the initial Christian assembly after Pentecost, under strong prophetical impulse; and the organizational Church of the Pastoral epistles.

To summarize in another way: is the ministerial role of women today to be prophetical and outside of priestly structure; priestly within the hierarchical organization; or a combination of priest-prophet in order to maintain for today the eucharistic tradition of the Roman Catholic Church?

Select Bibliography
Josephine Massyngberde Ford, "Biblical Material Relevant to the Ordination of Women," *Journal of Ecumenical Studies* 10 (Fall: 1973), pp. 669-699.
Andre Lemaire, "The Ministries in the New Testament. Recent Research," *Biblical Theology Bulletin* 3 (June 1973), pp. 133-166.
Krister Stendahl, *The Bible and the Role of Women*. Philadelphia: Fortress, 1966.
Carroll Stuhlmueller, "Women Priests: Today's Theology and Yesterday's Sociology," *America* 131 (Dec. 14, 1974), pp. 385-387.

5
Ordination: What is the Problem?

Rosemary Radford Ruether

ROSEMARY RADFORD RUETHER, Ph.D., is a member of the American Theological Society, on the Editorial Board of JOURNAL OF RELIGIOUS THOUGHT, as well as contributing editor of CHRISTIANITY AND CRISIS and THE ECUMENIST. Rosemary serves on the Board of Advisors of the Society of Priests for a Free Ministry. Her publications have been numerous and have included articles and books addressing the role of women: LIBERATION THEOLOGY (Paulist-Newman), RELIGION AND SEXISM (Simon and Schuster), FROM MACHISMO TO MUTUALITY: ESSAYS ON SEXISM AND WOMAN-MAN LIBERATION, coauthored with Eugene Bianchi (Paulist), and THE NEW WOMAN/NEW EARTH: SEXIST IDEOLOGIES AND HUMAN LIBERATION. Currently, Rosemary Radford Ruether is Associate Professor at Howard University School of Religion and Preceptor in Theology at Inter-Met (Inter Faith Metropolitan Theological Education) in Washington, D.C.

To address the ordination of women, we must first have a clear understanding of what the impediments to women's ordination have been. Briefly, the source of women's exclusion from Church leadership is simply that both Judaism and Christianity existed within a patriarchal society which rigidly excluded women from public professional life and justified this through an ideology of woman's generic inferiority. The voice that tells women to be silent in church and to be saved by bearing children is simply the reflection, in the religious assembly, of this patriarchal social system. Moreover, religious doctrine itself becomes a sanction for this social system, creating myths and statements that make women's inferior and auxiliary existence appear to be the "order of God's creation," rather than being, as it is, the fallen disorder of injustice created by sinful humans.

Symbols Which Oppress

Patriarchy not only pervades specific dictates about women, but also creates an entire symbolic edifice of reality that reflects the social hierarchy of male dominance and female submission. The symbolism of God as a patriarchal male, and nature as passively female; the portraying of the Messiah as a warrior, king and judge, lord over a passive, female Church; the same symbolism of minister as ruling male over a passive, feminized, infantilized laity, is simply the projection on the level of theology, ecclesiology and ministry of this same patriarchal hierarchy of male over female. The challenging of male dominance, therefore, challenges the entire symbolic language of order, hierarchy, power, lordship and authority in religion, as these have been shaped by patriarchy.

Can structures so deep-rooted be changed? The answer we must give is that they must be, for the sake of the Gospel itself. The Gospel, rooted in the unitary personhood of all humans, in the image of God, restored in Christ, is about the liberation of humanity from all orders of oppression and idolatry. Male dominance must be recognized as simply one of those systems of injustice that is to be overcome by the Gospel. Dressed up in the language of God, Christ and the Church, male dominance becomes idolatry, the projection of the vanities of human egoism and unjust power upon the very face of God. For that reason it is truly anathema, and all Christians, male and female, must come to look upon it with the horror and disgust it deserves, rather than continuing to cower before its presumptive authority.

A Mighty Fortress: Patriarchy

Yet, pragmatically speaking, we cannot underestimate the extreme difficulties that exist in making such changes in that branch of Christianity known as the Roman Catholic Church. Politically speaking, there are no representative structures by which the desire of changes by the majority of Roman Catholics can be enforced upon the hierarchy. Moreover, those persons who hold power for change are elderly Italian male celibates; in short, persons whose entire personal, social and cultural experience most totally removes them from understanding the issues of women or contact with changing cultures where women are playing different roles. From the perspective of women's rights, a more unrepresentative leadership could hardly be imagined.

The mobilization of the women's religious orders, therefore, is crucial to any hope for change. Lacking democratic representation, the women's religious orders represent a large institutional body of women, vital to the maintenance of the Church's ministry, quasi-autonomous, holding considerable potential power. There is the danger that mobilizing from this base will tend to exclude other types of qualified women who are not nuns. There should be a conscious effort to overcome the traditional dividing of women between religious and lay, married and unmarried.

There is also the long conditioning of religious women to docility and the many ways the male hierarchy has succeeded in limiting their financial and institutional autonomy. There is the still further question of whether religious women as a body would wish to see their orders clericalized in the same manner as male monastics. Has not the very autonomy of many women's orders, which allowed them to democratize rapidly and upgrade their own communities in the 1960s, been partly the result of the anomalous position of women in the Church? Not being clerics, women religious had a certain freedom to move. If women would be asked to sacrifice that independence as the price of ordination, it might be a dubious exchange.

If women use the religious orders to fight for ordination, they must orchestrate this carefully to maintain the independence that these orders presently have. Nevertheless, despite these problems, the women's religious orders are a major institutional base for a strategy for ordination of women.

Doctrines Bolster Status Quo

The second major impediment to changing the practice of excluding women from ordination in the Roman Catholic Church is authority and tradition—however contrary this authority and tradition is to the meaning of the Gospel. This is not, first of all, an argument over what Jesus did or Paul said. These arguments have already been sufficiently satisfied in other highly biblical churches which have decided that the true meaning of the Gospel calls for a change in the tradition of excluding women from ordination. For Roman Catholicism the very possibility of asking such questions about the tradition falls back on the prior question of the immutable or infallible character of the teaching authority of the Church.

Quite simply, what Archbishop Bernardin said, in the name of the American Catholic hierarchy, is that anything they have been doing for a very long time belongs to the ordinary magisterium (the teaching authority, or teaching body of the Church, viz. bishops) of the Church which is *de facto* infallible. Any questioning of such a deep-rooted tradition must therefore challenge this concept of authority.

As Hans Küng clearly realized, when the Pope rejected any changes on birth control, even when recommended by the majority of his own special commission, no changes on any important topic can come about in the Roman Catholic Church unless a new concept of teaching authority is developed. This new concept would have to allow for the fact of fallibility and incompleteness in what the Church taught in the past. For Roman Catholics, this impasse over unchanging authority is likely to be the primary impediment to considering the ordination of women. It may be so strong as to preclude even the possibility of considering theological or scriptural reasons to the contrary.

Ordination: Valid Goal or Outdated Symbol

Finally, women themselves must consider whether they want or need to be ordained. There is good reason to think that the present clerical and institutional structure of a Church so constituted is demonic and itself so opposed to the Gospel that to try to join it is contrary to our very commitments. One must also ask by what right this caste of bishops regard themselves as exclusive possessors of the power to ordain, and those whom they have ordained, the exclusive possessors of the power to consecrate? Historically speaking, no such offices were established by Jesus. All ministry (and there are at least two distinctly different types of ministry within the New Testament Church itself) must be regarded as the historical creations of the Church.

It is the Church which created the various types of ministry, not the ministry which created the Church. Any Christian community gathering together with the intention of being the Church of Christ has the power to celebrate the Lord's Supper as an expression of their common life; that community has the power to designate particular persons to represent it in the sacramental actions of the Church to itself, and to pastor the community.

As a first step for women asking what they want in ordination, I suggest that they must demystify their minds of the false idea that priests possess sacramental "power" which the community does not have. The sacramental power of the priest is nothing else but the sacramental expression of the life of the community itself in Christ, which the community has designated him or her to express for, and to, the community. The alienation of sacramental life as a power tool to be used over and against the community is the basis of all false clericalism; such clericalism is deeply rooted in sexist symbols of domination and passivity. Women cannot ask to be ordained without questioning fundamentally this concept of clericalism.

This is not to suggest that the Church should not designate particular persons to represent its sacramental life, mandate specific educational and spiritual qualifications for such persons, and make such offices a fairly permanent status. But it is essential to remember that it is the community itself that does this. Priests and bishops are to be the representatives of its life and power, not its masters who alienate this life and power, and reduce the community to subservience.

Far-reaching Consequences

The struggle for the ordination of women in the Roman Catholic Church will be a long and frustrating one, with no immediate success forseeable. We cannot afford to condemn numbers of women to a long fight to attain a life and ministry they do not have. Rather, we must recognize that the full life and ministry of the Church of Christ are already ours. When a brother or sister confesses to us, we already have the power to forgive. When two or three gather together in Christ's name, we already have the fullness of the Eucharist.

If we seek to put some women in that historical form of the ministry which has evolved in the Roman Catholic Church, it is not because we seek something we do not have, but because we wish to give to this clergy something that they do not have. By adding women to their number, we want to overcome the idolatry of sexism in the Church which supports all other kinds of ideologies of power and domination. We seek to help them rediscover the very nature of ministry, not as an alienated power and domination, but as the service of Christians to each other in the building up of a community of brothers and sisters.

From this perspective, the very process of seeking the ordination of women in the Roman Catholic Church, and the enormous changes in consciousness such a process will entail about the very nature of Church, ministry and the Gospel, constitute perhaps one of the most important means for the continuing renewal of this Church.

6

Moral Imperatives for the Ordination of Women

Margaret Farley, R.S.M.

MARGARET FARLEY, R.S.M. is a member of the Sisters of Mercy, Detroit Province. She received her M.A. in Philosophy at the University of Detroit, and her M.Phil. and Ph.D. in Religious Studies at Yale University. Her publications in ORIGINS, JOURNAL OF RELIGION, and REFLECTION explore the various areas of ethics—especially sexuality, commitment and man-woman relationships. Margaret is a member of the Executive Board of the American Society of Christian Ethics, the American Academy of Religion, and associate editor of the JOURNAL OF RELIGION STUDIES IN RELIGIOUS ETHICS. She is currently Associate Professor of Ethics, Yale Divinity School.

I. THE MORAL QUESTION

I think I understand the reluctance of many women in the Church today to allow the issue of ordination to the priesthood to become central in an overall questioning of roles for women in ministry. That is to say, I understand a concern to challenge the very meaning of ministry in the Church and to reform the patterns of ministry so that women will not be caught in structures which continue to fail to liberate either women or men. I especially understand a concern to press beyond an egalitarian ethic to an ethic which recognizes that equal access to institutional roles is not sufficient to secure justice if the institutions and roles are themselves oppressive to persons as persons.

I nonetheless wish to argue that the question of the ordination of women to the priesthood must indeed be central to any considerations of roles for women in the Church, and that the many moral imperatives which confront the Church regarding women and ministry un-

35

avoidably converge in the imperative to ordain women to the priesthood. The office of priesthood, in fact, offers a particularly potent
focus for addressing directly the sources of sexism in Christian
thought. Reasons and attitudes which have kept women from the office of priesthood are remarkably similar to reasons and attitudes
which continue to keep them from full participation in the general
priesthood of the faithful.

There are some fatal strategic errors which women can make,
however, in confronting the issue of ordination. They may, for example, challenge the present form which the office of priesthood takes in
the Roman Catholic Church, yet fail to challenge it precisely in the
aspects which have heretofore closed it to women. Thus, a challenge
to a hierarchical concept of orders which does not reach to the problem of sexism as such may result in a democratization of the priesthood which still fails to consider leadership as an appropriate role for
women. Such a failure would be akin to the one wistfully observed in
some countries by women who thought that the demise of capitalism
would be sufficient to eradicate sexism in society, but who have found
it as alive and well after socialist revolutions as before.

Further, women may make the mistake of not taking seriously
the power of the symbolic meaning of priesthood in the Roman Catholic Church. Unless the inner elements of the symbol of priesthood
cease to be alien to women, no effort on the part of women to share
fully in the life and ministry of the Church can be finally successful.
Thus, for example, it will not do for women to press for a form of ordained ministry which is only an extension of their present private
roles in teaching, healing, and providing for social welfare. As important as those roles are, they can be expanded and even officially
blessed without ever touching the underlying barriers to equality and
mutuality between women and men in the Church. Something can be
learned in this regard from women in other Christian churches where,
in at least some instances, ordination was opened to women with
deceptively little struggle. Formal barriers to ordination fell when
women proved themselves competent in various social ministries of
the Church. As long as women did not aspire to move into the symbolic center of the life of the churches—represented by preaching and
teaching—there was relatively little objection to their ordination. The
real issues were never joined, however, until it became clear that ordination might entail granting to women not only responsibility for
caring for children and other women and the sick, but responsibility

for tasks which were assumed to require powers of full critical intelligence.[1]

Fundamental theological and cultural presuppositions which lie at the root of women's exclusion from ordained ministry can, then, remain intact if ministry is redefined and restructured without shattering the gender-specification which has attached precisely to the content of the historically developed meaning of priesthood. But what are the inner elements in the meaning of priesthood which must be addressed specifically if the possibility of ordination is to be open to women in a way that conduces to full equality and mutuality in the life of the Church? Women from other churches have suggested that these elements are importantly different in a church such as the Roman Catholic Church "where orders and ordination are still principally understood in terms of public sacramental ministry."[2] I am doubtful that finally the elements of meaning that have been penetrated by sexism are really so different in the different churches, though it is surely true that they are intensified and given a unique emphasis in a tradition which intertwines patriarchy and the public mediation of grace as closely and deeply as does the Roman Catholic Church.

In any case, in the Roman Catholic tradition the office of priesthood combines the tasks of making visible the relation of human persons to God, and rendering present God's self-revelation to human persons. The priest symbolizes what is true of the Church as a whole and each individual member of the Church. Ordained to the community, the priest's function is to realize and to serve publicly, "officially," the meeting between God and the human person which characterizes the Christian life. On almost any model of the Church which still proves fruitful for describing and interpreting the life of the Church, at least three elements emerge in the meaning of ordained ministry which are particularly crucial to understanding both the problems and possibilities for the ordination of women.[3] These are the elements of (1) leadership, (2) representation—of God to human persons and human persons to God and to one another, and (3) the capacity to enter and to stand in the presence of God, in the realm of the sacred.

These elements are crucial not because they are mistaken or false or even inadequate (however much they may need serious critique when they are embodied in forms which inhibit the life of the Church or when an overemphasis on one rather than another causes distortion in ministry and in the life of the Church); they are crucial, rather, because they have been judged in the past as unable to be affirmed of women. They must be reappraised, then, not so much in themselves, as from the vantage point of better understandings of the nature and role of women. It is, I suggest, only by juxtaposing our understandings of the nature and role of women with these three elements of the inner meaning of priesthood that we shall begin to see the moral imperatives confronting us regarding the ordination of women.

II. THE MORAL SITUATION

To experience a moral imperative is to experience an unconditional claim upon one's action. Though the question of ordaining women is a concern of more and more persons in the Church, I am not sure that it has gained sufficient clarity to issue in experiences of moral obligation on the part of many. When it comes to specific concrete action in this regard, the Roman Catholic community as a whole is at best at the point of asking "what ought we to do" regarding the ordination of women. But if we are serious in asking the moral question "what ought we to do" regarding the ordination of women in the Roman Catholic Church, then we must be about the task of clarifying the theological understandings which bear on this question, the moral principles which are relevant to it, the capabilities and responsibilities of persons who have choices to make in its regard, and the context out of which options for action now arise.[4] In order to contribute to this task, I would like simply to describe what I will call the "moral situation" presently obtaining in the Roman Catholic community vis-a-vis the ordination of women.

By "moral situation" I mean something at once less and more than what is ordinarily meant by moral "context." There is not, on the one hand, the opportunity or the need here to include a full description of, e.g., societal factors which impinge on the contemporary experience of the Church, or a careful analysis of the complex dynamic between conflicting views current within the Church, or a comparative study of the varying needs of the Church in different economic and geographical settings. On the other hand, the "moral situation" in the Church regarding the ordination of women cannot be understood at all without examining the present status of theological understandings regarding women and priesthood, or without taking into account the effects of the contemporary experience of women on their perceived capabilities and responsibilities for action. Hence, the moral situation which I will describe is a situation in which (1) past understandings of the nature and role of women as alien to the inner meaning of priesthood are contradicted by present understandings of both woman and priesthood; and (2) the continued affirmation of past understandings by a continued refusal to ordain women results in harmful consequences for individuals and for the Church as a whole. I shall try to focus my description of the confrontation between past and present understandings in terms of the three elements in the inner meaning of priesthood which I have suggested above—namely, the elements of leadership, representation, and sacralaty.

A. UNDERSTANDINGS FROM THE PAST

1. Women and Leadership

However the leadership role of the ordained priest varies from century to century or from culture to culture, it remains an important element in the concept of priesthood. When the Church is perceived largely as an institution, the priest is expected to administer or to "govern" in some way. If the Church is understood primarily as a community of persons, the priest still functions as a "congregational leader," catalyst, or facilitator. When the Church is thought of as sacramental or as the proclaimer of the Word of God, the priest's leadership is the leadership of the mediator, the inspirer, the prophet. Not even a view of the Church on the model of "servant" removes the element of leadership from the role of the ordained priest. For service in such a context is precisely a special form of agency meant to help in the transformation of individuals and society.[5]

It is perhaps obvious how the element of leadership in the role of priesthood has been itself a major stumbling block to the ordination of women. Centuries of excluding women from the priesthood mirror centuries of belief that women cannot appropriately fill roles of leadership—whether in the family, church, or society. Arguments for relegating women to subordinate roles are well known, so that we need only recall briefly the appeals to Scripture, to biology and anthropology, to theories of Christian love and justice, which have served to ground those arguments. Whether it was because Eve was thought to be derivative from Adam, or female infants only misbegotten males, or women subordinated to men as a punishment for original sin; or whether it was because women were thought to be essentially passive not active, emotional not intellectual, destined to contribute to the human community through reproduction not production; always the conclusion came that women were to be followers not leaders, helpers not primary agents, responders not initiators.

Furthermore, Christian theological ethics offered principles of love and justice which systematically excluded the possibility of criticising the hierarchical relation between men and women. Granted interpretations of women's "nature" as inferior, there was no question of violating the principle of giving "to each her due" when women were placed in subordinate positions. Given notions of "equal regard" which affirmed persons as equal before God but not equal before one another, gradations among persons based on gender differentiation could not be ruled out. Given a concept of "order" in which one person should hold authority over others, justice was served precisely by the maintenance of a hierarchy—whether in the family, church, or society—in which a male person stood at the head.[6]

If priesthood entails leadership, then on the strength of past understandings it is clear why women could not be priests. They could not govern nor administer; they could not be decision-makers nor public teachers; they could not even be servants in a way that implied an equal share of responsibility for the life of the community.[7]

2. Women and Representation

The judgment that women could not be leaders in the church was inseparable from and perhaps rendered inevitable by the more fundamental judgment that women could not represent God to human persons nor human persons to God.[8] Christian theology for centuries refused to attribute the fullness of the *imago dei* to women. All persons are created in the image and likeness of God, but men were thought to participate in the *imago dei* primarily and fully, while women participated in it secondarily and partially. The Judaeo-Christian God was wholly transcendent, neither male nor female. But when a human analogue was looked for, such transcendence was portrayed in masculine terms. It was, after all, masculinity that stood for strength in relation to feminine weakness, fullness in relation to emptiness, spirit in relation to body, autonomy in relation to dependence.[9] No wonder, then, that men could be understood as representatives of God, but women as only lovers of God. No wonder that public witness of God's self-revelation seemed appropriately given only by men, and authorization for relating to the community as the human manifestation of God's providence and power seemed to be given only to men.

Not only could women not represent God to the Christian community, they could not represent the generically human—before God or before the community. The use of the masculine to refer to the human (whether in theology or liturgy) always implied that women were a special kind of human being, never able to represent humanity as such, never in fact sharing in the fullness of the human. Thus, even as lovers of God they could not stand for all human persons, could not sacrifice for all human persons, could not hold the prayer of all human persons. It is not, then, by chance that no one perceived the contradiction (or even the irony) in such assertions as *Pacem in Terris* "human beings have . . . the right to follow a vocation to the priesthood. . . ."[10]

3. Women and the Sacred

Finally, there were reasons other than essential inferiority or failure to share fully in the *imago dei* that kept women from fulfilling the role of the priest. The office of priesthood always implied the privilege and the responsibility of entering into the sphere of the sacred, of touching the most sacred thing, of mediating sacramentally the grace which was poured forth from the life of the godhead itself.[11] While all persons in the Church dwell somehow in the city of God, are somehow transformed by grace, and are somehow sources of grace to one another, it is the priest whose "office" symbolizes Christ's leading of the whole Church into the inner sanctuary, and who bears the symbolic weight attached to special sacramental agency.

Once again, however, throughout the tradition of the Church, men rather than women seemed the only appropriate subjects for so sacred a responsibility. Women could not be given the symbolic role of entering the holy of holies because they continued to be associated with images of pollution and sin. Ancient myths identifying woman with chaos, darkness, mystery, matter, and sin echoed clearly in Christian interpretations of concupiscence, of the body as defiled, of sexuality as contaminating, and thence of woman as temptress, as a symbol of evil.

Hopelessly entangled in the prohibition of women from the office of priesthood are not only myths of the Fall and Stoic fears of passion as the enemy of contemplation, but also ancient blood taboos and views of childbirth as defiling. However vaguely such notions remained in the consciousness of Christians through the centuries, this understanding of women became theoretically entrenched in sophisticated theologies of original sin, in anthropological theories of higher and lower nature, of mind and body, rationality and desire, and in spiritualistic eschatologies.[12] But there is no need here to repeat in detail what has now been so often rehearsed regarding woman as a special agent of evil.

B. DISSONANCE IN THE PRESENT

If there still linger today fears of women as symbols of evil or judgments of the basic inferiority of women to men or refusals to find in women the fullness of the *imago dei*, nonetheless past understandings of the nature and role of women have come into sharp conflict with a growing new self-understanding on the part of women. Both women and men have come to challenge the pastoral adequacy and the theological accuracy of past interpretations of the nature and role of women and of the patterns of relationship called for and possible to women and men. There is a growing perception of a "new order" in which all the arguments which maintained the essential inferiority of women or the relevance of sex-differentiation for hierarchically determined roles in the Church or society are judged to be simply false, and all the laws and structures that relegated women *qua* women to subordinate roles and to circumscribed spheres are judged to be simply wrong.

1. Correcting Untruths

(a) *Leadership and Representation:* Theology (consistent with its method of extrapolating from biological and socio-psychological data in order to interpret the nature and role of women) today has overwhelming evidence to the contrary of its former conclusions regarding leadership roles for women. Old claims regarding the intellectual superiority of men, the passivity of women's role in reproduction, the innateness of gender-specific divisions of labor, etc., are no longer tenable. New exegetical studies of Scripture offer more "seriously imaginable" ways of construing the meaning and use of both Old and New Testament texts vis-a-vis the relation between men and women.[13] And new theories of society render anachronistic a view of "order" which depends utterly on the unity achieved through one male at the head of every community of persons. Leadership roles, then, are no longer in principle closed to women.

Nor is it the case that women can any longer be thought to be less able to represent the generically human than are men. On the one hand, neither men nor women hold the whole of humanity within themselves; and neither men's experience nor women's experience can be universalized without some limit.[14] On the other hand, both women and men know themselves to be autonomous in a radical sense, responsible for their own lives, capable of and called to the realization of the fully human which characterizes their being. If women's experience today has told them anything it has told them that they, no less than men, must lay claim to their identity as human persons, resisting the temptation to remain forever without selves. Rilke's projection of a time when "there will be girls and women whose name will no longer signify merely an opposite of the masculine, but something in itself, something that makes one think not of any complement and limit but only of life and existence: the feminine human being," is according to many Christian women here at hand.[15]

Similarly, reconstructive efforts regarding the theology of the *imago dei* challenge the notion that God can be represented only or more fittingly by men. A more adequate understanding of the nature of human persons, male and female, largely dispossesses theology of the possibility of yielding to women only a derivative share in the image of God. Equally important in this regard are efforts to look again at the nature of God as it has been revealed by and interpreted by the Christian community. Despite the limitations to any attempts to attribute either masculine or feminine imagery to God,[16] it is probably the case that past problems in women's serving as representatives of God cannot be overcome without a process wherein women can know themselves and be known, *qua* women, as images of God.

Hence, important efforts have been made to look anew at the use of feminine imagery in God's self-revelation through Scripture. Beyond this, grounds have been offered from traditional trinitarian theology (where the Christian community has attempted to articulate its understanding of the inner life of the godhead) for naming each of the persons of the Trinity feminine as well as masculine. Attempts to find a feminine identity in the third person of the Trinity, the Holy Spirit, are well known.[17] Such efforts do not, however, exhaust the possibilities for discovering a "feminine" principle in God.

"Fatherhood" is the image traditionally used for the first person of the Trinity, and "sonship" for the second. But only in an age when the male principle is thought to be the only active principle, the only self-contributing principle, in human generation, is there any necessity for naming the first person "father" and not also "mother." And only in an age when sons are given preeminence as offspring is there any strong constraint to name the second person "son" and not also "daughter."

Further, given the long history of efforts to avoid subordinationism in the doctrine of the Trinity, it is clear that "fatherhood" and "sonship" cannot carry the whole burden of imaging the equality and unity of the two persons. Augustine went to images of mind, self-knowledge, self-love, and memory, understanding, and will, to try to express a triune life in which all that the Father is is communicated to the Son, and all that the Son receives is returned to the Father, so that their one life is a life of infinite mutuality and communion, the life of the Spirit. In such a relationship, it is not impossible to understand the first and second persons as masculine and feminine principles, in each of whom there is infinite activity and infinite receptivity. Infinite giving and receiving coincide in one reality constituted by utter mutuality.[18]

Femininity, then, expresses as well as sonship the relation of the second person to the first. And receptivity is revealed at its peak to be infinitely active and in no way passive. In any case, a model of relationship is revealed which is not hierarchical but marked by total equality and infinite mutuality. Such is the model offered for relationships in the Church—including relationships between women and men.

The conclusion of such ponderings is not that God must be imaged as feminine and not masculine, but that it is a serious distortion to image God in exclusively either masculine or feminine terms. From this it follows, however, that it is false to think that God cannot be represented by women as well as men, and hence equally false to conclude that on such grounds women are to be excluded from the office of priesthood.

(b) *Symbolism and the Sacred:* The invalidity of the symbolic connection between body and evil, sexuality and evil, and hence woman and evil, has become clearer and clearer as the history of this symbolism has been more and more starkly disclosed. Such disclosure surprised and even shocked many contemporary women, though it rang bells in long dismissed memories and provided missing pieces to long standing puzzles. Given an awareness of the history of the symbolic connection between woman and evil, it has been as easy to assert its falsehood (and as difficult to eliminate it from the collective unconscious and the implicit consciousness of persons) as it was in other times to assert the falsehood of a connection between evil and matter. On the basis of women's own experience of themselves, simple denials have seemed self-evidently true, though backing has not been wanting in the form of doctrines of creation or theologies of baptism or evidence from the behavioral sciences regarding the tendency of men to project fears of the evil within themselves on an "other."

De-symbolization is a more difficult enterprise, however, than can be accomplished by simple denial or even reasoned argument. Thus, studies in the symbolism of evil have helped to provide clues for the gradual transformation of symbolic structures. Paul Ricoeur's analysis, for example, of the consciousness of evil unfolds a possible evolution (in the individual and the community) from a sense of defilement (symbolized by bodily stain) to a sense of sin (symbolized by the breaking of a personal bond) to a sense of guilt (symbolized by the captivity of one's own will).[19] Now it is at the level of a sense of evil as defilement that the human body, and human sexuality, and woman, have functioned as symbols of evil. But the sense of defilement is, according to Ricoeur, a pre-ethical, irrational, quasi-material sense of "something" that contaminates by contact, that leaves a symbolic stain. Belief in the defilement of sexuality as such, then, or the uncleanness of woman as woman, is pre-ethical and irrational. Once a reflective process is introduced whereby the blind sense of defilement is subjected to criticism, ideas of the defiling nature of sexuality yield to judgments that wherever there is fault in the realm of sexuality it must be understood rather as an offense against a personal bond and as a failure in human freedom. Thus does there cease to be the entailment of ideas of the defiling nature of woman.[20]

Analyses such as those of Ricoeur give women a rational base from which to challenge vague feelings among both men and women that women are indeed somehow less suited than men to enter the realm of the sacred. Such a base becomes especially important when the challenge is directed to the continued exclusion of women from the ordained sacramental ministry.

2. Preventing Harm

The dissonance between past and present understandings of priesthood and women presents a particular kind of question of truth or falsehood. The continued choice on the part of the Church not to ordain women symbolizes the continued affirmation of what, from a present theological perspective, is a false interpretation of the nature and role of women. But such a continued affirmation not only engages the Church in speculative falsehood; it also entails harmful consequences for individuals in the Church and the Church as a whole. Such consequences are complex and multiple, but it may be sufficient here to describe briefly only four of them.

1. The first can be focused through an event which took place in a parish in Detroit. The parish council decided not to consider the question of introducing altar girls into the liturgical celebrations of the parish. Interestingly enough, it was women on the council who opposed it. Their reason for opposing it is of even greater interest, for they maintained that "If we let the girls do it, we will never be able to get the boys to do it again." It is possible to dismiss such reasoning as simply taking realistic account of the ways in which preadolescent girls and boys relate to one another. I suspect it represents something much more profound than that, however. It is at least analogous to what would be a general fear that an opening of ordination to women would result in an ultimate transfer of the role of priesthood from men to women. This might be predicted either on the basis that women, after all, are more religious than men (a myth not without its ironies), or that any social role loses status when it is opened to women. It is surely true that parish congregations tend to be constituted by a majority of women. One might conclude, then, that it is important to continue to grant access to the priesthood only to men, for only if they are granted sole rights to leadership will men participate actively in the life of the Church at all.

There is some insight to be gained regarding this, however, from the observable fact that the churches whose clergy (and hence leadership) are most totally male are the churches whose congregations tend to be more largely female. This is not surprising if we consider that where the clergy-congregation relationship is conceived of on the stereotypical model of masculine-feminine polarity (where, therefore, the congregation is characterized as led, guided, cared for, taught, governed, receptive, docile, passive), it is difficult for men to identify with the congregation (for it conflicts with their identity formation as male and offers a role for which they have no preparation) and relatively easy for women to identify as members of the congregation (for it fits the identity they have internalized and offers a role for which their conditioning provides an affinity).

What emerges from such observations is the strong suggestion that fullness of shared Christian life by both men and women in the Church cannot be had as long as the ordained ministry is characterized as male and the Church *qua* congregation is characterized as female. This means not only that images of priesthood as only masculine must be foregone, but images of the Church as only feminine must also be foregone or transformed. Where there is not collaboration between men and women at the level of leadership, there will not be true collaboration within the Church as a whole. Only with mutuality of relationships at all levels in the Church will we be able to open to a Christian life which is characterized by creative union, by a life which is modeled on the life of the triune God. As long as we fail to do this, we inhibit the life of the faith, and both women and men are harmed.

2. Since the continued exclusion of women from the ordained priesthood powerfully symbolizes the maintenance of false interpretations of the nature and role of women, it prevents changes in patterns of relationship between women and men not only within the Church but in all dimensions of human life. Thus, for example, it encourages the exclusion of women from leadership roles in society, inhibits full participation by women in the self-determination of society,[21] and retards the possibilities of new understandings of structures of justice and patterns of shared life and love in the institution of marriage.[22] Despite the continued move forward of culture and society without the church, the life of faith and human life in general is inhibited, and men and women are harmed.

3. Since what the nonordination of women symbolizes is so powerful, its failure to come to terms with sexuality and the symbolism of evil constitutes a failure on the part of the Christian community to integrate the powers of human life in the wholeness of the Christian life. If Ricoeur is right in insisting that

> it is not from meditation on sexuality that a refinement of consciousness of fault will be able to proceed, but from the nonsexual sphere of existence: from the relations created by work, appropriation, politics. It is there that an ethics of relations to others will be formed, an ethics of justice and love, capable of turning back toward sexuality, of re-evaluating and transvaluing it[23]

then to miss the opportunity of introducing considerations of justice into the inclusion of women in the ordained sacramental priesthood is to miss the opportunity of raising by indirection the pre-ethical to the ethical, the concern for the pure to a concern for fidelity to personal bonds, the fear of passion to a sense of freedom subject to principles of justice. To miss such an opportunity is at least to harm by omission; to continue to undergird an unreflective belief in the relation of woman to evil is clearly to harm by commission.

4. Finally, feminist theologians have begun to suggest that new work must be done on a theology of sin—work which takes into account the cardinal tendency of women not to the sin of pride but to the sin of failure to take responsibility for their lives, for becoming personal selves, for using their freedom to help make a better world.[24] To continue to refuse ordination to women is to reinforce this tendency—by reinforcing a view of woman which identifies her as follower not leader, responder not initiator. To do so is to harm women, and inevitably also to harm men.

III. THE MORAL IMPERATIVE

When the Roman Catholic community reflects on the question "what ought we to do" regarding the ordination of women, it has the same sources of moral illumination that it has for any other ethical reflection on how its faith is to be lived. It must look to its tradition, to the Scripture and theology which are part of that tradition, to other disciplines which can inform its theology, and to its own contemporary experience as a Christian community. We have explored some of the sources of which it must take account, seen some of the places of insight and some of the places of impoverishment of insight, discovered some of what must be incorporated and embraced and some of what must be transformed or abandoned. Through all, I have implicitly assumed that part of the richness of the Roman Catholic tradition of theological ethics, of moral thought and moral teaching, is the refusal to retreat to voluntarism, and the insistence that laws and policies should be inherently intelligible, should make inherently good sense in the Church's efforts to love truthfully and faithfully. What, then, is the answer to the question "what ought we to do" regarding the ordination of women in the Roman Catholic Church? Two general imperatives, it seems to me, are already clear: First, the Church ought to open its ordained sacramental ministry to women. It ought to do so because not to do so is to affirm a policy, a system, a structure, whose presuppositions are false (for the nonordination of women is premised on the denial in women of a capacity for leadership, a call to represent God to the community and the community to God, and a worthiness to approach the sacred in the fullness of their womanhood). It ought also to do so because not to do so is to harm individual persons and the Church (by choking off the life of faith which is possible in a Christian church modeled on the life of God; by perpetuating unjust patterns of relationship between women and men; by failing to speak a word of healing to persons as yet fragmented in the powers of their own selves; and by reinforcing inadequate notions of freedom and destiny for women and for men).

Secondly, women in the Church ought to seek ordination—for the same reasons that obligate the Church to ordain women, and because some women will have received a unique imperative by the power of the Holy Spirit and from the Christian community in which they find life. They should seek it without bitterness (though they will know the meaning of Naomi's complaint, "Call me not Naomi, for that is beautiful; but call me Mara, for that is bitter"). They should seek it in spite of weariness (though they can say, too, "I am so tired . . . and also tired of the future before it comes,"[25] and though they are subject to the cardinal temptation to weaken and not to struggle forward in freedom and responsibility). They should seek it in a way that does not alienate them from one another, whatever their pasts and whatever their present contexts. They should seek it because now ripens the time when they must say to the Church, for all women, words reminiscent of the words of Jesus Christ to his disciples (under the continued query for a revelation of his true reality), "Have we been so long with you, and you have not known us?"

Notes

1. See the brief but relevant observations in this regard by Beverly Wildung Harrison, "Sexism and the Contemporary Church: When Evasion Becomes Complicity," in Alice L. Hageman (ed), *Sexist Religion and Women in the Church: No More Silence!* (N.Y.: Association Press, 1974), p. 200.

2. *Ibid.*, p. 204.

3. I would argue, for example, that these three elements are all present in some form in each of the models of the Church offered in the typology which Avery Dulles draws in *Models of the Church* (Garden City, N.Y.: Doubleday & Company, Inc., 1974).

4. In other words, the now famous "four base points" of Christian ethics are relevant here as elsewhere. See James M. Gustafson, "Context vs. Principles: A Misplaced Debate in Christian Ethics," *Harvard Theological Review*, vol. 58 (April, 1965), pp. 171-202.

5. See Dulles, chap. 6 (especially his discussion of the relevant positions of Hans Kung, Richard McBrien, and Yves Congar); see also Karl Rahner, "On the Diaconate," *Theological Investigations*, vol. 12 (N.Y.: The Seabury Press, 1974), p. 72.

6. Thomas Aquinas offers one of the clearest theories of the created order in this regard. See, for example, *Summa Theologiae* I, 92, 1; 96, 3; *On Kingship* 2, 17-20; *Summa Contra Gentiles* III, 123, 3-4.

7. See *Summa Theologiae* II-II, 172, 2.

8. Of course, everyone in the Church has always been thought to manifest God in Jesus Christ in some way. Women, however, were not considered capable of manifesting God to such a degree that they could serve to do so at a symbolic level.

9. I have treated this question in fuller detail in my article, "New Patterns of Relationship: Beginnings of A Moral Revolution," *Theological Studies*, vol. 36 (December, 1975).

10. *Pacem in Terris*, section 15 (Paulist Press, 1963).

11. This is true, it seems to me, even when the cultic aspects of priesthood are considerably deemphasized.

12. The fact that woman has also been placed on a "pedestal," revered as a special bearer of virtue, etc., has served to reinforce rather than to counter her position of inferiority and even her association with evil. After all, one who is on a pedestal has little force in appealing for elevation from inferior status. And one who is expected to be especially virtuous can be made to feel evil by the simple fact that she cannot fulfil unrealistic expectations.

13. "Seriously imaginable" is a condition offered by David Kelsey for theological interpretations of Scripture: see *The Uses of Scripture in Recent Theology* (Fortress Press, 1975), chap. 8. Its function is well illustrated by such efforts as those of Robin Scroggs, "Paul and the Eschatological Woman," *Journal of the American Academy of Religion*, vol. 40 (1972), pp. 283-303; Elaine H. Pagels, "Paul and Women: A Response to Recent Discussion," *Journal of the American Academy of Religion*, vol. 42 (1974), pp. 538-49; Phyllis Trible, "Eve and Adam: Genesis 2-3 Reread," *Andover Newton Quarterly*, vol. 13 (March, 1973), pp. 251-58.

14. This point has been especially well delineated by Judith E. Plaskow in *Sex, Sin and Grace: Women's Experience and the Theologies of Reinhold Niebuhr and Paul Tillich*. Unpublished dissertation, Yale University, 1975. See esp. pp. 8-11.

15. Rainer, Maria Rilke, *Letters to a Young Poet*, trans. M. D. H. Norton (N.Y.: Norton, 1962), p. 59.

16. Such limitations include importantly the need for continual affirmation of the transcendence of God beyond either masculine or feminine characteristics and the continual reminder of the danger of rigidifying stereotypical notions of masculinity and femininity.

17. See, for example, George Tavard, *Woman and the Christian Tradition* (University of Notre Dame Press, 1973).

18. I have expanded on these notions in two other articles: "New Patterns of Relationship: Beginnings of a Moral Revolution," *Theological Studies*, vol. 36 (December, 1975), pp. 640-43; "Sources of Sexual Inequality in the History of Christian Thought," *Journal of Religion* (April, 1976).

19. Paul Ricoeur, *Symbolism of Evil* (N.Y.: Harper & Row, Publishers, 1967).

20. See article cited above, "Sources of Sexual Inequality in the History of Christian Thought."

21. Leaders and groups in the Roman Catholic Church were among those who, for example, opposed women's suffrage (see the Sophia Smith Collection of Documents of the Catholic Bishops against Women's Suffrage, 1910-1920).

22. Those who favor new patterns of relationship between women and men are often accused of being against the family and for such procedures as abortion. In fact, under some unexamined old patterns of relationship the family has come upon hard times, and abortion is often symptomatic of deep-seated problems in heretofore accepted structures of society. New patterns of relationship which are based upon principles of equality and mutuality will, indeed, mark a change in some models of the family (for no longer will a man be considered the sole head of the family). If, however, equality and mutuality prove more fruitful as bases for relationship (because more true to the reality of the persons involved), then the family which incorporates those principles will be less threatened in modern society than will other models of family. Thus will the "liberation" of women and men serve to support, not destroy, family life. Similarly, a society in which women are not left with the whole burden of child-bearing and child-rearing (but where women and men share these human experiences and responsibilities), will at least move toward being a society in which abortion is no longer offered as the solution to problems which it cannot finally solve. I have considered this possibility in my article, "Liberation, Abortion and Responsibility," *Reflection*, vol. 71 (May, 1974), pp. 9-13.

23. Ricoeur, p. 29.

24. I have been much influenced in this view by the work of Judith Plaskow, *Sex, Sin and Grace: Women's Experience and the Theologies of Reinhold Niebuhr and Paul Tillich* (Yale diss., 1975).

25. Doris Lessing, *Martha Quest* (London: Panther Books, 1972), p. 7.

7

A Theologian Challenges
Margaret Farley's Position

George Tavard

REV. GEORGE H. TAVARD was born in Nancy, France, and was ordained a member of the Augustinians of the Assumption, 1947. He received an S.T.D. in Lyon, taught theology in Surrey, England and was assistant editor of DOCUMENTATION CATHOLIQUE in Paris. His present work includes consultant to the Pontifical Secretariat for Unity of Christians, a member of the Anglican-Roman Catholic and Lutheran-Catholic Dialogues, both internationally and in the U.S. He has published books in German, French and English, the most recent in English, WOMEN IN CHRISTIAN TRADITION (University of Notre Dame Press). Father Tavard is currently Professor of Theology at the Methodist Theological School in Ohio.

I certainly appreciate Sister Margaret Farley's paper, particularly in its concern to show that nonordination of women is harmful, not only to the women who aspire to the priesthood, but to the Church as a whole. In all our endeavors in whatever touches on the structures of the Church, the point of view of the whole should always, I believe, predominate. This is necessary if our conclusions are not to give the impression of special pleading.

Although I generally agree with her conclusions, I am not so sure, however, that the case has been well made. And I suspect that, if I had not already reached a theological position on the matter, I would not be convinced by the proposed argumentation. At least, I would be negative to some important aspects of it. In general, I believe that it is nonproductive or dysfunctional to rely on a historical argumentation, or on an interpretation of the past, which is doubtful or shaky. Often we judge the past in the light of the present and of

52

what we would like the future to be; and then we turn around and we criticize the present in the light of what we have said about the past. Criticizing a general argument of which we find, it seems, some specific instances in Sister Margaret Farley's paper, I would say that to blame the Church for oppression of women in the past does not make sense if the women of the past did not think they were oppressed. Oppression is not an objective state. It is a subjective response to a situation. Certain objective conditions make oppression possible. But when we try to assess them, we should not, and ultimately we cannot, superimpose our own subjectivity on that of our ancestors as we read their lives and study their living context.

Concerning "Leadership"

After stating this general principle of historical methodology, I will say a few words on what I take to be the three lines of argumentation of the paper, leadership, representation and "the sacred."

I suggest first that the paper suffers precisely on this point when it asserts the leadership potential of women. I have theological problems with the notion that leadership is one of the constitutive elements of priesthood. But the question I wish to raise does not touch on whether this is the best approach to priesthood. Rather, accepting the approach adopted, I ask if it is true that "these elements are crucial . . . because they have been judged in the past as unable to be affirmed by women." I raise this question in relation to "leadership." Margaret Farley states: "Centuries of excluding women from the priesthood mirrors centuries of belief that women cannot appropriately fill roles of leadership, whether in the family, church or society."

But the centuries in question, which I take to include the Middle Ages, did accept the leadership of abbesses, with quasi-episcopal jurisdiction over the priests in the territory of their abbeys. On this point, the evidence adduced by Joan Morris, in her book, *The Lady Was a Bishop*, is unimpeachable. The title is a mistake, for the lady was never a bishop. But the information given in the book is extremely valuable. We cannot have it both ways. If there were exempt abbesses, then the Church did recognize the leadership of women in some areas of public life. It was only with the Renaissance and with the French Revolution—that is, with events that weakened the sense of the Christian tradition—that the leadership of women as abbesses was questioned and eventually done away with.

The leadership of women in public life was also recognized in reigning queens who were duly crowned. And as the coronation ceremony often (I have not fully investigated the matter, so I dare not say always) included anointing with holy chrism (the oil used also for baptism, confirmation and ordination), there was some theologizing that Kingship or Queenship were quasi-sacraments which somehow shared the dignity of the sacrament of Orders. The one major exception to the leadership of reigning Queens was of course the Kingdom of France. But when the unwritten and half-forgotten Salic Law was invoked for the first time and became a principle at the end of the Capetian monarchy, this was not based on the idea that women cannot lead; it was a political maneuver destined to make sure that the crown would not fall into the hands of the English pretender, Edward III, who claimed it through his mother. It had nothing to do with women; it had to do with Englishmen.

Likewise, on the positive side, one can make a long list of women whose leadership was recognized in fact, such as Joan of Arc or Catherine of Siena, or Brigid of Sweden, or Mary of the Incarnation. The working of the feudal hierarchy was much more fluid than we are told. Margaret Farley writes: "If priesthood entails leadership, then, on the strength of past understandings, it is clear why women could not be priests. They could not govern nor administer. . . ." As a matter of fact, they could govern and administer; and in many cases, they did. One ought to reverse the sentence, with a slight modification: "If priesthood entails leadership, then on the strength of past experience, it is clear that women could be priests."

Concerning "Representation"

Concerning the notion of "representation," I have theological difficulties with the idea that the priest "represents" God. That the priest, in some activities, represents the risen Christ ought to be enough. Even the Popes—with the exception of Innocent III—have not commonly used the title of *Vicarius Dei; Vicarius Christi* has been quite enough. However this may be, I have other problems with Margaret Farley's argumentation concerning the *imago Dei*. "Christian theology for centuries refused to attribute the fulness of the *imago Dei* to women." This, I contend, is a considerable oversimplification of the theological tradition on the point, with the result that the argument based upon it remains unconvincing.

The Christian tradition on the *imago Dei* is not unanimous. The

Greek tradition is different from the Latin one. But the Latin tradition, to which I will limit my remarks, is not adequately formulated in "Moral Imperatives for the Ordination of Women." Thomas Aquinas affirms clearly that women and men share equally the essence of the *imago Dei*, for the image of God resides in the intellectual nature of human beings, which is the same for women as for men (I q.93 a.4, ad 1; a.6, ad 2). Men and women differ, for Thomas Aquinas, in secondary or accidental aspects of the *imago Dei*. This accidental aspect is that man is created—as Thomas Aquinas thinks on the basis of what he reads in St. Paul, or better, of what he reads into St. Paul—"as the principle and the end of woman, as God is the principle and the end of all creatures" (1 q.93, a.4, ad 1). One may of course find fault with this. I would see it as an erroneous sacralizing of the pattern of social relationships with which Thomas Aquinas was familiar. But to overlook the nuances of the tradition on the *imago Dei* does not help the case for the ordination of women. Thomas Aquinas insists: "The *imago Dei* is common to both sexes, because it resides in the *mens*, (Ed: The intellectual nature of human beings.) in which there is no distinction of sexes." (I q.93, a.6, ad 2.) The doctrine of St. Bonaventure is practically the same: "As to its essence, the image consists principally in the soul and its faculties, as these are destined to turn to God; and in this matter there is no distinction of male and female. . . ." The difference appears, for Bonaventure, in regard to the *bene esse* or the clarity of expression of the image: here the soul "is ordered and related to the body." The distinction of sexes and the social roles of both affect the way in which the image is found in each sex. It is "in a higher way" in the male, but, as Bonaventure adds, "not because of what regards the essence of the image itself, but because of adjunctions to it." (C.S., II, dist. XVI, a. 2, q. 2.) One can make a case for the social origin and nature of these adjunctions, so that it is not the theology of the *imago Dei*, but its sociology, which has been detrimental to women and which has negatively affected the question of ordination of women. This would be, in my judgement, a better case than one based on an over-simplified account of the *imago Dei* tradition.

Concerning the "Sacred"

The last point I will make concerns *women and the sacred*. Here, I have no quarrel with the relationship that is hinted at by Margaret Farley between priesthood and the sacred. For I personally define the

essence of priesthood, not in relation to leadership or to representation, but in relation to the sacraments and especially the Eucharist.
I hold for a profoundly cultic priesthood, from which other functions
may flow according to the needs of the times. Indeed, I see priesthood active in the four areas of worship, proclamation, education and
service; but worship alone defines the essence of priesthood.

My difficulty here concerns what is said by Margaret Farley
about the sacred. It is more difficult to pinpoint and to document
than my previous arguments, but it may reach deeper. The point is
this: I do not see that either the religious tradition of mankind as a
whole has excluded women from cultic functions because women are
"associated with images of pollution and sin," or that the Church has
continued in the same line. The association of women with blood
taboos is obvious in the Old Testament tradition; and this, in Jewish
cultic and ethical conceptions, has left its mark on the place of
woman in the Temple and in the Synagogue. But the "ancient myths
identifying woman with chaos, darkness, mystery, matter . . .", to
which allusion is made, do something quite different. They do not associate woman with sin, but with another realm of the sacred. They
associate woman with the sacredness of the chtonian deities. And for
that reason, both the Greek and the Roman mythologies and religions reserved to women some high religious functions that men
could not fulfill. It is not from this that the Christian tradition inherited the notion of "woman as temptress, as symbol of evil." It
inherited the popular belief, which underlies many folk traditions and
some of the great cultures of humankind, that there are two realms of
the sacred, two types of the numinous, the yin and the yang, earth
and heaven, and that these can be, should be, united, but cannot be,
should not be, confused, because if they are complementary, they are
not identical. The sacredness of the altar and the sacredness of the
home are twin concepts, but the twins never meet.

This raises an important question for us. But the question is not
whether we should do away with "sophisticated theologies of original
sin, anthropological theories of higher and lower nature, of mind and
body, rationality and desire, spiritualistic eschatologies." I experience
higher and lower nature every day. I am caught between rationality
and desire. One can make a good case for each of such views without
touching the question of ordination of women. What is relevant—in
the related yet opposite concepts of the sacredness of the altar and the
sacredness of the home—is that we need to define our own anthropol-

ogy. Does a Christian anthropology see womanhood and manhood as two distinct complementary ways of being human that cannot be reduced the one to the other? If so, one can make a good case for two functions in the Church. And in this case, the sacerdotal function goes naturally to the male, because *melior est conditio possidentis*. (Ed: Because he already has it; our closest idiom would be "possession is nine-tenths of the law.") It is easy to refute the belief that women are inferior. But this does not take us very far. For it is not the view that one finds in ecclesiastical circles. The view is that there exist providentially predetermined roles for woman and for man. And this is much more difficult to refute. The alternate question remains: does a Christian anthropology see womanhood and manhood as abstractions which imperfectly fit the living beings called women and men? Does it hold that in practice each human being is in some ways and in varying degrees both female and male, so that it is up to each one to define, before God, one's own self and one's own function in the Church and in society? I personally think that on this basis we can make a much more solid argument for the ordination of women.

This, I believe, should be the question before us. Until we have answered it, we cannot present a good case, whether for or against, the ordination of women.

8

The Dialogue Continues

Margaret A. Farley, R.S.M.

George Tavard, as the author of one of the most important studies which we now have on the role of woman in Christian thought, has himself offered some very convincing arguments for the ordination of women.[1] I thus take very seriously his concern to make the best case possible in this regard. Whatever is the best case, however, I should want to continue to insist on the importance of taking into account the kinds of considerations I have already suggested. The following five points, then, may help to clarify my position:

First: It has not been my intent to argue either that (a) all of history offers one wholly consistent pattern of events and ideas, or that (b) the responsibility which the Church has had for the direction of events and ideas in the past is such as to render it blameworthy.[2] It has been my intent, rather, (a) to raise up those aspects of the history of Christian thought and belief which remain explicitly or implicitly as barriers to the ordination of women, (b) to consider the loss of validity of those ideas and beliefs in the face of present understandings of the nature and role of women, and (c) to assess the harm entailed by continuing to affirm what are essentially false ideas and beliefs. I have sought to do these three things in an effort to discern a moral imperative regarding the ordination of women. If I am right in concluding thus to a clear moral imperative, then it is true that the question of present and future blameworthiness on the part of the Church is at stake.

Second: I would not want to argue, as Father Tavard suggests, that leadership is an "adequate conception of priesthood." Broadly understood (that is, with the wide meaning I have allowed it vis-a-vis many models of the Church and of ministry), it is a necessary but not sufficient element in the meaning of priesthood. Even if one considers the central element of priesthood to be the role of the priest in the Church's life of worship (as does Father Tavard), it seems to me that that role is itself a special kind of leadership role. Leadership, representation, and participation in the sacred need not be (and, in fact, may not ever be) separate roles which the priest fulfills; they are, rather, logically discernible aspects of the role of priest (hence, elements in the meaning of priesthood) which may indeed modify one another or be combined with one another in a variety of ways.

Third: The fact that in the history of Christianity women have fulfilled some leadership roles does not, it seems to me, gainsay the fact that the overall weight of the history of Christian thought has been in the direction of a denial of leadership roles to women. From the pastoral letters of the early Church to the *Apostolic Constitutions* of the fourth century to the scholastic position in the thirteenth century to what I would insist are widespread implicitly accepted views not yet left behind today, women are considered subject to men—ordained to obey not to govern, to help not to lead, "for man is the head of woman."[3]

The position of some abbesses in the Middle Ages, the reign of some queens, and the charismatic leadership of some individual women are exceptions to the overall rule which placed women in auxiliary roles, subject to men. Indeed, they are frequently the kind of exceptions which prove the rule. The refusal to allow the jurisdictional power of abbesses to grow or even to remain (and the refusal to allow them full power of Orders) was finally due to the fact that arguments against women's suitableness for such power prevailed. It is difficult, moreover, to forget how hard some kings tried and to what lengths they were willing to go in order to beget sons and so to avoid leaving their realms in the hands of daughters. And it is not difficult to recall that it was Joan of Arc's insistence on wearing men's clothing that contributed finally to her destruction.

Fourth: It is true, as both Father Tavard and I have indicated, that the doctrine of the *imago dei* was generally applied to all persons *qua* persons—and hence to women as persons. Yet it is precisely the refusal to accord to women *as women* the fullness of the *imago dei* (that is, not only in its essential aspect, but in its accidental aspects as well) that is the point at stake. The nuances of the tradition on the *imago dei* are such that finally woman *qua* woman remains a secondary image—because she participates less fully in human nature itself.[4]

Tavard is right, I think, in attributing a "social origin" to the way in which women are accounted for in the theology of the *imago dei*. Theology, however, is quite capable of incorporating sociologi-

cally based ideas into itself; and in this instance, it incorporated societal definitions and norms in a way that reinforced what it might
otherwise have served to correct.

Fifth: Father Tavard's concern to deal with the "two realms" of
the sacred is an extremely important one. I agree fully that a long
tradition of interpreting the masculine and feminine as complementary principles has provided a strong rationale for assigning to men
and women separate but complementary roles. I also agree with the
suggestions Tavard has made here and elsewhere that such gender-
differentiation of roles is based upon an inadequate understanding of
human persons, both men and women.

While ancient and modern myths and theories of the comple-
mentariness of women and men need serious critique, such a critique
will not substitute for a similar effort to deal with myths and theories
which identify woman with evil. Father Tavard has himself well documented some aspects of the history of this latter problem.[5] The fact
that the tendency to associate woman with evil has not been completely eliminated in our own day is evidenced in such contemporary
experiences as the refusal of some persons to receive the Eucharist
from the hands of a woman extraordinary minister. To say that this is
simply an expression of the belief that women belong in the private
sphere of the sacred and not the public is to miss the judgment in the
experience that women are somehow here unworthy and a source of
contamination.

Indeed, the "two realms" theory of the sacred will not finally be
demythologized without a careful analysis of the points at which it
has become intertwined with the belief that women are somehow associated with evil. Thus, for example, when Father Tavard asserts
that a good case can be made for "anthropological theories of higher
and lower nature, of mind and body, rationality and desire," he
misses both the point that such theories have been associated with
polar gender-assignments (which are at the root of the "two realms"
theories) and that frequently one pole of each of these dualities has
been judged less good than the other (and, yes, even more likely to be
marked by evil than the other). Similarly, with "another realm of the
sacred," they have also been associated with evil (the influence of
philosophical concepts of reason and order is, for example, un-
mistakable in Christian theories of virtue). The association of woman
with disorder and so with evil has itself contributed to the "two
realms" theory by serving as an impetus for placing women in cir-

cumscribed spheres (the home or the cloister)—thereby introducing order into the sexual lives of men.

Notes

1. George Tavard, *Woman and The Christian Tradition* (University of Notre Dame Press, 1973), pp. 211-219.

2. In other words, I am simply not taking up the question of the blameworthiness of the Church in the past. I leave that question to other persons and to other occasions. I would, however, take some issue with Tavard's view that oppression is only subjective. Recent social theory has shown quite convincingly that the worst forms of oppression are those which make the oppressed think that their way of existence (as oppressed) is the way that is right and just. It is true, of course, that both oppressed and oppressors may have no explicit awareness of the oppression (as oppression).

3. See, for example, *Apostolic Constitutions* I, 8; *Summa Theologiae* I, 92, 1 ad 2.

4. In some representatives (e.g., Gregory of Nyssa) of the Greek tradition of the doctrine of the *imago dei* the problem is less serious, for man *qua* male is also not considered as relevant to the *imago dei*. In the Latin tradition, however, maleness is given special participation in the *imago* of God. This is especially true in the doctrine taught by Thomas Aquinas; see *ST* I, 93, 3; 93, 4; 92, 1 ad 1 (where Aquinas details accidental and essential sharing in the *imago dei*—a distinction which then works nicely to give the primary and full share to men as men). For an especially helpful analysis of the doctrine of the *imago dei* in the patristic era, see Rosemary Radford Ruether, "Misogynism and Virginal Feminism in the Fathers of the Church," in *Religion and Sexism* (N.Y.: Simon and Schuster, 1974), pp. 150-183.

5. See Tavard, 105 and *passim*.

9

The Justice of the Gospel Narrative

Emily Clark Hewitt

EMILY CLARK HEWITT, Episcopal priest, canonical resident of New York Diocese, is currently a student at the Harvard Law School, having completed her M.Phil. at Union Theological Seminary. Emily has worked with the Upward Bound Program of Cornell University. Besides being Assistant Professor at Andover Newton Theological School, 1973-75, she worked as consultant in urban education, theological education and women in ministry. She was ordained to the Episcopal Priesthood in Philadelphia, 1974. Emily is a founding member of the National Episcopal Women's Caucus, and has published in areas of education and church life, including WOMEN PRIESTS: YES OR NO? with Suzanne Hiatt (Seabury Press), and an article in WOMEN AND ORDERS (Paulist).

Margaret Farley has made the topic of the "moral imperatives for the ordination of women" the occasion for a penetrating look at ethical decision-making, at the nature of the priesthood, at our understanding of the Trinity and at what women can bring to a renewed ministry. What she has to say is important precisely because so many of the questions she has addressed will continue to be of consuming interest long after the present problem of opening holy orders to women has been removed.

To affirm the imperative of opening holy orders to women is to affirm justice and the Gospel against a series of stubborn objections no longer tenable. What is the imperative of justice here? In the Roman Catholic Church itself one finds teachings that could point only to the inclusion of women in Holy Orders. What else is one to conclude from what one reads in *Gaudium et Spes*?

With respect to the fundamental rights of the person, every type of discrimination, whether social or cultural, whether based on sex, race, color, social condition, language or religion is to be overcome and eradicated as contrary to God's intent.

What is the view of the New Testament? We find no qualification or limit to Paul's teaching on the implications of baptism:

> For as many of you as were baptized into Christ have put on Christ. There is neither Jew nor Greek, there is neither slave nor free, there is neither male nor female; for you are all one in Christ Jesus. (Gal. 3:28)

The Church does not have to make up moral imperatives for opening Holy Orders to women. They exist and have existed since Jesus came into Nazareth preaching the good news. (Luke 4:16-19) Despite this fact, there is outspoken opposition. Much of the opposition—perhaps most of it—comes from those who ought best be acquainted with the moral and Gospel imperatives. Why is it that those learned in theology—scholars, priests, and prelates of the church—have done so much to fashion arguments against opening Holy Orders to women?

Dean Krister Stendahl, now of Harvard Divinity School, who was instrumental in opening the priesthood to women in the Church of Sweden a generation ago, has noted and reflected on this problem. His answer, in brief, is that seeing the moral imperative is too simple for many of those who are learned in theology. He says

> The church wants to speak in distinctly Christian terms. But justice and the concern for justice is universal, a common human urge. That may be the reason why questions of plain justice have had a difficulty in becoming Item Number One on the church's agenda. It does not sound "Christian enough." So Christian theologians have lost themselves in often penetrating and sometimes perverse reflection on distinction and polarity and subordination when it comes to male and female. Simple calls for justice and equality [are] branded with the damaging designation "secular" or "worldly" or "political." The call for justice is a call for first things first. (Cf. "Enrichment or Threat," *Sexist Religion and Women in the Church*, ed. Alice L. Hageman. (New York: Association Press, 1974), pp. 118-119.)

The exercise that we must do is to name the arguments of those learned in theology for what they are—red herrings put forward to obscure the clarity of the moral imperative. Naming demons is squarely in the New Testament tradition. Their name in this case, too, has biblical precedent—Legion.

Let me illustrate with a few examples. First, the justice issue, which is raised in a clear way by the quote from *Gaudium et Spes* to which I referred earlier. The issue here should not be easy to obscure. But recently I saw a manful (if I may say so) effort to obscure it. A Roman Catholic Archbishop tells us that ordination is not a "justice" issue because ordination is not a "right."[1] What he misses is the fact that no one is asserting that ordination is a right. What *is* being asserted is that the opportunity to test one's vocation is a right. And that right is being denied. The Archbishop's comment does not meet the issue because it *cannot* be met.

On the scriptural side, women are told that they cannot be ordained because Jesus chose only males to be his disciples. This precedent, we are told, shows Christ's will for the composition of the clergy—and that composition is male only. But the precedent argument proves too much. If the precedent of the composition of Jesus's disciples were really taken seriously, we should exclude from orders not only women, but also Gentiles. (Indeed, if one is to take seriously the important distinctions in first century Palestine, perhaps it would be more important to exclude Gentiles!)

We are told by theologians that women are "improper matter" for ordination. This means that women cannot receive the indelible sacrament of Holy Orders. Let us leave to one side the assumptions of biological inferiority that have buttressed this argument. In theological terms, the logic of the argument is that women should not be baptized either, since Holy Baptism is also an indelible sacrament. Indeed, I know of no scriptural or theological arguments against women in Holy Orders that can be maintained without at the same time undermining the Church's teaching that salvation extends to both sexes.

When all such red herrings have been met, there is still one more argument to address. We are told that those who persist in asserting the moral imperative to ordain women have failed to heed the imperatives of love and reconciliation in Christian teaching. "Reconciliation," "love," "peace"—"shalom"—those words that so much inform Christian life and visions of the future—mean nothing unless each and all include justice. This is a time to heed the biblical warnings against those who cry peace in order to lead God's people astray! (Micah 3:5)

The moral imperative of ordaining women is clear, direct, simple —perhaps, too simple. Yet it must be urged. It is on the same simplicity—the simple promises of the good news—that we stake our lives.

Note

1. Cf. The Bernardin statement in Appendix A.

10

The Church in Process:
Engendering the Future

Anne Elizabeth Carr, B.V.M.

*ANNE ELIZABETH CARR, B.V.M. received an M.A. in the-
ology from Marquette University and an M.A. and Ph.D. in
Christian Theology from Chicago Divinity School. Anne taught
at Mundelein College, Indiana University and is currently at the
University of Chicago. She is Associate Dean of the Divinity
School at the University. Anne has published various articles
and reviews, and is now doing research on transcendence and
freedom, and in the area of the work and method of Karl
Rahner.*

Voices urging the ordination of women in the Roman Catholic
Church make it apparent, despite authoritative advice to the contrary, that the issue is not untimely, intramural to the hierarchical institution nor peripheral to the major business of the Church; it is central to the very shape of Catholicism for the future. The urgency in
these voices from all parts of the community challenges theology to
present the evidence to the Church and to call it to fidelity to its own
message in its most visible expression, the ministry.

In my understanding, theology must always conjoin two sources,
the Christian tradition and our common human experience, in expression that is adequate and appropriate to both. It must be faithful to
the Christian message as found in the New Testament and the living
tradition of the Church, especially its central religious affirmations,
and responsive to the contemporary situation in which the Gospel is
proclaimed and witnessed.[1] Thus I will try to correlate here (1) the
significance of the Christian tradition on the Church and its ministry
with (2) the experience of women, as reflected in the contemporary
women's movement within and on the boundaries of the Church.

Women's experience has much to say to the Church, as the Church and its tradition have much to say to women, if (3) an authentic model of the Church is to be engendered for the future.

There is some tension between these sources for our reflection this weekend. The Christian message is that in the life, death and resurrection of Jesus, all humankind is redeemed in principle through the miracle of God's self-gift and word to us. In the sending of the Spirit, we are joined in communion such that the social distinctions of class, race and sex are overcome. Equality, freedom in the Spirit, and love of one another are the hallmarks of the Church, the body of Christ, the people of God. In this communion we women are told we share fully in its life of faith through baptism. Nevertheless, we experience a disease with the structures which embody our participation. The Church has not, in its human structure, accepted women as sharing equally and fully in its life. We, as Christians, are no longer willing to gloss over this inconsistency between faith and life. Thus we call for recognition of our full personhood and redemption in Christ in sacramental ordination.

In quite a different sense of the word "tradition" (i.e., custom, *traditiones*), women are not considered suitable candidates for the ordained priesthood in the Catholic Church. We are expressly excluded in Canon 968, which reflects long-standing thought and practice in the Church. The arguments given for the exclusion of women from the ordained ministry, as for our inferior status in the life of the Church—God revealed in predominantly masculine imagery as Father; Jesus's maleness and that of the apostles he chose; women's role as different from (i.e., subordinate to) the male role of headship in the patterns of revelation; the societal subjection of women as a class; the evil, uncleanness and temptation of our sex—have been questioned and refuted logically and theologically. God is not sexual; Jesus's and the apostles' maleness corresponds to the sociological conditions of the ancient Near East and the traditions of Israel; the significance of Jesus is not his maleness but his humanness; women's roles in the Church have always been shaped by society; our sexuality is not evil or unclean, but good in the goodness of creation and sanctified in the sacramental life of the Church.[2]

Nevertheless, we are told to avoid discussion of the ordination of women because of "tradition." But we also know that *traditio* fundamentally means handing on the word of faith, indeed the reality of faith—the body of the Lord—in the preaching of the word, in pastoral service and liturgical expression.[3] Tradition is not a static past. And we find the seeds for a new model of ministry, which includes women fully, in the Church's understanding of the process by which tradition develops and lives when this is joined with the new experience of Christian women today.

Tradition as the Church in Process

Our age is profoundly aware of development and change in every dimension of experience. We know in our very bones that ours is not a static world, but a world of flux and relativity; consciousness of time and history pervades our relationships, politics, our institutions, even our deepest beliefs and values. Nowhere has the impact of this historical consciousness been felt more sharply than in the religious sphere where the formulas of faith and our notions of the Church, indeed their intrinsic meaning and truth, have been challenged.

The challenge of history, however, has also been an opportunity for rebirth: witness the Second Vatican Council's efforts to read the signs of the times. Describing itself as an interior mystery which no human language can directly comprehend, the Church used a variety of images, many of biblical origin, to express its own reality. Phrases like the "people of God" and "pilgrim Church" became as familiar as the more extrinsic "institution" and "society." According to Vatican II, the divine-human, visible-invisible Church, the very sacrament of Christ, is both interior mystery of communion and external sign of his presence in the assembly of believers on their march in history toward the kingdom of God.[4]

The awareness of historical change that marked the Church's self-understanding at Vatican II and its plural self-description were, to an extent, the result of historical studies of the Church's doctrine and practice. For historians demonstrate that different models were dominant at different times in the Church's past and that these issued in a variety of ministerial expressions.[5] Today we are aware of the pluralism of models of the Church among the Christian traditions and within the Catholic communion itself. Each is, in a different way, expressive of the fundamental mystery of the Church—the Church as mystical communion, as sacrament of Christ and of the world, as herald of the Gospel, as servant, according to one theologian;[6] or in the words of another, expressive of the Church's need to adapt itself more clearly to the times as a democratized, declericalized, open Church.[7] All models represent changing expressions of the Church's self-understanding as it adapts itself to its situation in history.

The Relative and the Absolute

The relationship of the Church to its changing historical setting poses the thorny question of separating the relative from the absolute, peeling the onion, to use a famous analogy. How far can the accretions of history be peeled from the core of truth? What changes can be allowed? The truth of the one Christian mystery is always embodied in human, temporal forms and simply is not available in its pristine essence.[8] So one Catholic theological argument goes: if the Church, i.e., the magisterium, allows a change, then it is allowable, and this is a "theological development" under the inspiration of the Spirit.[9]

We do not challenge this belief in the work of the Spirit. On the contrary, contemporary Christian women are sharply conscious of the way the Spirit breathes where the Spirit will. But we are also aware of another facet of historical consciousness, its dimension of freedom. We know that human freedom is the bearer of divine freedom in the world, that God's work is entrusted to the responsible and responsive freedom of limited, fallible women and men. The visible and human Church must strive, freely and with increased consciousness of its own history, to be adequate to its invisible reality, the enduring mystery of Christ, and precisely in doing so to be adequate to the exigencies of its times. For the revelation to which it witnesses is for people, in their here and now situations. Because so many older forms of cultural and social life are crumbling, the Church can no longer depend on social forms developed in response to a past culture. It must find new forms appropriate to the present and future if it is to hand on its permanent message authentically and effectively to the coming age.[10] That such free adaptation is in fact traditional is clear in the history of the ministry (or the priesthood).

Plurality from the Beginning

For "no major Roman Catholic ministerial office in its modern form can be found in the New Testament—pope, bishop or priest."[11] Rather the scripture describes a plurality of ministries in the Church. There were the functions of apostles, prophets, teachers, evangelists, admonishers for the preaching of the Gospel; the functions of deacons and deaconesses, the distribution of alms, those who cared for the sick, the widows who served the congregations; there were presiders, overseers, shepherds who led. Each of these functions is understood in the Pauline churches as a gift of the Spirit, a share *(clerus)* in the authority of the risen Lord, a charism or calling from God for service to the congregation.[12] There is evidence, in fact, of three models of what we call priesthood, i.e., leaders of the Eucharist in the very early Church: the hierarchical (the apostles and the bishop or presbyters), the charismatic-prophetic (prophets and perhaps teachers), and the communitarian (natural or appointed leaders who presided in the absence of the apostles).[13]

According to the New Testament, there is only one priest and mediator, Jesus Christ. Never is the word "priest" *(hieros)* used for an individual who holds office in the Church.[14] The entire people of God, all believers in fundamental equality, and as a whole, constitute a royal priesthood. "All Christians are priests" in having direct access to God, in offering spiritual sacrifices, and in the preaching of the word. Likewise, baptism, the Lord's supper, and absolution are given to the whole Church.[15] Several scholars have suggested that from a New Testament perspective the word "priest" might be dropped as an exclusive term for those who have specific ministries in the Church, because all believers are priests.[16] Others insist that the relatively late awareness of the Eucharist as sacrifice accounts for the absence of the word "priest" and for the gradual but appropriate emergence of the vocabulary of priesthood in relation to the Christian celebration.[17]

What about church office? Again, there is no word in the New Testament for office; rather an ordinary, nonreligious term is used, *diakonia*, ministry or service, as in serving at table.

Apparently Jesus himself had set a standard which was not to be put aside. It is characteristic that the same logion of Jesus about serving appears six times, in various forms, in the gospel tradition (controversy among the disciples, Last Supper, washing of the feet): the highest should be the server (table server) of all.[18]

Hence there is no office among the followers of Jesus constituted simply according to law and power, like that of state officials; nor is there any office which derives simply from knowledge and dignity, like that of scribes. This is not to deny authority in the Church. But New Testament authority receives its legitimation from service, and develops as a function of *leadership* in the congregation.[19] It derives fundamentally from the risen Christ through those commissioned by him to witness to the resurrection.[20]

Not all New Testament ministries are of equal importance. One group of charisms is more private in nature, others more public and permanent, and some are appointed. Most important are the apostles, witnesses of the resurrection who received a personal commission from Jesus to proclaim the Gospel and who spoke with his authority.[21] Beyond the apostles, upon whom the Church is built in "apostolic succession," the most striking evidence is of a plurality of congregational structures. Paul's churches particularly appear to be "associations of free charismatic ministries." After Paul's death, however, when the expectation of an imminent parousia ended, a system of presbyter and overseer took effect which included a special calling to the ministry of leadership through the imposition of hands.[22]

A complicated development in the post-apostolic era led to the presbyters becoming the sole leaders of the congregation, over against the more charismatic prophets and teachers; the monarchical episcopate emerged in which the original collegiality of overseer and presbyter became that of one overseer with his presbyters and deacons.[23] As the Church spread from the cities to the country, the overseer who had originally been president of a congregation became president of a whole church district, a diocese, in our terms a bishop. This development was legitimate and functional, and indicates that neither Jesus nor the apostles imposed any absolute forms of ministry.[24] The young Church freely adapted to its new situation in society as it attempted to unify the Church and preserve its authentic message after the death of the original witnesses.

It is important to note two elements in this development: (1) The increasing tendency toward institutionalization, uniformity, and a fixed structure of ministry in the presbyteral model is achieved through an increase in the power of one of the members and the decrease in the significance of other ministries, "by a greater emphasis on pastoral authority at the expense of the service of the word" which had had unchallenged priority in the earliest phases of New Testament ministry.[25] (2) And because of the looser charismatic structure of the Pauline churches, and the indication of several models of Eucharistic leadership, there is no reason for not allowing other routes to the ministry; rather, there is good argument for remaining open to all the possibilities that existed in the primitive Church. "The New Testament does not allow the canonization of one congregational structure alone,"[26] and while its own models need not be slavishly imitated, certain elements must endure even in radically different situations. One theologian suggests the ministry of leadership must (a) be a service to the congregation, (b) follow the norm of Jesus, (c) be faithful to the apostolic testimony, (d) reflect a plurality of functions, ministries and charisms.[27] Another suggests two: (a) service of the word, (b) service of unity, adding that "the forms and structures of these services are adaptable and can be changed as required."[28]

Societal Models Emerge and Dominate

As early as the second century, ministerial forms took on the pattern of the Roman civil service with the bishop as the civil head of a region, and presbyters and deacons as lower officials. The medieval class of clerics derives from a series of earlier changes: in the fourth century, the granting of special privileges, immunities and titles; in the fifth, traditional clothing and monastic tonsure; in the sixth, the increasing requirement of celibacy; in the eighth, Latin as the clerical language, special training, and later the breviary.[29] Thus "sociological factors contributed to the rise of a special caste . . ., underlined by the privileges allotted them in civil law" and these "spiritual men" came to be understood as of higher moral value than the laity, with whom they were often seen in contrast rather than unity.[30] Theologically, this class of clerics was understood as distinguished by the single cultic power of offering the sacrifice of the mass, to the diminishment of the New Testament centrality of preaching the word and of the priesthood of all believers in Christ's one priesthood.[31] It is obvious that the historically conditioned character of these practical and theological developments cannot and has not been considered normative or irreversible. There is no strong argument against new structures of ministry from the historical development of the priesthood.

This can be seen clearly when we compare the statements of the magisterium on the priesthood. The Catholic view of office was fixed at the Council of Trent, which emphasized a visible priesthood with exclusive powers in relation to the sacrifice of the mass and penance, an indelible sacramental character and the existence of a hierarchy of bishops, priests and deacons.[32] These dogmatic decisions confirmed the medieval priesthood, with its emphasis on the cultic powers of the priest, the mass as a sacrifice, and the consequent overshadowing of the service of the word and the priesthood of the faithful.

As we know, Vatican Council II returned to a New Testament viewpoint, even as it retained and enriched many traditional structures. While affirming an official priesthood in the Church, it reunited the liturgical-cultic function of priesthood with the prophetic service of the word and pastoral leadership,[33] righting a balance of ministerial tasks that had been askew not just since Trent, but since the second century. With the restoration of the diaconate as a permanent function, the Council underlined the diversity of ministries in the Church.[34] Finally, when we align these views of ministry with the *Constitution on the Church*—the whole Church as the people of God, a collegial ministry of service in the priesthood of the entire community of believers, the importance of its charismatic element, and of the local congregation[35]—we see a response to a new historical and cultural situation that at the same time preserves fidelity to the original sources of the Christian message.

Trent and Vatican II demonstrate the Church in process and the divergence of operative models of its self-understanding. While Trent polemically intensified an institutional model against protestant biblical notions, Vatican II, in a nonpolemic context, consciously returned to New Testament and patristic sources in its self-configuration. And newly aware of its own historical relativity, it produced the *Pastoral Constitution on the Church*, affirming that the human race is involved in a "new stage of history," "a true cultural and social transformation."[36] Eugene Kennedy remarks that the Council fathers "had caught hold of the dominant truth of our time: man's institutions are challenged either to renew themselves or to suffer slow but sure disintegration."[37] Part of the social and cultural transformation of which Vatican II spoke ten years ago was the international women's movement, which from its inception had its voices in the Church, voices raised in protest at the Council itself, which refused to allow a woman to read a paper before the assembly and tried to bar women journalists from attending Council masses or receiving communion during its meetings.[38]

The Experience of Women

The cultural situation to which Christian tradition must be correlated today is the growing and questioning "experience of women," in our case, women in the Church. Like women in the general society, women in the Church experience a new emergence into fuller personhood, central to which is an awareness of mutuality and equality with men that seeks to overcome sexual stereotyping and generally passive role models for women. The message of Jesus, transmitted in the apostolic testimony, has taken on new power for women as we search for an expression of our full Christianity that is adequate to our experience of ourselves and to our cultural situation in society. The discovery of gifts and talents of intellectual, pastoral and personal leadership has forged a variety of ministries in which women today express a new yet very traditional Christian charism. It is a call for service to the Christian congregation and the world that includes the experience of a vocation to the sacramental ministry as well as other ministries in the Church. This experience of vocation on the part of women is traditional in that women have always been involved in the Church's ministry. But while this tradition of female service is long, it is sketchy and often unclear; the roles of women in the Church for the most part seem to have reflected the position of women in society.

Contradictory Evidence

Women are the products of a contradictory tradition, and the strange history of our position in the Church has been widely documented. This history is central to an understanding of the experience of Christian women today. In the Bible, for instance, there is a group of statements which proclaim our equality in creation and redemption. Gen. 1:27 declares "God created man in the image of himself, . . . male and female he created them," an obvious statement of equality. Gen. 2, in which man's rib is the origin of woman, is the account used by Paul and the tradition following to justify the subordination of women. More significant to women, however, is the implication of equality in the words, "This at last is bone from my bones and flesh from my flesh"—woman described as the completion and even perfection of creation.[39] Gen. 3 tells of the curse, woman's subjection because of sin. But "the inferiority of woman is presented as a deterioration from the primitive and unspoiled condition" of creation and man is cursed too.[40] Gal. 3:28, which has become the "women's text," indicates that indeed salvation, i.e., restoration and reconciliation, has come: "All baptised in Christ, you have clothed yourselves in Christ, and there are no more distinctions between Jew and Greek, slave and free, male and female, but all of you are one in Christ Jesus."[41] A final text from Paul, I Cor. 11:11-12, is especially interesting because it occurs in the middle of his statement about women keeping their heads covered and their creation as "the reflection of man's glory" and "for the sake of man": "However, though woman cannot do without man, neither can man do without woman, in the Lord; woman may come from man, but man is born of woman —both come from God." Following this statement of equality, the argument (about woman's head covering when she prophesies or prays in public) ends abruptly with Paul's assertion, "it is not the custom with us!"[42] This last phrase indicates clearly the distinction between theological affirmation and arguments derived from sociological conditions, from custom.

These texts from the Old and New Testaments surround the record of the Church's memory-image of Jesus himself, an amazing record given the historical context. For the pattern is one of Jesus's disregard for the social inferiority and uncleanness of women. Jesus, against social and religious custom, had women friends and helpers, discussed religious matters with Jewish women (who were forbidden to study Torah), broke the blood taboo by acknowledging the faith of the woman with the issue of blood, and the double taboo against talking to women in public and against Samaritans in the incident of the woman at the well. Jesus's pattern was responsive to the times, to the experience of women, and counter-cultural [43] And it was the pattern of the early Christian congregations, in which women played an active role in the ministries or functions of deaconesses, prophets, and in the orders of widows and virgins.[44] This freedom for women, however, diminished as it became apparent in the Church that the return of the Lord was not going to happen immediately, as the Church forgot, or ignored, the theological equality of women in accommodating itself more permanently to its cultural setting. Thus we have to separate the theological and enduring truth of salvation from its cultural matrix, just as we do with Pauline texts which justify slavery.

For a pattern of theological affirmation and cultural equivocation endures throughout post-apostolic Christian history. It becomes more complicated as the fathers and medieval theologians attempt to justify theologically the culturally inferior position of women. Thus we have a frank record of misogynism as the fathers identify women with sexuality and sin (why woman is identified with sex any more than man is a logical conundrum) even as they recognize our redemption in their glorification of virginity and lofty praise of Mary,[45] and the record of the "equality of souls but inequality of sexes" in medieval theology, the title of a recent essay which concludes with the imperative to recognize that the categories underlying medieval theological and psychological accounts of sex (and therefore of women) are as time-bound and relative as the dogmas of Aristotelian biology.[46] The author of this study detects the core of Christian revelation enduring in the medievals' assertion of the moral equivalence of the sexes in marriage, never given full cultural expression but never quite lost. Incidentally, she warns us against the acceptance *today* of an easy notion of "different but equal": "Under every bush of 'complementarity' . . . espy a hierarchical cosmology and a rationalized subordination of women."[47] Finally, the historical-theological subordination (indeed humiliation) of women is intensified and given systematic legal status in canon law.[48]

In the Church's "conquest" of the West it adopted the power models of its culture. And while there are interesting exceptions indicating the theological equality of women (ordained deaconesses until the eleventh, and some say eighteenth century, women martyrs, saints and abbesses whose spiritual and intellectual gifts caused male observers to remark that they had transcended their sex to become truly "men"), the acquiescence of the Church to the cultural oppression of women was almost complete.[49] The most charitable interpretation is that it was also unconscious.

New Consciousness

Today that interpretation is impossible. The position of women in secular society has shifted so radically that the Church, in its public statements, has taken notice. The *Pastoral Constitution on the Church*, for example, states that women have been ". . . denied the right and freedom to choose a husband, to embrace a state of life, or to acquire an education or cultural benefits equal to those recognized for men." And it teaches that "with respect to the fundamental rights of the person, every type of discrimination, whether social or cultural, whether based on sex, race, color, social condition, language or religion, is to be overcome and eradicated as contrary to God's intent."[50] And *Pacem in Terris:*

> it is obvious to everyone that women are now taking a part in public life. This is happening more rapidly perhaps in nations with a Christian tradition, and more slowly, but broadly, among peoples who have inherited other traditions or cultures. Since women are becoming ever more conscious of their human dignity, they will not tolerate being treated as inanimate objects or mere instruments, but claim, both in domestic and in public life, the rights and duties that befit a human person.[51]

Statements can be multiplied, but just let us add the recent words of Pope Paul on the International Women's Year: "What is most urgent is . . . to labor everywhere to have discovered, respected and protected the rights and prerogatives of every woman in her life—educational, professional, civic, social, religious—whether single or married."[52]

These official statements follow in the wake of the early modern popes resisting the inroads of the enlightenment and the industrial and medical revolutions on the traditional role of women. While some progress was made, the modern Church resisted until very recently the full equality of women. Our place was in the home or in traditional religious life, and emancipation was a sad result of the dechristianization of modern society.[53] And yet, as *Pacem in Terris* states, the secular emancipation of women took place first and more rapidly in Christian societies. Why? Could it be that the message of the Gospel, submerged in oppressive cultural forms, acted as a leaven in surprising ways? Some women would like to think this is the case, that the emergent call for our full humanity is not anti-gospel and anti-Church, but arises precisely from the Gospel itself preserved in the living tradition of the Christian community.

This, I think, is a serious issue for us and for authority in the Church. Some feminists maintain that the Christian Churches are the ultimate bastions of feminine oppression, constituted by patriarchal systems and mythologies reaching far back to ancient Near Eastern forms. Patriarchy is so deeply embedded in Judaeo-Christian traditions that both doctrine and practice are "beyond redemption."[54] Others claim that the substantive Christian message can be separated from patriarchal forms and language. Among the latter are women who have moved into the Church's plurality of ministries, who find their source of feminine hope in the actions of Jesus and the message of the Gospel, who experience their own liberation and call to the Church's ministry as the action of grace.[55]

Women faithful to their own experience, to conscience and common insight, have banded in a new sisterhood, a "fourth world." We in the West see our relationship to other oppressed groups in the world, and the consonance of our joint demands for liberation, justice and peace. We recognize, at the same time, that our oppression is not the same as that of the third world;[56] we know that we participate in the oppression of class and race even as we struggle against the oppression due to sex.[57] We recognize therefore that women's issues are part of all social issues relevant to justice in the world. We recognize further that even in the West, our sisterhood is torn by the issues of abortion, radical separatism, anti-male hostility, that our emancipation into new freedom is not without the loss of many old securities, that we risk isolation, loneliness, ridicule. Women ask what word the Church has for us today and whether it can possibly mediate the Gospel to women without their full participation in its ministry.

The Pain and the Options

We know that our own experience has to be the fundamental source for our reflection as we shape our future,[58] that "as in every liberation movement in history, the freeing of women must be principally the work of women" for "no oppressor willingly hands over his power (or what he thinks is power) to his restive vassal."[59] Will sisterhood be able to emerge into a community of women *and* men?[60] Or will serious women drop out of the Church, withdraw their energies because no support, no home is to be found there but only tokenism, half-way gestures, pious words in solemn assemblies of men? How many of us would agree with the statement that ". . . at this point in history the church is in the somewhat comical position of applauding women's legal, professional, and political emancipation in secular society while keeping them in the basement of its own edifice?"[61]

Some among us maintain that answers to the dilemmas of women are indeed found in the Christian tradition, in its Gospel of reconciliation, its political and liberation thought, its theologies of religious transcendence. These are women and men who have urged the Church, authorities and congregations alike, to think and act in new ways, to choose imagination over the violence of authoritarian structures of power, prestige and caste.[62] We ask the Church, its all-male hierarchy and its male-dominated diocesan structures, not just to permit our thinking in new ways but to join with us, to demonstrate that the power of the Gospel is strong enough to reverse the pattern of history where "no oppressor ever willingly handed over what he thinks is power." It seems that in our heightened consciousness of the past and our responsibility for the future a "grand option" is imminent. The Church can choose freely to affirm fully the personhood of women, or it can continue to equivocate in a way that is intolerable to our human and Christian experience.

A Model of the Church

It seems clear that the developing tradition of the Church and its ministry should be correlated with the experience of contemporary women in such a way as to legitimate female ordination. The variety, flexibility and charismatic structure of New Testament ministries offer ample precedent for the recognition of the pastoral service, natural and charismatic leadership, and the service of the word which many women are already performing and for the calling women already experience to sacramental ordination. Conversely, the experience of women in the Church—their liberation to fuller personhood—could be used to open up a richer image of the Church and of its ministry, quite in continuity with the New Testament and the renewal initiated by Vatican II. The full affirmation of women's ministry would reverberate on the whole Church, on men in the Church and on the Church as a male institution; and the Christian tradition could be more fully searched through the sacramental participation of women to illuminate the Christian experience of women today.

Fuller Sign in Sacrament

Rather than a "theology of women" in which we are a special case, an oddity to be accounted for, the correlation of the Church's tradition with the experience of women might result in a new theology of the Church as sacrament. As the sacrament of the incarnation of Christ into all of humanity, the Church would fittingly express the duality and mutuality of the human sexes and its service to both by male and female ordination. It would be a fuller sacrament of the one priesthood of Christ in the whole people of God and of the apostolic witness of the message of Jesus to both men and women if both men and women participated in all its ministries. It would be a clearer sacrament of the transformation of the priesthood from medieval to New Testament patterns begun at Vatican II: the transformation of the clerical priesthood into a ministry of service, the uniting of the cult to the ministry of the word, the service of the unity in which there are no patterns of domination but the collegiality of all Christians in the plurality of functions. New routes to the ministry would thus be opened, uniting charismatic and communitarian leadership with appointed ordination. And the eschatological nature of the Church would be more clearly signalled in today's society: the new order of things promised as the Church moves in history toward the kingdom of God.

As sacrament of God's self-gift for the reconciliation of all persons, the Church would embody the Christian message of equality, freedom and love as a causally effective sign to itself and to the world. This sacrament would include the Church as institution in a sign of its care for ordered and efficient planning in the organization of *all* its personnel, women and men, for pastoral action and for an effective and authentic mission founded on apostolic testimony and succession. The institutional-legal side of the Church would not dominate, however, but would signal its mystery, the interior communion of women and men in Christ and the Spirit, a pilgrim people together in exodus toward the reign of God. Internally, it would sacramentalize its message in the preaching of the word, proclaiming the Gospel in the variety of pastoral ministries, and in the breaking of the bread and other liturgical gestures which flow from and move toward the Eucharistic celebration, all shared by women and men. As such, it would be the sacrament of the word, proclaimer of the Gospel to which it is bound, a message and a God whose continuing revelation it does not control. Finally, it would be an authentic sign as servant, not only lending its strength to the forces of healing and reconciliation in the world but *leading* by its prophetic determination to deal with the roots of injustice and oppression, rather than symptoms. The Church's criticism of policies and attitudes which deny the dignity of individuals and peoples, classes, races and sexes would have the power of authenticity only if it had seen carefully to its own house.

New Expression of Old Tradition

Such a Church would be a sacrament of its own tradition, of its fidelity to the Gospel and to its times. It would be traditional in its concern for the authentic handing on of the word to both women and men, and would signal this in its willingness to relinquish outdated forms, worldly securities, titles, honors and prestige, the better to conform to the tradition of the poor and crucified Jesus.[63] It would be traditional in this larger sense by breaking with "traditions" as it has broken with them in the past—in reversing its stands on usury, persecution of heretics, the single reception of penance, the vernacular liturgy, slavery, war, racism, crusades against Moslem and Jew, democracy, socialism, communism, modern science, philosophy, history and exegesis—and developing a more sensitive conscience in areas where it clings to outmoded social forms and theological arguments. Going against traditional practice has been called for many times and is especially now, in a Church newly conscious of its sinfulness, past and present, of the times it has sided with the rich and powerful over the poor and powerless, with vested interest over truth in scholarship.

Tradition, like the word of God, is a two-edged sword; it can mean betrayal as well as handing on.[64] Lest it betray its own word, the Church would reject its own misogynist traditions, in which women are considered less than fully human, less than fully redeemed, as well as those symbolic traditions in which we are glorified and removed as more than human.

In this Church, ministry would also be a sacrament, indeed a revelation of its faith and values.[65] Because it would include, in its pastoral, liturgical and social expressions, a full representation of classes, races and sexes, it would witness to belief in "neither Greek nor Jew, slave nor free, male nor female." It would reveal ministry as service, especially of the powerless, and as oriented toward the fullness of its own life in word and sacrament. Signalling the importance of the variety of ministries in its liturgical life, it would at once make clear the importance of its liturgical life for all its ministries.[66] Recognizing that Christian salvation is essentially sacramental and that the service of the word is integral to the sacraments, none of its official ordinations would be closed, on principle, to any members of the priestly people engaged in the ministry of the word. The mutual involvement of men and women in the sacramental ministry would be an intrinsic sign of the service of unity required by the Gospel.

Women today are already engaged in this ministry of the word and in pastoral service. We share in caring for the poor, the hungry, the sick, the elderly; we administer social service agencies, perform pastoral functions in parishes, prisons, campuses; we teach children, young people and adults and have joined our brothers in pastoral and theological reflection and in the preaching of the word; we counsel and give retreats. Our assumption of these ministries reflects our status in secular society, where the emancipation of women has opened the educational and cultural opportunities closed to us in the past. The old theological arguments against the ordination of women rested on our subjected position in society, our ignorance. And, yes, they made some sense in the past. They obviously do not make sense today. In the patriarchal ancient world, only men could perform the functions of leadership because only men had the necessary authority and mobility. Now, when the subjected, ignorant woman of the past has ceased to exist, at least in many parts of the world, when a new cultural environment means equally educated, mobile, theologically and pastorally competent women, no obstacle prevents the church's recognition.[67]

Indeed, women's ministry is already recognized by the Church, but only as an auxiliary service. Women are allowed to help, to volunteer, to work in limited ways, to have a miniscule representation in the decision-making bodies of dioceses and parishes, and often are not adequately paid. As long as women are barred from full recognition and completion of the service many are already fulfilling, barred in fact from the liturgical functions usually assigned to eight-year-old boys, the language of the Church is unfortunately clear in what it is saying to women and to the world about women. In the theology of sacrament, language clarifies the ritual action which in turn infuses the words with deepened meaning. In the attempt to purify our everyday language of sexist overtones, we recognize its power as reflector and shaper of attitudes and beliefs. We in the Church strive to purify our religious language of the implications of patriarchal dominance, to find new words for God. When the Church's language, its gestures and its actions become a real sacrament, sign and cause of the Gospel affirmation of "neither male nor female," it will use its fullest human vocabulary in speaking to our experience today.

The Church giving official recognition to the ministry of women will be more than the ordination of those who already experience God's call and who are personally suitable and adequately prepared. It will be more than recognition that in certain areas women ministers are already acceptable to the people of God. It will be a sacramental word, a gesture of loving acknowledgement to all women in the Christian community and to the world of its commitment to women as full citizens in its own realm and to the societal liberation of women in all spheres. It will be speaking its truth boldly and become a really credible sign of its concern for fully half the human race under the sign of the Gospel. It will be a sign of its recognition of the charismatic working of the Spirit in the Church, a sign that its sacramental life is bound to that Spirit and not to canon law or the cultural conditions of the past.

New Reality of Church and Ministry

The ordination of women will not mean admission to the clerical caste, as some fear,[68] or as the defensive jokes and cartoons—ridicule of the issue—suggest. Rather it would further the transformation of the priesthood: by admission of those who have traditionally only served, the sign will be clear. It will help to transform the ministry from a predominantly cultic role to a ministerial one, from a symbol of prestige to a symbol of service, releasing the imagination of half the Church's population into fuller operation as the Church moves into the future.[69] The priesthood will no longer be a male-dominated club with restricted membership, a bureaucratic hierarchy, but an open, collegial spiritual service of unity. Nor will ordination do away with the variety of functions in the Church. Only some ministries appropriately call for official appointment and sacramental ordination. But those women who have led a community in prayer on campuses, in homes for the aged, in hospitals, prisons, neighborhoods, who have counseled retreatants in their own discovery of God or the experience of reconciliation recognize that the ability to celebrate the eucharistic meal, to baptize new life into the Church, to give absolution is the appropriate sacramental expression of the liberating action of Christ's grace in their ministries. For our tradition, in which sacramental experience is central,[70] the ordination of women will be a sign of the Church's attentiveness to the concrete experience of its people, of its awareness of where God's grace is working in people's lives, where the authentic ministry of the word is occurring.

Emphasis on historical consciousness and on tradition raises the question of whether women seek ordination because of developments in the secular sphere or in the Church.[71] Clearly it is because of both —the Church reflects its culture even as it transcends culture as a prophetic voice. But there is a distinction between the women's movement in the Church and in society. In the secular sphere, women justly demand equal rights, and affirmative action programs insure and protect those rights. In the Church it is different. In a certain sense, no one has rights or even powers. The priesthood belongs to the whole Church. And all of us, women and men, are receivers and sharers. The grace of God in Christ and the Spirit is pure gift, unowed, incomprehensible benevolence. Intrinsic to the whole pattern of sacramental mediation of grace in the Church is that it cannot be hoarded, claimed, deserved. Nor is it rare or intermittent. It is given freely as it is received freely. The ordination of women in the Church is an appropriate sign in our time of the generosity and freedom of Christian grace.

Finally, there is the issue of what is "pastorally prudent." Are people ready for this? Will it be a stumbling block to faith for the community? Will it appear that the Church has been wrong in the past if it now goes against so enduring a practical tradition? And from the perspective of women, will it appear that women are merely being used, once again, this time to fill the places of thousands of departed men? Certainly not all people are ready. For some (including some women) the very idea is distasteful, and this reaction reflects the depth of the cultural taboo—the feeling that women's reproductive processes are unclean, or that women represent the temptation or evil of sex, or that women cannot bear the authority of leadership, be theologically competent, or be trusted with significant functions in the Church. All of these taboos have been disproven, but they remain. The gradual ordination of women to the diaconate and priesthood will be a profoundly educational sign of the human and theological truth of the matter. The ordination of women cannot be a stumbling block to faith because an authentic faith must recognize the full personhood of women, that we are not lesser human beings, auxiliaries, instruments, as the language of the Church on the "use" of women in discussions of sexuality used to suggest. Women look for a new language, not a sign that we are suddenly useful because of the shortage of men but that the new ministries we perform are genuinely needed by the Church.

The Church: Entrenched or Response-able?

Breaking this long tradition will not mean an admission that the Church was wrong in the past, but simply the admission that it adapted itself to taken-for-granted social patterns in secular society. The Church is not, and never has been, a static entity; its tradition is a living Church in process. And a significant part of the Church's experience in modern times is a new awareness of its own historical process. This awareness makes it more responsible for its decisions, attitudes and gestures as it conforms to the demands of the Gospel in new times. A Church responsible for its freedom and responsive to its own tradition and the contemporary situation cannot ignore the experience of half its membership, and half the world to which it claims to be a sacrament of Christ. Will its environment remain "an unhealthy climate for women?"

The insight is already available for the Church to recognize the ministry of women through sacramental ordination. The issue is not peripheral but reflects the Roman Church's whole posture toward people, women and men, and toward the central human questions of the future. The ordination of women will not solve all the problems of the Church's mission; it is no panacea. It will simply be a very effective symbol, sign and cause, of the Church's intention to engender a future in which it struggles to become the sacrament of the full personhood of all people in the grace of Christ.

Notes

1. See Karl Rahner, "Theology and Anthropology," *Theological Investigations* IX, tr. Graham Harrison (New York: Herder and Herder, 1973), pp. 28-45; Paul Tillich, *Systematic Theology* I (Chicago: University of Chicago Press, 1951), pp. 3-5; David Tracy, "The Task of Fundamental Theology," *Journal of Religion* 54:1 (Jan., 1974), pp. 13-18.

2. See Emily C. Hewitt, "Anatomy and Ministry: Shall Women Be Priests?" *Women and Orders*, ed. Robert L. Heyer (New York: Paulist Press, 1974), pp. 39-55; Emily C. Hewitt and Suzanne R. Hiatt, *Women Priests: Yes or No?* (New York: Seabury Press, 1973), pp. 57-70.

3. Cf. Karl Rahner, "Scripture and Tradition," *Theological Investigations* VI, tr. Karl H. and Boniface Kruger (Baltimore: Helicon, 1969), pp. 98-103.

4. Cf. "Dogmatic Constitution on the Church," *The Documents of Vatican II*, ed. Walter M. Abbott, S.J. (New York: Guild Press, 1966), pp. 14-37.

5. Cf. Rene Laurentin, "The New Testament and the Present Crisis of Ministry," *Office and Ministry in the Church*, Concilium 80, ed. Bas Van Irsel and Roland Murphy (New York: Herder and Herder, 1972), pp. 7-18; Richard McBrien, *Church: The Continuing Quest* (Paramus, N.J.: Newman Press, 1970), pp. 5-21; Avery Dulles, *Models of the Church* (New York: Doubleday, 1974), pp. 7-30.

6. Dulles, pp. 43-96.

7. Karl Rahner, *The Shape of the Church to Come*, tr. and intro. Edward Quinn (New York: Seabury Press, 1974), pp. 56-63, 93-132. In describing such a church, Rahner advocates the "relative" ordination of married men, and of women, in relation to particular Christian communities.

8. Cf. Richard McBrien, Review of Haye van der Meer, *Women Priests in the Catholic Church? Commonweal* 101:2 (Oct. 11, 1974), pp. 44-45.

9. Cf. Committee on Pastoral Research and Practices of the National Conference of Catholic Bishops, "Theological Reflections on the Ordination of Women," *Review for Religious* 32:2 (March, 1973), p. 221.

10. Rahner, *Shape of the Church to Come*, p. 24.

11. John McKenzie, "Ministerial Structures in the New Testament," *The Plurality of Ministries*, Concilium 74, ed. Hans Kung and Walter Kasper (New York: Herder and Herder, 1972), p. 13.

12. Hans Küng, *The Church* (New York: Sheed and Ward, 1967), pp. 385; 393-406.

13. Geffrey Kelly, "Priesthood in the Context of Brotherhood," *Priestly Brothers* (Wheaton, Maryland: National Assembly of Religious Brothers, 1975), p. 11. On the question of who presided at the Eucharist, see Myles Bourke, "Reflections on Church Order in the New Testament," *Catholic*

Biblical Quarterly 30:4 (October, 1968), pp. 499-507; Raymond Brown, *Priest and Bishop. Biblical Reflections* (New York: Paulist Press, 1970), pp. 40-45. Bourke distinguishes the first two models and implicitly allows for the third.

14. Brown, p. 13.

15. Küng, pp. 370-380. But see also Brown, pp. 14-15, who maintains that I Pet 2:9 "does not primarily concern priestly function (in particular, cultic sacrifice) but priestly holiness. . . . One cannot argue from the royal priesthood of Christians against the existence of a Christian specialized cultic priesthood." Brown argues that all Christians share in priesthood through baptism and confirmation but that the ordained priesthood is a different thing.

16. Hans P. Küng, *Why Priests?*, tr. Robert C. Collins, S.J. (New York: Doubleday, 1972); Alexandre Ganoczy, " 'Splendours and Miseries' of the Tridentine Doctrine of Ministries," *Office and Ministry in the Church*, p. 84.

17. Brown, pp. 16-20; Kelly, 7; 16, nn. 3, 4. See also Bourke, 505 on the New Testament appropriation of the Jewish ordination rite in relation to the celebration of the Christian Eucharist, and Daniel Donovan, "Brown, Küng and the Christian Ministry," *The Ecumenist* 10 (September-October, 1972), pp. 88-94, on their divergent approaches to issues of priesthood and ministry.

18. Küng, *Why Priests?*, p. 39.

19. *Ibid.*, pp. 39-40; Peter Kearney, "New Testament Incentives for a Different Ecclesiastical Order?" *Office and Ministry in the Church*, p. 57. See Brown, pp. 27-28, on the notion of service as primarily service to Jesus Christ.

20. Bourke, pp. 495-498.

21. *Ibid.*; McKenzie, pp. 14-15.

22. Küng, *The Church*, pp. 405-406, Bourke, pp. 504-505.

23. Bourke, p. 503.

24. Ernst Niermann, "Priest," *Sacramentum Mundi* 5 ed. Karl Rahner et al. (New York: Herder and Herder, 1970), p. 97.

25. Andre Lemaire, "From Services to Ministries: 'Diakoniai' in the First Two Centuries," *Office and Ministry in the Church*, p. 48.

26. Küng, *Why Priests?*, p. 49.

27. *Ibid.*, p. 50.

28. Lemaire, p. 48; cf. Kearney, pp. 61-63.

29. Küng, *Why Priests?*, p. 55.

30. Niermann, p. 99.

31. *Ibid.*

32. Ganoczy, pp. 75-86.

33. "Decree on the Ministry and Life of Priests," *Documents of Vatican II*, pp. 538-546.

34. "Decree on the Church's Missionary Activity," *ibid.*, p. 605; cf. "Constitution on the Church," *ibid.*, p. 55.

35. "Constitution on the Church," pp. 24-37, 77, 30, 50.

36. "Pastoral Constitution on the Church in the Modern World," *ibid.*, p. 202.

37. Eugene Kennedy, *The People are the Church* (New York: Doubleday, 1969), p. 25.

38. Sister Albertus Magnus McGrath, O.P., *What a Modern Catholic Believes About Women* (Chicago: Thomas More Press), p. 5.

39. George H. Tavard, *Woman in Christian Tradition* (Notre Dame: University of Notre Dame Press, 1973), p. 8.

40. Mary Jo Weaver, "Women in the Church: Some Historical Perspectives," unpublished paper.

41. See Constance F. Parvey, "The Theology and Leadership of Women in the New Testament," *Religion and Sexism: Images of Women in the Jewish and Christian Scriptures*, ed. Rosemary Reuther (New York: Simon and Schuster), pp. 132-136.

42. *Ibid.*, pp. 125-218; McGrath, pp. 29-42.

43. Cf. Krister Stendahl, *The Bible and the Role of Women* (Philadelphia: Fortress Press, 1966); Alicia Craig Faxon, *Women and Jesus* (New York: United Church Press, 1973); Leonard Swidler "Jesus Was a Feminist," *Catholic World* (Jan., 1971), pp. 177-183; Rachel Conrad Wahlberg, *Jesus According to Woman* (New York: Paulist, 1975).

44. Charles R. Meyer, "Ordained Women in the Early Church," *Chicago Studies* 4:3 (Fall, 1965), pp. 285-309; *Man of God: A Study of the Priesthood* (New York: Paulist, 1975), pp. 58-85.

45. Rosemary Ruether, "Misogynism and Virginal Feminism," *Religion and Sexism*, pp. 150-183.

46. Eleanor Commo McLaughlin, *Religion and Sexism*, pp. 213-266.

47. *Ibid.*, p. 260.

48. See Clara Maria Henning, "Canon Law and the Battle of the Sexes," *Religion and Sexism*, pp. 267-291.

49. Mary Daly, *The Church and the Second Sex* (New York: Harper, 1968), pp. 95-98.

50. *The Documents of Vatican II*, pp. 227-228.

51. John XXIII, *Pacem in Terris* (New York: The American Press, 1963), No. 14, p. 14.

52. *The National Catholic Reporter* 11:29 (May 16, 1975), p. 5.

53. Daly, pp. 107-117.

54. Mary Daly, *Beyond God the Father: Toward a Philosophy of Women's Liberation* (Boston: Beacon Press, 1973). In another vein, C. S. Lewis (*God in the Dock: Essays on Theology and Ethics*, ed. Walter Hooper (Grand Rapids: Eerdmans, 1970), pp. 230-239), maintains that patriarchal and sexual role models are so central to Christianity that their removal from doctrine and practice would result in a new religion.

55. See, e.g., Letty M. Russell, *Human Liberation in a Feminist Perspective* (Philadelphia: Westminster, 1974); Alice L. Hageman, ed., *Sexist Religion and Women in the Church* (New York: Association Press, 1974); Sarah Bentley Doely, ed., *Women's Liberation and the Church* (New York: Association Press, 1970); Arlene Swidler, *Woman in a Man's Church* (New York: Paulist, 1972).

56. See June O'Connor, "Liberation Theologies and the Women's Movement," *Horizons* 1:2 (Spring, 1975), pp. 103-113.

57. Rosemary Reuther, "Women, Blacks and Latins: Rivals or Partners in Liberation Theology," address given at the University of Chicago, May, 1975.

58. See Karl Rahner, "The Position of Woman in the New Situation in which the Church Finds Herself," *Theological Investigations* VIII, tr. David Bourke (New York: Herder and Herder, 1971), pp. 75-93.

59. Harvey Cox, "Eight Theses on Female Liberation," *Christianity and Crisis* 31:16 (Oct. 4, 1971), p. 199.

60. Rosemary Reuther, "Sexism and the Theology of Liberation," *Christian Century* 90:49 (Dec. 12, 1973), pp. 1224-1229.

61. Mary Daly, *The Church and the Second Sex*, pp. 202-203.

62. Dorothy Donnelly, C.S.J., "The Gifted Woman: New Style for Ministry," *Women in a Strange Land*, ed. Clare Benedicks Fischer, Betsy Brenneman, Anne McGrew Bennett (Philadelphia: Fortress Press, 1975), p. 90.

63. Cf. Sister Marie Augusta Neal, "Social Encyclicals: Role of Women," *Network Quarterly* 3:2 (Spring, 1975).

64. Russell, p. 73.

65. Gregory Baum, "Ministry in the Church," *Women and Orders*, pp. 57-66.

66. Cf. Karl Rahner, "Priestly Existence," *Theological Investigations* III, tr. Karl H. and Boniface Kruger (Baltimore: Helicon Press, 1967), pp. 239-262.

67. Cf. Haye van der Meer, *Women Priests in the Catholic Church?* (Philadelphia: Temple University Press, 1973).

68. Ann Kelley and Anne Walsh, "Ordination: A Questionable Goal for Women," *Women and Orders*, pp. 67-74.

69. Mary Daly, *The Church and the Second Sex*, p. 207; Nelle Morton, "Preaching the Word," *Sexist Religion and Women in the Church*, pp. 29-45.

70. Cf. Anne E. Patrick, "Conservative Case for the Ordination of Women," *New Catholic World* 218:1305 (May/June, 1975), pp. 108-111.

71. "Theological Reflections on the Ordination of Women," p. 219.

11

Women's Ordination: Effective Symbol of the Church's Struggle

Richard McBrien

RICHAM IP. MCBRIEN, Professor of Theology at Boston College, is the author of CHURCH: THE CONTINUING QUEST and THE REMAKING OF THE CHURCH: AN AGENDA FOR REFORM. He is the Director of the Institute for the Study of Religious Education and Service.

From the outset, I should say that I agree with Professor Carr's paper in whole and in almost every part. I shall necessarily focus upon those parts (or better: those parts of parts) which I should want to question, qualify or even dissent from. Our sense of fundamental agreement, however, should not be obscured in the process. Indeed, I shall also underline some points with which I find myself particularly sympathetic. My critical comments are listed not necessarily in order of importance but according to the sequence in which the material appears in the previous article.

How "Central" Ordination?

There is at least a trace of inconsistency between statements made in the opening and closing paragraphs of Professor Carr's paper. There is a claim at the beginning that the ordination issue is "*central* to the very shape of Catholicism for the future," but the end of that article states that "ordination of women will not solve all the problems of the Church's mission; it is no panacea." Insofar as there may in fact be some ambivalence here, I want to support the latter judgment over the former. I do agree fully with the concluding judgment that the admission of women to ordination would be "a very effective symbol . . . of the Church's intention . . . to become the sacrament of the full personhood of all people in the grace of Christ"; and I correspondingly want to qualify the initial suggestion about the issue's centrality. The central issues for Christians today are not unlike those identified by Dietrich Bonhoeffer in 1944: how can Christ be Lord even of those with no religion, and what is to be the place of the Church in this new situation? The ordination question is logically, or theo-logically, a subordinate issue within the second major question, but a subordinate issue of great, even urgent, historical and practical importance.

While I agree that our theology proceeds according to a bipolar course, that is, conjoining both Christian tradition and our common human experience, I notice that the pole of "common human experience" is reductively identified with "the experience of women, as reflected in the contemporary women's movement within and on the boundaries of the Church." If the Church is indeed to pursue the bipolar method of theological reflection, then one cannot restrict "common human experience" to women, and, *a fortiori*, to women identified with the "contemporary women's movement within and on the boundaries of the Church." I say this without prejudice to Harvey Cox's belief, cited in the previous article, that "the freeing of women must be principally the work of women."

Vatican II: Ambiguous or Directive?

From my viewpoint, Professor Carr renders an excessively kind judgment upon the Second Vatican Council's concept of ordained ministry when she proposes that the Council "returned to a New Testament viewpoint, even as it retained and enriched many traditional structures." The point was that the Council tended to reunite the liturgical-cultic function of the priesthood with the prophetic service of the word and pastoral leadership, and it restored the diaconate as a permanent function within the Church.

But the Council also is the source of that ambiguous, and often quoted, text that the common priesthood of the faithful differs from the ministerial or hierarchical priesthood "in essence and not only in degree" (*Lumen Gentium*, n.10). Moreover, the Council continued to act upon the assumption that there is indeed a clear-cut New Testament blueprint for the various ordained ministries of the episcopate, the presbyterate, and the diaconate, a position from which Professor Carr, and the various scholars she cites, vigorously dissent. Finally, the Council never once hinted at the question of the ordination of women. On the one hand, the Council clearly condemned discrimination throughout the world based on sex (*Gaudium et Spes*, n.29), but did not even acknowledge the existence of a problem of discrimination within its own borders, and specifically with regard to the exclusion of women from positions of significant pastoral leadership.

The Lone Frontier

I am not persuaded that "The Church in Process: Engendering the Future" effectively and finally deals with the now lonely negative argument from the traditional practice of the Church. It reappears most recently in the statement issued by Archbishop Bernardin in the name of the Administrative Board of the National Conference of Catholic Bishops.* Though an excellent case has been made for the intrinsic possibility of such ordinations in the light of ample evidence of flexibility and change within the history of the Catholic Church itself, the Bernardin argument (or perhaps better: the counterargument) is not directly addressed; namely, how do we account for the fact that in the Church's entire two thousand year history women have in fact never been ordained to the priesthood or presbyterate?

My own response has been that this counterargument is itself out of step with our traditional ascetical insistence upon seeing all reality "subspecie aeternitatis" (Ed: from God's eternal point of view; or, in the light of God's plan). The fact that the Church has not ordained women to the priesthood during its first two thousand years of existence would be a serious problem if indeed the history of the Church were about to end or were at least past its half-way mark. But suppose we do not in fact collectively pollute ourselves to death before the year 20,000. How will the first two thousand years of the Church's existence appear to some of our successors in the faith in the year 19,975, for example? Will we not look a bit like the "early Church" to them? And do we not now justify and accept changes, even substantial changes, in the discipline of the Church if they were made "long ago" in the second, or third, or fourth centuries—and even later? We readily acknowledge the need and the inevitability of a period of consolidation in the history of so intricate and so complex a multicultural and multinational institutional reality as the Christian Church. Who is to say, looking at matters "subspecie aeternitatis," that we are not still in such a period of youthful consolidation? The argument from the constant practice of the Church, in other words, may be an argument with which to contend, but it is not insurmountable and we ought not to suggest by our silence that we are utterly perplexed by its challenge.

Where Are the Perimeters?

Finally, I am concerned about Professor Carr's reluctance to articulate her own position *vis-a-vis* the views of some contemporary feminists to whom she occasionally refers. I have in mind specifically the views associated with my colleague, Professor Mary Daly, that "the Christian Churches are the ultimate bastions of feminine oppression, constituted by patriarchal systems and mythologies" and that "patriarchy is so deeply embedded in Judaeo-Christian traditions that both doctrine and practice are beyond redemption."

Later in her presentation, Professor Carr proposes that the best ecclesiological base for the correlation of the Church's tradition with the experience of women would be the theology of the Church as sacrament, and specifically as "the sacrament of the incarnation of Christ into all of humanity." But it is the view of Professor Daly and other post-Christian, if not anti-Christian, feminists who agree with her, that Jesus's maleness is an insurmountable barrier to women's acceptance of the central Christian mystery of the Incarnation. She speaks indeed of the problem of "Christolatry."

I suggest that those of us committed to the ordination of women cannot rest content with the cataloguing of opinions. "Some say, on the one hand, . . . but others say. . . ." I think it is clear from the entire context of Professor Carr's paper that she does not, in fact, accept the anti-Church, Christolatry hypothesis. But one should not have to infer something so important from a contextual analysis.

We cannot ignore the lesson of the defeats of equal rights amendments in both New York and New Jersey. The margin of defeat—and the defeat was overwhelming—was supplied in large measure by women themselves. Rightly or wrongly, the advocates of the equal rights amendments were perceived as antimarriage, antifamily, and even as proponents of lesbian life styles. If we do not make clear to our more conservative critics within the Church that the argument for the ordination of women does not depend in the slightest degree on the anti-Church, anti-Christian views of some radical feminists, and indeed that we explicitly reject such views, then we cannot complain that we have been forced to bear burdens not of our own making.

Three Affirmations

There are three points of particular agreement with which I should like to conclude. First, I should want to endorse the selection of the sacrament model as the ecclesiological starting-point and foundation for an argument in favor of the ordination of women. The sacrament model is more effective than any other, in my judgment, in getting at the heart of the Church's distinctive reality and mission.

I should also want to applaud the observation that the oppressed in one situation may themselves be oppressors in another. "We know that we participate in the oppression of class and race even as we struggle against the oppression due to sex." All just causes, in other words, are always themselves in need of conversion and repentance. The final Kingdom has come neither for them nor for their opponents.

Finally, I should urge that Professor Carr's concluding sentences be allowed to echo and reverberate throughout the entire North American Church: "The ordination of women will not solve all the problems of the Church's mission; it is no panacea. It will simply be a very effective symbol, sign and cause, of the Church's intention to engender a future in which it struggles to become the sacrament of the full personhood of all people in the grace of Christ."

If that be our central affirmation, then we have set ourselves a course that is at once theologically sound and pastorally realistic.

Note
    *cf. Appendix A.

12

Women Apostles: The Testament of Scripture

Elizabeth Schüssler Fiorenza

ELISABETH SCHÜSSLER FIORENZA studied at the University of Wurzburg and the University of Munster which culminated in a Licentiate in Pastoral Theology, 1963, and a Doctorate in Theology (New Testament) in 1970. Her professional involvements have included Associate Editor of the CATHOLIC BIBLICAL QUARTERLY, JOURNAL OF BIBLICAL LITERATURE, and HORIZONS. Her research and publications have dealt with many areas of Church life, especially the role of women in the Church. Her books (in German) present the priesthood according to the New Testament, and another work addresses ministries of women in the Church. She is currently Associate Professor of theology at the University of Notre Dame.

St. Bernhard is reported to have been praying before the altar of the Madonna. Suddenly Mary opened her mouth and began to speak. "Be silent, be silent!" St. Bernhard cried in desperation: "Women are not allowed to speak in church!"[1] Despite papal and episcopal warnings, we have today broken the silence. Our speaking is compelled by the vision of church expressed in Gal. 3:28 and it is strengthened by a new experience of sisterhood. Since I am by trade an historian, theologian and teacher of the New Testament, my response is decisively determined by the study of early Christianity. Insofar as I have experienced myself as "sister among sisters," it is inspired by the vision of sisterhood or brotherhood which the New Testament calls ecclesia. The fundamental condition of this ecclesial community is pronounced in Mt. 23:8-10:

But you are not to be called rabbi,
For you have one teacher and you all are brothers (and sisters).

And call no one of you on earth "Father"
for you have one father who is in heaven

Neither are you to be called leaders,
for you have one leader, the Christ.

We can safely assume that the author of the Gospel of Matthew
would have extended the list of forbidden titles if he had known mon-
signors, bishops, cardinals or popes.

If we ask what a new understanding[2] of the history of primitive
Christianity could contribute to the theological quest for women's
leadership in the Church, I would like first to look at women's role in
the early Church and then to point out some conclusions in order to
further corroborate the theological ramifications of Professor Anne
Carr's presentation.

Nascent Christian Community

Studies of the socio-cultural conditions[3] of the nascent Christian
movement have shown that sociologically speaking it represented a
socially and religiously deviant group similar to other sectarian
groups in the Judaism of the first century. In distinction to the Sect
of Qumran and the Pharisees, the Jesus movement in Palestine was
not a cultic-exclusive but an inclusive group.[4] It rejected the priestly
laws of Jewish religion and attracted the outcast of its society. Jesus's
followers were not the righteous, pious or powerful of the time, but
tax collectors, sinners and—women, all those who were cultically
unclean and did not belong to the religious establishment or the pious
associations of the day. The inclusive character of Jesus's message
and fellowship made it possible later to broaden the Christian group
and to invite gentiles of all nations into the Christian community
which transcended Jewish as well as hellenistic societal and religious
boundaries.

The theological self-understanding of this early Christian movement is best expressed in the baptismal formula Gal. 3:27-29.[5] In
reciting this formula the newly initiated Christians proclaimed their
vision of an inclusive community. Over and against the cultural-
religious pattern shared by Hellenists and Jews alike, the Christians
affirmed that all social, political and religious differences were abo-
lished in Jesus Christ. The self-understanding of the Christian community eliminated all distinctions of religion, race, class and caste,
and thereby allowed not only gentiles and slaves to assume full leadership in the Christian community but also women. Women were not

marginal figures in this movement but exercised leadership as apostles, prophets, evangelists, missionaries, offices similar to that of Barnabas, Apollos or Paul.[6]

The controversies of Paul with his opponents prove that the leadership of *apostles* was most significant for the nascent Christian movement. According to Paul, apostleship is not limited to the twelve. All those Christians are apostles who were eyewitnesses to the resurrection and who were commissioned by the resurrected Lord to missionary work (I Cor. 9:4). According to Luke only those Christians were eligible to replace Judas who accompanied Jesus in his Galilean ministry and were also eyewitnesses to his resurrection (Acts 1:21). According to all four Gospels women fulfilled these criteria of apostleship enumerated by Paul and Luke. Women accompanied Jesus from Galilee to Jerusalem and witnessed his death (Mk. 14:40 par). Moreover, women were according to all criteria of historical authenticity the first witnesses of the resurrection, for this fact could not have been derived from Judaism nor invented by the primitive Church.[7]

That these women were not left anonymous but identified by name suggests that they played an important role in the Christian movement in Palestine. Their leader appears to have been Mary Magdalene[8] since all four Gospels transmit her name, whereas the names of the other women vary. Thus, according to the Gospel traditions women were the primary apostolic witnesses for the fundamental data of the early Christian faith: they were eyewitnesses of Jesus's ministry, his death, his burial and his resurrection.

An unbiased reading of Rom. 16:7 provides us with one instance in the New Testament where a woman is called apostle. There is no reason to understand Junia as a short form of the male name Junianus, when Junia was a well-known name for women at the time. M.J. Lagrange, therefore, suggests that Andronicus and Junia were a missionary couple like Aquila and Prisca.[9] Both were fellow prisoners of Paul. They were Christians before Paul and outstanding figures among the "apostles."

From the very beginning prophets played an eminent role within the early Christian movement. Since they functioned as inspired spokespersons for the resurrected Lord, their authority is based on divine revelations. Paul repeatedly mentions the prophets directly after the apostles. He values the gift of prophecy higher than that of glossolalia. Despite the appearance of false prophets, the prophets still had great authority at the end of the first century as the Apocalypse and Didache indicate. According to Did. 13: 1-7 prophets have the prerogative in the leadership functions at the celebration of the Eucharist. Paul as well as Luke and the Apocalypse[10] document that women exercised leadership as prophets in early Christianity.

Finally, the references to women's leadership in the nascent Christian movement do not limit their activity to the circle of women, nor do they evidence ascetical tendencies (such as Encratite groups which encouraged celibacy and the renunciation of marriage). We know definitely that Prisca was married, whereas we do not know the marital status of women like Mary, Phoebe, Euodia, or Tryphena. These women were not yet defined by their societal sex-roles nor by their relationship to men. Indeed, women's leadership in the primitive Christian community was exceptional not only by the standards of Judaism or the Greco-Roman world, but also by those of the later Christian Church.

Gradual Cultural Compromise

The process of cultural adaptation and ecclesial institutionalization however, progressively limited women's role and influence. Since Jesus did not leave his followers a blueprint for the organization of his community, the early Christians assimilated structures and institutions of Judaism and Hellenism. Whereas in Paul's time leadership roles were still diversified and based on charismatic authority, the process of institutionalization set in gradually toward the end of the first century. In the second and third centuries the leadership shifted from itinerant missionaries to hierarchical offices, from apostles and prophets to local bishops and ruling elders, from charismatic leadership to traditional forms of authority. Whereas the various New Testament authors do not understand Christian leadership in a cultic sense and therefore apply the title "priest" only to Christ and to all Christians, the second and third century documents begin at first to liken Christian ministry to that of the Old Testament or Hellenistic priesthood and then gradually identify Christian leadership with the hierarchical priesthood and cultic sacrifices of Jewish and Greco-Roman religion.[11]

This structural solidification and cultic hierarchization meant at the same time, however, a patriarchalization of the Christian ministry and Church. This process necessarily had to eliminate more and more women from ecclesial leadership roles and had to relegate them to subordinate "feminine" tasks. The more Christianity adapted to the societal and religious institutions of the time and, thus, became a genuine segment of the patriarchal Greco-Roman culture and religion, the more it had to relegate women's leadership to fringe groups or to limit it to roles defined by gender. The orders of deaconesses and widows for example no longer served the whole community but mainly ministered to women.[12] No longer all women exercised leadership functions but only those who, as virgins and widows, transcended sex-roles.

Patriarchy Defined Women's "Place"

A feminist history of the following centuries could demonstrate how difficult it was for the ecclesial establishment to suppress the call and spirit of freedom and responsibility among Christian women.[13] It achieved the elimination of women from ecclesial leadership and theology through woman's domestication under male authority in the home or in celibate communities. Those women who did not comply but who rather were active and leading in various Christian communities were as heretics eliminated from mainstream Christianity. Hand in hand with the elimination and repression of the emancipatory elements within the Church went a theological justification for such a suppression of women's leadership and the patriarchalization of church office. The trajectory of the Pauline tradition which stresses the submission of women on theological grounds reflects this reactionary, patriarchal evolution of the Christian Church. Whether or not Paul himself initiated this patriarchal reaction is discussed by scholars.[14] Certainly, however, the theological justification of the elimination of Christian women from the leadership of the Church was able to claim the authority of Paul without being challenged. Further, the misogynist statements of the Church Fathers and later theologians are not so much due to a faulty anthropology as they are an ideological justification for the discrimination against women in the Christian community.

Even though my review of the early Christian development had to be rather sweeping, it nevertheless demonstrates that it is invalid to deny ordination to women on scriptural grounds. Jesus called women to full fellowship and the Spirit empowered them as apostles, prophets and leaders in the early Church. If the Church is indeed built on women, apostles and prophets, then it must also acknowledge women as the successors of the apostles and prophets. Such an acknowledgement would mean a radical transformation of the present hierarchical male structure of the Church. In my conclusion, I should therefore like to point out three steps which we have to take if we want to recover the full apostolicity and catholicity of the Church.

Call to Conversion

The admission of women to the full leadership of the Church requires the official confession that the Church has wronged women and has to undergo, therefore, a radical conversion. As the Church has officially rejected all national and racial exploitation and publicly renounced all antisemitic theology, so it is now called to abandon all forms of sexism by rejecting a theological and institutional framework which perpetuates discrimination and prejudice against women. In the document on the Church, the Vatican Council has affirmed the vision of church pronounced in Gal. 3:28: "Hence there is in Christ and in the Church no inequality on the basis of race or nationality, social conditions or sex."[15] Yet the context of the conciliar statement reflects the discriminatory praxis of the Church insofar as it maintains the equality of all Christians only with respect to salvation, hope and charity, but not with respect to ecclesial office and power. An analysis of the Christian tradition and history, however, indicates that church and theology will transcend their own ideological sexist forms only when women are granted not only full spiritual, but also full ecclesial, equality. The Christian Churches will only overcome their discriminatory and oppressive past tradition and present praxis if the very base and functions of this tradition and praxis are changed. If women would be admitted to full leadership in the Church, the need would no longer exist to suppress the Spirit who moves Christian women to participate fully in theology and ministry. Church leaders and theologians who do not respect this spirit of liberty and responsibility among Christian women deny the Church its full catholicity and wholeness.

Transformation of Hierarchy and Church

In my book on ministries of women in the Church (twelve years ago) I maintained that women have to demand ordination as bishops first, and only after they have obtained it, can they afford to be ordained deacons and priests.[16] Women have to become visible on all levels of the Church; they have to be priests, bishops, cardinals and popes, they have to be involved in formulating theology and church law, in issuing encyclicals and celebrating the liturgy, if the Church should truly become a community of equals before God and the world. Moreover, those women, who as teachers, theologians, assistant pastors, religious educators, counselors or administrators already actively exercise leadership in the Church, have to insist that their ministry is publicly acknowledged as "ordained ministry," if women's leadership should not fall prey to the pitfalls of the present clerical, celibate and hierarchical form of the Catholic priesthood.[17] The ordination of women can not simply mean their addition and integration into the clergy but implies a psychological, structural and theological transformation of the Church. The Christian community no longer should be split into an active leadership of male dominance and a passive membership of female submission, but should be a community of persons who are all called and entitled by God to active participation and leadership in the mission of the Church. Equal ordination is the test case, but the transformation of a celibate priesthood, a hierarchical church and a male-clerical theology is its unconditional prerequisite and consequence.

New Christian Sisterhood

The demand of women for ordination has to be rooted in a theology and praxis of sisterhood, which is not based on sexual stratification. Even though women were never ordained, traditional Roman Catholic Church theology and structure divides women into two classes: nuns and laywomen. The true Christian perfection and ideal is represented by the consecrated virgin. Only among those who are the brides of Christ true Christian sisterhood is possible. Distinct from women who are still bound to sexual desires and marital dependency, the biological virgins in the Church, subject to ecclesial authority, are the true "religious women." As the reform discussions and conflicts of women congregations with Rome indicate, dependency on ecclesial authority is as important as biological virginity.

Only when this deep psychological, theological and institutional split between Roman Catholic women is healed and overcome will the ordination of women lead to a new wholeness and catholicity of the Church. Otherwise the ordination of some nuns who evidence a great dependency on church authority will lead not only to a further clericalization and hierarchization of the Church but also to an unbridgeable theological and metaphysical split between women and women. Our most pressing task is therefore, in my opinion, to build a universal sisterhood, which would bridge the traditional gap between women and women in the Roman Catholic Church. Women who wish to be ordained should be rooted and supported by such a sisterhood, but also be responsible to such a sisterhood, if ordination should not become tokenism, but engender the transformation of the Church toward the vision expressed in Gal. 3:28.

Notes

1. Cf. L. Scanzoni and N. Hardesty, *All We're Meant to Be*, Waco Texas, 1974, p. 60.

2. For the discussion of a feminist hermeneutic see my article "Feminist Theology as a Critical Theology of Liberation" in the December 1975 issue of *Theological Studies* no. 36 (1975), pp. 605-26.

3. For the most recent analyses, cf. J.G. Gager, *Kingdom and Community. The Social World of Early Christianity*, Englewood Cliffs, 1975. G. Theissen, "Legitimität and Lebensunterhalt. Ein Beitrag zur Soziologie urchristlicher Missionäre," *New Testament Studies* 21 (1975), pp. 192-221.

4. For a comparison of the Qumran and the early Christian community see my forthcoming article "Cultic Language in Qumran and in the New Testament" in *Catholic Biblical Quarterly* (37) April 1976.

5. Cf. R.A. Scroggs, "Paul and the Eschatological Woman," *Journal of the American Academy of Religion* 40 (1972), pp. 5-17; W.A. Meeks, "The Image of Androgyne," *History of Religion* 13 (1974), pp. 165-208; H.D. Betz, "Spirit Freedom and Law: Paul's Message to the Galatian Churches," *Svensk Exegetic Arsbok* 39 (1974), pp. 145-160.

6. For a more detailed analysis see my article "The Role of Women in the Early Christian Movement," *Concilium* 7, January 1976 (English version not yet published).

7. This is obvious when we observe that already the writers of the Gospels attempt to downplay the importance of the women's witness and that the traditional formula in 1 Cor. 15:3-5 does not even mention women as witnesses of the resurrection.

8. The apocryphal gospel literature presents Mary Magdalene's leadership role as equal if not superior to that of Peter. See Hennecke-Schneemelcher, *New Testament Apocrypha I*, Philadelphia, 1963.

9. M.J. Lagrange, *Saint Paul. Epitre aux Romains*, Paris 1916, p. 366.

10. The attack and slander of the author of the Apocalypse against "Jezebel" demonstrates that the prophet had a considerable authority in the community of Thyatira.

11. For an exegetical and theological discussion of the notion of priesthood in early Christianity see my book *Priester für Gott*. Neutestamentliche Abandlungen 7, Münster, 1972, pp. 4-60; A. Lemaire, "The Ministries in the New Testament, Recent Research," *Theological Bulletin* 3 (1973), pp.

133-166; M. Houdijk, "A Recent Discussion about the New Testament Basis of the Priest's Office," *Concilium* 80 (1972), pp. 137-147; J.L. Mohler, *The Origin and Evolution of the Priesthood*, New York, 1970.

12. See A. Kahlsbach, *Die altehristliche Einrichtung der Diakonissen bis zu ihrem Erlöschen*, Freiburg, 1926; G.J. Davies, "Deacons, Deaconesses and the Minor Orders in the Patristic Period," *Journal of Ecclesiastical History* 14 (1963), pp. 1-15; J. Danielou, *The Ministry of Women in the Early Church*, Buzzard, 1961; R. Gryson, *Le ministere des femmes dans l'Eglise ancienne*, Duculot, 1972.

13. For bibliographical references see K. Thraede, "Frau," in *Reallexikon für Antike und Christentum*, Stuttgart, 1973, pp. 197-269.

14. Cf. Winsom Munro, "Patriarchy and Charismatic Community in Paul," In Plasko-Romero, *Women and Religion*, 2nd ed. Missoula, 1974, pp. 189-198; W.O. Walker, "1 Cor. 11:2-16 and Paul's Views Regarding Woman," *Journal of Biblical Literature* 94 (1975), pp. 94-110.

15. Dogmatic Constitution on the Church, IV.32 cf. W.M. Abbott and J. Gallagher, *The Documents of Vatican II*, New York, 1966, p. 58.

16. Elisabeth Schüssler, *Der vergessene Partner, Grundlagen, Tatsachen und Möglichkeiten der beruflichen Mitarbeit der Frau in der Heilssorge der Kirche*, Düsseldorf, 1964, pp. 87-94.

17. Cf. the various articles in R.J. Heyer, ed., *Women and Orders*, New York, 1974.

13
Models for Future Priesthood

Marie Augusta Neal, S.N.D.

SISTER MARIE AUGUSTA NEAL, S.N.D. is presently professor of sociology at Emmanuel College, Boston, and visiting professor of sociology and sociology of religion at Harvard University Divinity School. Her Ph.D. was obtained at Harvard University. Sister Marie Augusta Neal has been involved in research and publications dealing with the renewal in religious life and life in the Church since 1955. She was the Director of Research for the Conference of Major Religious Superiors of Women's Institutes, and has been a Member of the Archdiocesan Commission on Human Rights, Boston. She served for three years as area chairperson for the Governor's Commission on the Status of Women in Massachusetts.

Naming God
> O the depth of the riches
> and wisdom and knowledge of God!
> How unsearchable are the judgments and how
> inscrutable are the ways of God!
> For who has known the mind of God
> or who has been the counselor of God?
> Or who has given a gift to God
> that they might be repaid?
> For from God and through God
> and to God are all things.
> To God be glory for ever. Amen.

> (Romans 11:33-36)

When we pray we should pray like this, without pronouns; for right now God has no pronouns. The symbols of God are symbols of love and power. The power symbols of God have been used to mandate oppression of poor people; the love symbols, the oppression of women and children. Lord and Master relate to servants and slaves, King and Sovereign to subjects bound beneath burdens of human oppression. Father relates to son, often forgetting even to name the daughter or naming her as sex object available to the guest to save the self or the son. The Great Warrior becomes leader of armies, killer of peoples, taker of captives, ravager of the lands—lands now awaiting restoration to the people. The Judge of the Nations becomes protector of laws and treaties which designate some nations as slaves and servants of other nations. Providence and Shepherd maintain people in crippling dependency. Men, in the name of God, have violated all these relationships by acting as if they were gods, as agents in social relations that are exploitative of people in the interest of dominant groups. All these names, then, must go. Now, as in the early days, God has no name but Yahweh. And that name is not to be taken lightly.

As long as life includes the experience of things beyond our control—such as birth, death, transitions from stage to stage, illness, sorrow, loss and the fear of loss—a faithful people will still search for meaning. People will feel called and dedicated to the search for God, beyond the God named by the society that presently gathers to celebrate, beyond the comfort and the challenge provided by the God so named. Yet needed are people to celebrate God's presence and lament God's absence. Within the Catholic tradition, who will they be? What will they do? How will they be related to the other people? This is the problem we face now.

Relation of Priesthood to Societal Problems

As women who have reviewed our history and in it those societal patterns our predecessors generated . . . as women reflecting on our experience as women in a sinful world . . . as women called by our Church to take action against injustice . . . as women longing to return to the altar where our gifts are lying ready for the sacrifice . . . we are considering models for future priesthood, for common prayer, worship, preaching and sacramental service. We want to dwell in the house of God forever, with goodness and mercy following us all the days of our life (Psalm 23, vv. 5 and 6). We call on God to help us build the house because we do not want to labor in vain.

That house is society. It always has been society. At present something is radically wrong with our society. This is manifest in the fact that, despite our enormous wealth, we cannot provide for our people. The only solution we seem to devise is to destroy those people who are perceived as different from ourselves or to enslave them in our interests, and then to call upon God to witness to the truth of what we do. We cannot seem to hear the cries of the people unless we rephrase what they say, but then the meaning is changed and the problem submerged. This is why we need new models of priesthood. Our priests, their good will notwithstanding, celebrate the life of a social class as if it were the life of all the people. No matter what the cries of the people, the seminary goes on the same way. Any modification of services occurs within the same narrow range, extending at most to a little left of center.

Rooted as we are in custom and good intention, we cannot see the plight of the two-thirds of the world that lives below subsistence level despite the fact that we have a technological potential that could, but does not, address that problem. We are still focussing our service on the alleviation of the *results* of poverty when the times call for an elimination of its *causes*. Though we say we respect life, we still purchase health services like commodities on the open market. It is not the extent of one's illness, but one's ability to pay, that determines who will receive care. It is the ability to pay that determines whose teeth receive attention, whose security is assured, who lives and who dies. We say we respect life, but our largest production-and-exchange commodity is lethal weaponry for the destruction of people. We say we respect life, but we celebrate the liturgy for the military coup that overturns the people's government. We say we respect life, but our system of justice is least adequate in the treatment of rape.

Our models of priesthood reflect our sense of justice. Before whom does the rapist confess his sin, seek absolution and repent by spending his life caring for his progeny? Who counsels the unwed father? Who counsels the heads of single-sex male households as they care for the lives of their many children born of women who did not assent to their conception? Where are the day-care centers for the children of fathers who spend eight hours or more at their offices, too long a time to be away from their primary responsibilities, the children they alone chose to generate? Where are the cohorts of priest-counselors striving to create the society that will accept its primary responsibility—to use the commonwealth for the health, education and welfare services that people need rather than for the military and police protection which does violence to those who break the rules that protect the property of the rich but not the lives of the poor? I say the priest-counselors because, holding the keys of the confessional, they alone know what the faithful name as their sin; they alone can test these conceptions of sin against the societal evils that generate human neglect; they alone can know whether confession is used to slough off guilt for immediate and individual failings, or to make atonement for the human exploitation that violates God's creation and destroys the society. I ask the questions rhetorically, because these counselors do not exist. They do not exist because none hear those sins. Those sins go unconfessed because most of them are still unnamed. Unnamed, the guilt for them can scarcely enter the consciousness of the perpetrators. Only recently have we had a word for social justice; how much less for social sin (Ferree).

Adam, Eve and Population Size

The story of Adam and Eve is correctly labeled a myth (Vawter). A myth is a story of people that has for its purpose to unfold a part of their world-view, or to explain a practice, a belief or a natural phenomenon (Webster's Dictionary). We know now that myths are people's accounts of their origins, generated many years after their beginnings, and describing life not as it should be but as it is (Daly). Myths are rationalizations of the status quo. In that sense they are true.

In the myth of our origins, a woman seeks the knowledge essential for the development of life. God forbids that knowledge. The serpent (the devil) urges her to achieve it magically, by eating forbidden fruit. She urges her mate, from whom she is made, magically to achieve this knowledge also. He agrees and they eat the forbidden fruit. God reprimands them by sending them out of the garden into the wilderness, instructing them to increase and multiply and to fill the earth and subdue it, making the city out of the wilderness. They do all this.

Today we view the completed task. The world is filled with their progeny and the city is all over the land. It is a special kind of city. It has been made by cutting down the forests, using up the energy stored under the earth, fashioning objects for the use of some at the expense of others, providing some with services and neglecting others, making objects that wear out easily and using assembly lines for reproducing them, building highways, waterways and airways to facilitate the exchange of goods, providing schools to train people for the jobs that make the system work, and socializing people to fit into the system.

In worship centers, for periodic gatherings of members who believe in God, a blessing is asked for this life and work. At these gatherings, the focus is on heaven hereafter for the poor, moral discipline for the workers and, for the rich, gratitude for the good life. There is little understanding that this division of worship and labor keeps the system going in the interests of those advantaged by it; advantaged, that is, by the current division of labor and employment.

Most of us are caught up in the maintenance of the city. However, since the city no longer provides for the needs of the people, more and more are becoming disenchanted with the church—that is, with the place where the people gather as a moral community to affirm what is good and what is evil (Durkheim). The prophets cry out that the city is structured in evil, but the priests do not hear because they are walking along the road to Jericho and they are busy about many things. They are lonely because their way of celebration is no longer relevant and, being lonely, their concern becomes narrowed to their own interests, their survival problems, (as noted in the National Opinion Research Center, "American Priests"). That circumstance is understandable, but it is part of the decaying city. While the prophets cry out about the state of the city and while the world becomes an interdependent system, faceless and godless, the priests write books about the local community. But there are people everywhere ready to build the new city. There is new life among people—in the Third World reaching out to take what is rightfully theirs; there is new life among women rediscovering their identity as persons; there is new life among youth, ready to begin a new century. For *this life*, we need a *new society*. And for the new society we need new models of priesthood.

We need to review the myth of our origin, examine what its interpretations have led us to think about ourselves, listen to the words of our prayers and the intent of our sacrifices, and recognize the truth of what we find. Our worship legitimates the structure of our society to the degree that it rejuvenates our energy, recreates our will to continue, or focuses our attention on personal reform. When our worship calls for continuation of a social structure that causes oppression, those who experience the oppression withdraw from the worshipping community. They either drift haphazardly, or join a new organization if there is life elsewhere to which they can redirect their energies and where they can find communal support.

Who are they who have withdrawn from the assembly as distinct from those who want to continue as in the past? Youth, blacks, women and Third World peoples are meeting separately. Do we as women have models for priesthood that are models for society that have meaning beyond our own self-interest? Do we as women have models that are models for life and development that respond to the cries of the people in a credible and lasting way—credible to us, to the world of oppressed people, to the God whom we serve but cannot name?

Two Proposals

The God of history as we know him (and he is a "him" in history) originates for us in the Bible, and the God of the Bible originates among the peoples of ancient Babylon. The biblical record up to the years after Jesus traces a developing refinement in the ideas of God as mighty warrior, father, creator and trusted faithful companion (Kaufman). The Catholic Church includes tradition as well as the Bible as a legitimate source of ideas about God, because it recognizes that there is a development in our ideas about God as society changes; it recognizes, that is, that our ideas about God are related to our ideas about the just society. We need not stop here to review how central to the Judaeic-Christian tradition is the mandate to create and sustain the just society. However, suffice it to say that it was the mandate (incorporated in the Hebrew Scripture) of justice for all people—strangers, neighbors and family alike—that made of the Jews a people for the world, and their inspiration is the base of the Gospel which Christians try to realize today.

Today we face the World City as another Babylon, city of sin. As women we observed the international year of women in 1975; we see in the United States a most powerful and self-conscious people thinking of itself as having an errand into the wilderness. Warned by the models of priesthood embedded in this New Babylon, we have some symbols available for beginning the task of making *new models* of priesthood, where we don't go into wilderness but come back into the community. This paper will name but two dimensions of this new venture: 1) a process for mandating new models of priesthood that links directly with the sacred tradition; and 2) a proposal for a societal change rooted in a neglected Gospel mandate.

The First Proposal: Toward a Re-Structuring of the Magisterium
During the meeting September 9-10, 1975 in Washington, D.C., of the National Conference of Catholic Bishops, Bishop Joseph L. Bernardin, head of that Conference, *restated* the Church's teaching that women are not to be ordained to the priesthood. He clearly indicated that his position was a re-statement.* He located "the strong theological argument" not in Scripture where, it is quite clear, it does not exist, but in tradition, indicating that it is "necessary to the life and practice of the Spirit-guided Church" where "the constant practice and tradition of the Catholic Church has excluded women from the episcopal and priestly office." He states further that "theologians and canonists have been unanimous until modern times in considering this exclusion as absolute and of divine origin." He concludes from this that "the constant tradition and practice of the Catholic Church against the ordination of women interpreted (whenever interpreted) as of divine law, is of such a nature as to constitute a clear teaching of the Ordinary Magisterium of the Church. Though not formally defined, this is Catholic doctrine." "*This reason*," he adds, "is of ponderous theological import," and *for this reason* "a negative answer to the possible ordination of women is indicated." But Bishop Bernardin's statement did not remain closed to the dynamic of time. He further states: "The well-founded present discipline will hold the entire field *unless and until a contrary theological development* takes place, leading ultimately to a clarifying statement from the Magisterium."

Contrary theological developments are already taking place. The most striking of these is the development of the theology of liberation —a body of theological reflection grounded in the experience of oppression caused by basic want and exclusion from the resources of health, education and the services needed for human development. This is a new theology that addresses itself not to the support of projects for the alleviation of human suffering, as did earlier theologies, but rather to the elimination of the causes of physical poverty. This new theological reflection is done from the point of view of the oppressed and not from the speculative abstraction of the man of leisure and scholarly training. Moreover, this theology from the point of view of the oppressed suggests a corresponding theology from the point of view of the advantaged, namely, a theology of relinquishment; so that, when the poor reach out to take what is rightfully theirs, there will be some consecrated hands ready and willing to lead the rich assembly in letting go of their hold on the treasures.

Both of these theologies, rooted in a process of conscientization, call into question the very structure of traditionally arranged communities of worship. The new theologies suggest that these traditional groups go to the altar, but only to leave their gifts there, in order to go off to be reconciled with their colleagues before beginning the priestly tasks of leading the assembly in prayer, worship and song. Whenever reflection on the conditions of life reveals the existence of injustice within the community of the faithful, this new theological development requires participation of the faithful in action for social change, before the presence of God be realized.

This same theological development keeps enlarging the community of the faithful to include more and more of the oppressed peoples of the world. The prophetic call to return the land to the people in the jubilee year, the fiftieth year, underscores the awful exploitation of humankind caused by the privatization of the land and its resources within economic systems whose production plans are rooted in unjustified assumptions about who is entitled to that land and those resources (cf. Leviticus 25:1-25, also Nozick, *Anarchy, State and Utopia*). This theology of liberation calls for the poor to reflect together on their grievances and to bring them to the community to find support. There they seek together what the faithful left the altar to achieve, namely, reconciliation. In this way new oppressions are discovered each time the community gathers; and, as it disperses, it is called to action to right the newly understood wrongs. Once the community names the grievance, it either bonds and binds itself to the resolution of the grievance, or else it goes away in new sin.

If the priesthood has as its function the offering of the sacrifice of the worshiping community as it realizes its moral solidarity in the community known as church, then the priest of the future, the very near future, will be in one of three places: (1) in the midst of these gathered theologians assembled with the poor, reflecting on the oppressions of their lives, hearing the new naming for the problems, bonding for action, reflecting together on action taken, and then, being reconciled, offering the Mass; (2) alone in the parish church awaiting the return of the faithful who left their gifts there in order to go and be reconciled with the oppressed; (3) contrary to the mandate of the Gospel, continuing to offer the regular services with the faithless who did not leave their gifts at the altar to go and be reconciled once injustice was revealed in the land. Who will the priests be in these various locations? It is not easy to say. However, should women choose priesthood, it would be an idle choice, it seems to me, if the first of the alternatives named here is not the one they choose.

In his official decree on behalf of the National Conference of Catholic Bishops, Bishop Bernardin announces that women are invited to assume greater leadership in the Church, that "their contributions are needed in the decision-making process at the parochial, diocesan, national and universal level," and that they are "in a very special way called to collaborate with all other segments of the Church in the essential work of evangelization." He goes so far as to say that "the Church will suffer, indeed it will be betrayed, if women are given only a secondary place in its life and mission." What would Bishop Bernardin's words mean in the face of continued exclusion of women from ordained priesthood? Either that ordained priesthood is secondary to the life and mission of the Church or that the future of the Church is to be one of suffering and betrayal. It is not enough, Bernardin goes on to say, simply to make statements. Statements must be matched by action to bring more women into the mainstream of the life of the local Church. Celebration of the Eucharist is in the mainstream.

Bernardin quotes the conclusion of Bishop John R. Quinn (speaking as Chairman of the Bishops' Committee on Pastoral Research and Practices) that "the ultimate answer must come from the Magisterium, and the current question is whether the Magisterium has already given a definite and final answer. At this level of doubt only the Magisterium itself can give ultimate clarification." This is a well-reasoned and fair position. It sets aside any claim to justify the exclusion of women on the basis of a divine plan (Quinn, items 5 and 6).

But what of the Magisterium? If, as Pope Paul VI reasoned, women's dignity and equality are rooted in "their filial (sic) relationship with God, of whom they are the visible image," then surely they can be received into the Magisterium as partners in decision-making at the universal level. Only when the Magisterium reflects the adult membership of the Church in accordance with its own directives will it be able to address adequately the issue of ordination for women. That issue cannot be adequately addressed by the existing process of decision-making, reflecting as it does the limited vision of an all-male perspective on the world. Bishop Bernardin acknowledges this deficiency in his statement that the contribution of women is needed not only at parochial, diocesan and national levels, but also at the universal level—that is, at the level of the Magisterium. The possibility that new models of priesthood will be mandated by the Magisterium lies in the participation of women in the staffing of that mysterious body. This, then, is my first proposal: that, as a mediate step toward ordination, places be sought for women within the Magisterium, the process of decision-making at the level of the universal Church.

The Second Proposal: Toward a Restructuring of Work Time and Reflection Time

The practice of priesthood is fashioned on the pattern of work and leisure in society. It is this pattern of work and leisure that is fostered in prayer and worship. What is the pattern presently being fostered? The present distribution of workers and unemployed has some people over-working, some not only have no work, but are idle, while service roles needing trained personnel go unaddressed and hence undone. The billion underemployed in the world could provide paraprofessionals for public health programs, literacy learning, rehabilitation and city renewal. The only objections are cost and status: cost means fitting into our current conception of the uses of money, and status reflects the jobs which we regard as of sufficient importance to warrant allocation of money. People's money is spent in large part on health, education and insurance against unexpected need. The limited manner in which we provide these life securities falls far short of what the three billion seven hundred million members of our world society need. Yet there are plenty of people between the ages of twenty and sixty to train themselves for these tasks. Within the present pattern of work and leisure, however, these tasks are imagined as peripheral and hence without status.

As women consider ordination to the priesthood, it makes sense for us to reflect on the pattern of work and leisure in society which is fostered in the worship and prayer of the faithful community. Given our previous experience with the division of labor, women could hardly begin to think about themselves as hearers of confessions, blessers of marriages, ordainers of deacons, priests and bishops, anointers of the sick, baptizers of new members, confirmers of youth, or breakers of eucharistic bread without intending to make of these events transitions to a more human society. Accordingly, I propose that women who are considering ordination commit themselves to the reinstatement of the workers' sabbatical.

My proposal is rooted in the 25th chapter of Leviticus, where God has Moses tell the people that each person should take off every seventh year from labor in order to reflect on the previous six years of life and to make decisions about the future. Women know well the need we have to reflect on what we have done, to provide time for service, for community and public action, to spend time with children, to be available beyond the call of duty, to enrich the quality of our lives with art and other forms of contemplation of the beautiful. Women know these needs because we know how it feels to be used as a commodity and as a container of commodities. It makes sense, then, that women would espouse the workers' sabbatical as our special contribution to the righting of the international injustice of taking from people the resources they need for human survival.

Let us consider more closely the possibilities for a more human society suggested by the workers' sabbatical. On a worldwide level, we have an enormous unemployment problem; yet millions of people could be working as para-professionals in public health, education and welfare services that would provide for human needs in programs that would resolve many a fiscal problem. This would require a little balanced imagination and the relinquishing of the profit motive. As one step toward a solution of that large problem, we could institutionalize the workers' sabbatical. According to this plan (guided by Leviticus), every adult between the ages of 18 and 60 (or whatever we institutionalize as the years for the common law of labor to apply) will not work during the seventh year. During that year, set aside for reflection and for a review of life and society, the adult will live on welfare, to which his and her labor will have contributed during the other years of work. That year of reflection may be spent in a monastery, a school, in public service, or in whatever way the individuals can best review the humaneness of their lives during the previous six years. Whether working in a business or profession, household or school, whether employed previously or not, whether prisoner or free, the goal will be for the sabbatical year to become the common practice for all adults of the society.

It will mean that each year approximately one seventh of the adult population of the land will be in reflection on the quality of the life of the community. It will mean that this body of people will be free to look at the conditions of our society, to take civic action for reform, to examine the uses of monies in the common interest. They will have time to examine their own consciences regarding the uses of human resources; they will have time to update their skills, to relax the tense hatreds customary in the struggle for survival. As they live on public welfare these persons will come to understand its workings, its purposes, and its forms. The funding for this form of life will come from the commonwealth. It will be sufficiently expensive to preclude large investments in military materials. It will enlarge the number of contemplative practitioners and vary the perspectives from which contemplation is undertaken, using the resources of monasteries and retreats. It will provide content that breaks through traditional definitions of normality. It will help to make us a more reflecting and compassionate people. It will provide for bursts of creativity, and for relinquishment of the cultural preserves of power.

Taught as a religious mandate, it will gain public interest because it is useful in the light of mechanization, the high level of unemployment and the rapid decay of the quality of our lives. We will soon learn to use our leisure in many different ways. We will learn how to reduce our work weeks so that we can, even when not on sabbatical, spend more time with families and friends, and begin to live more human lives. The workers' sabbatical will allow for the redistribution of parental responsibilities between married men and women, and add a communal dimension to the responsibility of single people for the children born into the community.

Having increased and multiplied and filled the earth, having invented a technology that could be used for human development—but is not—humankind is now in need of modes of humanization that affirm our personhood and provide for the full development of people's capacities. If our images of God have proven oppressive of the poor, of women and of children, if God's power and love have become distorted in narrow images of an aggressive sexuality that condone war, rape and extortion, this is because God has been made in the image of men. The decision-makers have forgotten their stewardship, and aspired to the prerogatives of God, as if they alone were made in God's image and likeness. Images of God which foster the life of all the people will be generated by the faithful community only when it is a community in which all the people can gather for life, when its priests are drawn from among men and women who acknowledge their accountability to all the people. If we need a new priesthood, it is because we need a new society. Along with the workers' sabbatical, Leviticus 25 mandates the jubilee year, a year for restructuring society, a year for restoring the land to the people. We need a priesthood

that can bless the restructured society. We need a priesthood to celebrate the restoring of the land to the people. We need women for this
priesthood.

*Cf. Appendix A.

Select Bibliography

Bernardin, J. L., Archbishop of Cincinnati, "The official position of the U.S.
Bishops concerning the ordination of women to the priesthood, Oct. 7,
1975." *Crux of the News*, October 13, 1975, pp. 5-6.

Daly, Mary, *Beyond God the Father* (Boston: Beacon Press, 1973).

Ferree, William, *The Act of Social Justice* (Dayton, Ohio: Marianist Publications, Mount Saint John, 1951).

Kaufman, Gordon, *God the Problem* (Cambridge, Massachusetts: Harvard
University Press, 1972).

National Opinion Research Center, *American Priests*. Prepared for the United States Catholic Conference, March, 1971.

Nozick, Robert, *Anarchy, State, and Utopia* (New York: Basic Books,
1974).

Quinn, John R. Bishop, "Theological Reflections on the Ordination of
Women." (1972) Report prepared by the Committee on Pastoral Research and Practices of the National Catholic Conference of Bishops.
Bishop Quinn is the Archbishop of Oklahoma City, and former Chairman of Bishops' Committee on Pastoral Research and Practices.

Riley, Thomas J. Bishop, "Women Priests? . . . Not Now," *Pilot*, Boston,
October 3, 1975. Vol. 146, no. 39, p. 1.

Vawter, Bruce, *A Path Through Genesis* (New York: Sheed and Ward,
1956).

14

Diversity of Gifts in the Future Priesthood

Dorothy H. Donnelly, C.S.J.

DOROTHY H. DONNELLY, C.S.J. holds an M.A. and Ph.D. from Catholic University and a Th.D. from the Pacific School of Religion at the Graduate Theological Union, Berkeley. She is full-time faculty member of the Jesuit School of Theology there. She has published in NEW CATHOLIC ENCYCLOPEDIA, NCR, COMMONWEAL and SISTERS TODAY and authored three books on leadership training, human communication and group dynamics. Her current writings deal with team ministry, prison reform and women's rights.

In responding to Sister Marie Augusta Neal, let me say that I find her first proposal regarding restructuring the Magisterium more realistic than her second one of the workers' sabbatical. In considering some of my own proposals for future models of priesthood, I realize they, too, may appear utopian. Yet I feel all these models call for our consideration. From the outset, let me say that there are exceptions to every model; there is no absolute theology. Each of us is called to create our own. That is part of the task ahead.

Theology of Gifts

The question of future models of priesthood is a deeply theological one. We are the victims of poor theology, a theology culturally conditioned—just as ours will be. Yet, I submit that we do need a new theology, a theology I call a "theology of gifts." Let me address some of the ramifications of such a proposed theology.

The shape of ministry in the future, I submit, will be that of *team:* the present pyramid of hierarchical ministry will become a circle. And along with a new "shape" of ministry, the Church will

116

need a new criterion for ministry—namely, response to human need.

Team Model

The pastoral team as a possible model for the ministry of the future would break through two stereotypes: a sexist one and a denominational, or religious one. These teams would strive to be woman-man teams, and they would strive to be ecumenical; that is, they would move ever out into the Christian community. I would assume that these teams would eventually be led by married couples. Those of us now considered "religious" would function as resource people according to our gifts.

Basis of This Model

There are certain presuppositions basic to this kind of theology of the gifts. First, we really believe and obey the fact that God calls the shots as to who has what gift in the Church. None of us can tell the Spirit what to do. She will do whatever She pleases; ours is to listen and obey. Secondly, we believe that gifts are given to particular individuals. Thirdly, we believe these gifts are given *for* the Christian community. (Gifts are not given as something to keep, as a possession. I personally do not like to see women thinking of ordination as a "possession," as something to own. If that occurs, then, as Ricoeur puts it, "symbol hardens into idol." "Gift" may not be the best word to express the reality; perhaps "manifestation of power" would be more accurate.)

We are called to discover the meaning of priesthood; we must ask the question relevant to the theology of the gifts: namely, which gift of the Spirit is confirmed by the sacrament of Holy Orders? That brings me to the fourth presupposition. In a divine economy of supply and demand of gifts for the community, a gift *may* be confirmed by the community (the community of the Church is the sacrament of the continuing ministry of Jesus on the earth). This raises an important consideration: perhaps we must be more discerning in what sacraments we seek. Is it Holy Orders we want for women? Originally, that sacrament was sacramentum ordinis (singular): the sacrament of order. The person receiving that sacrament was the one who had the gift of order for a congregation. That historical model poses one kind of gift which could be confirmed in the sacrament of Order. But is that the gift that women in ministry need? Is that the gift that those who serve need? We, as individuals and as a community, must discern whether this kind of serving needs a sacrament.

Jesus as Model

In considering models of future priesthood, we must consider the principle of serving, the Incarnation, which includes all of humankind (our being men *or* women is irrelevant to the invitation, the duty, to minister). Let's explore a bit further what it means to say that the work of the Church is to continue the serving of Jesus. If Jesus is the model, that means taking on his mind, his attitudes, his concerns. When we look at his life, we find Jesus calling for a continual change of heart (Luke 24). Not only our preaching but our work as well must be about a change of heart which leads to the forgiveness of sins. That is why each of us is responsible for our own theology—that's another way of saying we are responsible for our intellectual conversion: searching for a theology which explains our lived experience.

I believe this understanding illustrates why we do not need a theology of ministry, or a theology of priesthood, or a theology of serving. Each of these implies, at this moment in time, inequality—it cannot be avoided. I would propose that the more adequate theology would be a theology of sharing—sharing of gifts in groups. That's why the shape of this theology is a circle: to show more clearly the power of the Spirit moving about that group. And this is important to note: the power is not our own! We allow the Spirit to move, and this means we can *receive*. A theology of sharing of gifts supports receiving gifts as well as the giving of gifts. Our attitude and stand toward others is immediately changed by this realization.

Let's look again at Jesus, our model. It is precisely in the central mystery of our faith, what we call "paschal mystery," that we must find our model for today. Jesus lived a life of concern and caring, and he died—that is, Jesus disappeared, entered into the mystery of death and change so the Spirit might be released. It is precisely here that we must find our corollary for ministry and priesthood today.

Dying and Rising for Justice

As women, we turn to our brother-priests and invite them, "Don't be afraid to die, dear brother—to a role, a function which may no longer need such a form as yours. We foresee a new kind of interacting, a beautiful circle of ministry, of teams, where one can find identity as well as develop and receive the various gifts of the Spirit." Just as the bishops in centuries past gradually gave away their exclusive powers and functions to priests, priests must be about the same divesting today. This is dying; this is the paschal mystery.

But this dying-rising goes on in each of us. The very proportion of people participating in the Detroit Ordination Conference tells us something. Of the 1,200 taking part, 1,000 were members of women's religious communities, 100 brothers, seminarians, deacons, priests, and 100 single and married men and women. That statistic points out that religious women are the most advantaged, highly educated, privileged, prestigious group of women in the Church. As we (religious women) address one issue of justice (ordination of women) are we willing to be just? As we ask our brother-priests to enter into the dying-rising to new styles of ministry, the voice of the laity summons us, "Don't be afraid to die dear sister . . . to a position, a role, a caste, a unique privilege which has been yours alone among the women in the Church." The question of women's ordination raises a myriad of other concerns: are we ready to enter into our dying and rising to be people for others on the model of Jesus?

In the light of the needs of others, ordination seems not enough to ask for. "Priest" may be a word we no longer need for a century or so, until we develop the neglected gifts of our own brothers and sisters. Is it possible our pursuit of ordination might be a form of idol-worship? Let's answer three questions first, through study, consultation and sharing: who are we as Christians and what is our function in the Church and world? what does it mean to be Church in our time? and what is the present meaning of sacrament?

Two Strategies for New Models

What I propose is to say *yes* to whatever deaths we are all called to, so that we may *all* live more faith-fully as coservers, as brothers and sisters. I suggest that our motto be "S.O.L.—Stamp out the Laity!" From this moment on there are no laity, only baptized Christians—Christians seeking access to the discovery, use and testing of their gifts in community. So I ask: can we take the next seven years (a solid sabbatical) to assess our resources—money, land, capital, personnel, organizations—and then assign these resources to develop the gifts of those nonvowed and nonordained (as we understand those terms)? Will we attempt to restore the imbalance and inequality in the Church? Then Sister Marie Augusta's proposal for a representative Magisterium will be possible, because on that Magisterium will be married couples, lay women and men.

Secondly, in reallocating resources, let us plan, in two years, to sponsor a conference (similar to the Detroit Ordination Conference) in each of the states. Two years will allow time to have the laity involved in the organization and participation of such conferences. Let us resolve that each religious community of women and men will finance the attendance for a married couple, a single woman and man. In doing so, we may learn what it is to change our own hearts (and society's) through listening, receiving, fostering one another's gifts. Our goal is to develop an apostolic spirituality, a truly pastoral spirituality after Jesus's own model. If we learn what it means for us to share our gifts in community, then we can learn what it means to be truly a team.

In studying these areas and the ramifications of our conclusions, let us take both these questions and proposals to prayer. Let us know that, like Jesus, we serve with a power that is not our own, so that like him, we may disappear gloriously to rise again and to be with him always.

15
Practical Problems Facing the Future Priesthood

Eleanor Kahle

ELEANOR KAHLE has lived and worked in Toledo, Ohio. Her involvements have included ecumenical and Roman Catholic areas. Having attended Mary Manse College and the University of Toledo, been mother of six and grandmother of nine, she is currently the first lay women to be employed as Pastoral Associate in the Diocese of Toledo. She was the first Roman Catholic to chair the Ecumenical Celebrations for Church Women United in that area, and served as vice-president of that same organization. She has been secretary for the Women's Institute on Human Relations in Toledo, Board member of the Toledo Metropolitan Mission—Committee on the Aging, and founding member of Naim (an organization for widows). She has served as President of the Northwest Toledo Deanery, member of the Diocesan Council of Catholic Women, and member of the steering committee for the Diocesan Pastoral Council.

"Where are you going, my pretty maidens, where are you going?" they said. "We're going a'milkin', kind sirs," they said, "we're going a'milking." Does that quote from a western folk ballad sound ludicrous and facetious, especially as you compare it to everything that has been said previously? It was not meant to be funny, but rather meant to bring to your attention some very down to earth problems that must be faced as we consider models for future priesthood. I don't know how many of you come from a farm background, or a rural community, but those that do know that one of the most demanding, most earthy chores that has to be done is the "milkin'." It must be done every day, no holidays, no days off—it must be done "religiously" at the same time, in the same manner each time—and

121

when this chore is done well the end result is milk—one of the most perfect basic foods necessary for a good life. "Where are *you* going, my pretty maidens?"

Rectory—a Place To "Reside"

Are you going to that mysterious rectory to face the earthy demanding chores that must be dealt with every day, before we can begin to produce a food necessary for everlasting life? Under the present structure, the highest percentage of priests work in a parish. The parish, a geographical neighborhood, has at its heart a rectory. We all know the rectory as a place where records of baptisms, marriages and deaths are kept, where census cards are filed, where funeral and wedding arrangements are made, where many types of questions are answered, where counseling is done, where homilies are prepared, where collections are counted, and where the parish priest *resides* as well as ministers. Others, who work as professionals in church-related ministries, go to work each morning—to a school, hospital, office—to a place (a space) set apart for the performance of this particular task. After being in the place for a period of time—six, eight, ten hours as the case may be—they leave this place to go "home." Home might be the convent, an apartment, a room or a house. It is the place of residence, separated from the place where ministry is done. A place where we go to eat, sleep, relax.

Not so with the parish priest. The place of ministry and the home are one and the same. It is the thought of women invading this home that is causing so many problems at the parish level. If the present parish structure continues, the change of life style that would have to occur, if women were priests, is more threatening, more difficult to cope with, to accept, than the thought of women celebrating mass. Women have a tremendous responsibility to be sensitive to this earthy quandary, "What will we do with a woman in the rectory?"

A Place To Work

Let's look at the building problem realistically. In the 1950s-1960s during the building boom, bricks and mortar were put up everywhere. This erection of structures has now come to a halt. With the exodus of priests, the closing of parochial schools, many fairly new buildings are standing half-filled. When new associates—male or female—come to a parish, the logical process will be to fill up these partially filled buildings. A place from which to work, a landing place where you can be contacted, with which you can be identified is essential. The place where a parish priest works is the rectory. How will a woman fit into this situation? Will she share an office with "Father," a sitting room, a bathroom? Rectories were never built with women in mind (except maybe the housekeeper, who had little or nothing to say about the building). There's really no place for women. Will women be satisfied with an oversized closet, a storage room, an enclosed porch, a corner of the dining room, even a card table and folding chair set up in the hallway? Will the parish council finance committee agree to remodel for women when there are buildings standing empty? Privacy will be minimal. Not only must the pastor contend with the invasion of privacy of his "home," but also of his working place. How will he be able to treat a woman as an equal when first he must deal with his own feelings of resentment, animosity, yes, even rage?

Martha vs. Mary

And how about the housekeeper? The controversy between the Marthas and the Marys has been going on for almost 2,000 years, and it's still going on. Rarely will these dedicated devoted women, who for so long have been the only women in the rectory, understand what women priests are all about. Unlike the parishioners, she will know that you are NOT the president of the women's organization, the new secretary, or Father's cousin or aunt; but she won't know just exactly who or what you are—even if the pastor has explained to her beforehand. Will you be willing to assure her and reassure her that you are not there to mend Father's socks, peel potatoes or make the soup? It will be important to have her as your friend, as well as all other staff members, because you are going to need every bit of support and friendship you can get—especially from those with whom you share the daily chores.

Support of Laity

How about the support of the laity? Realizing that not all people will be on the same level of growth, of what worth will the knowledge, the training, the desire, the approval of the Magisterium be, if women are not accepted by the laity? What if Catholics reject the Body of Christ because women offer it? The uncertainty of the legality of baptism, the blessing of marriage, the absolution of sins, the validity of anointing, if done by a woman will cause the laity fear—and thus rejection.

Creating a Climate of Acceptance

As women prepare for the future, there is an important task that must be done RIGHT NOW. A climate of acceptance must be created among the laity, the acceptance of a woman in the rectory, a woman in the sanctuary—and this must be an immediate priority. Women must be the MOST of everything they can be right now—lectors, readers, extraordinary ministers, prebaptism instructors, pre-Cana advisors, those who take communion to the sick and confined. Women must be visible, vocal and viable—in all areas of parish life—until the sound of woman, the sight of woman, the feeling of woman is acceptable—yes, even taken for granted. This may mean a change in lifestyle, in priorities; it means "GO FORTH AMONG THE PEOPLE" building trust, love and acceptance. It means doing the ordinary things in an extraordinary way until the extraordinary way becomes the ordinary way.

Publicity

Equally important, people must know that there are women supporting ordination and ready for ordination. The average lay person has no idea that there are such women—knowledgeable, capable, ready to do more to keep the Church alive than they have done previously. Not only is there a responsibility for being good public relations people on the local level in order to create a climate of acceptability, women must be a publicity committee. The Detroit Conference was outstanding. The number of participants attested to that. But who attended? Those already involved, or already aware. If the results of the Conference receive widespread publicity, would a mustard seed be planted? I don't know. The time must be right for the planting, this we know. But the ground can be prepared at any time, all the time. And when God says the timing is right, the maidens will be ready to do not only the milking, but EVERYTHING that needs to be done that there might be food for everlasting life.

16

Strategies and Strengths to Confront the Barriers to the Future Priesthood

William R. Callahan, S.J.

WILLIAM R. CALLAHAN, S.J. ended a career with a Ph.D. in physics and experience with NASA Goddard Space Flight Center in Beltsville, Maryland, to work fulltime with spiritual renewal, and participative planning programs for the New England Jesuits. He functioned as Director of Social Ministries for that Province. Ordained in 1965, completing his S.T.L. in 1966, Bill's awareness of social need led him to co-found the CENTER OF CONCERN in Washington, D.C. He was principal author of THE QUEST FOR JUSTICE, 1972, editor of SOUNDINGS, 1974 and coordinator of the Center's Task Force on Women Religious in the Church, 1973. Priests for Equality was begun at his initiative in 1975, and with two others, Bill founded QUIXOTE CENTER, a justice center whose aim is to relate social concerns to religious experience. His work in giving workshops and writing center mainly on two areas: world hunger and the spirituality of liberation.

When the Jewish people approached the Promised Land, their way was blocked by the city of Jericho, which barricaded itself against them. Yahweh gave them the plan for entry. . . . For six days you will march around the city. On the seventh day you will go seven times around the city and when the ram's horn rings out, the whole people will utter a mighty cry. The wall will collapse then and there, and the people can enter the town, each person going straight ahead.

We people of the Catholic community are a people moving toward a promised land of equal opportunity for ministry and decision-making. A walled city blocks the way. Within those walls lies present access to the fullness of ministry and decision-making. Ordination is the only gateway into this town. Only men are allowed to pass. Authorities have mounted strong forces to guard this narrow passage.

Who, in a Church community which desires to live a life based on love and reconciliation, looks forward to storming such an entry? Yet who of us believes that the Spirit is suggesting we turn back, and with resignation trudge back to the desert of inequality, whence we've come? No! There is a land of greater promise ahead and we are called to enter it.

Perhaps the nonviolent way of Joshua offers promise. I will use that way to suggest two practical steps to be taken toward Sr. Marie Augusta's model of broadening decision-making and ministry.

One Possibility

The first plan deals with the ordination gateway to this city of ministry. I propose that creative tension be kept on these gates by 1. setting up an independent office of women to follow up the proposals and calls to action of the Detroit Conference, and 2. by means of a cooperative program of research and education. In this program, the people of the Church community would take up the major questions and obstacles which affect the sharing of ministry and decision-making in our Church. Teams could gather material and evaluate the biblical arguments, the theological reasoning, the argument from tradition, the questions of justice; other teams would interview and test the call of women who feel called to priesthood, and give a composite report of their caliber and preparation. Pilot programs of education and dialogue might test the readiness of the Catholic people for women and men sharing ordained ministry.

The resultant studies could be published, together with a public evaluation and recommendations. Might not such material serve well the Roman Catholic bishops, while effecting great consciousness raising among the people of the Church? Perhaps the dialogue and the gentle call of the Spirit might be heard by the guardians of the portal. Perhaps they would cast open the gates and welcome women in—you who are people who love the Church and seek to serve.

Jericho Image Provides Model

A second plan prepares for a possible longer struggle, and it addresses the critical question, "Why would women want to enter the present structured, highly clericalized city of present-day ministry?" Again, the witness of the Israelites offers an answer. The goal is not to break into and dwell in the Jericho of present-day ministry, but to clear the journey of the people for the land of shared ministry and service which lies ahead. The preparation for that land must be made while you (the nonordained) circle the city and gather forces for the great cry to come. You must build a powerfully voiced throng of ministers by seeking to summon forth the gifts of ministry present in each. Future ministry must acknowledge and celebrate the many gifts present in the community. Future ministry and decision-making must have new forms and settings in which these gifts may shine forth. Hence the days of marching about the walls of our clerical Jericho must be spent in training and in encouraging all people—men, women, married, single, members of religious communities—to build a sense of themselves as ministering people. Encourage one another to heal, preach, teach, interpret, reflect, celebrate, give counsel. The struggle for ministry is everyone's struggle.

Let all of these gifts be blended into a rising chorus of ministry. Round and round the city will tramp the growing throng of people whose gifts are being set free. Soon it will be time for the seventh day, when after the seventh circuit of the people that day, the ram's horn of love and the priestly trumpets will blow, a mighty shout of freedom in equality will be raised, and the walls of opposition to this voice of the Spirit will collapse. Not just through the narrow gates of ordained priesthood will people pass, but each person will be acknowledged and celebrated in the ministry and will pass straight ahead in accord with his or her gifts. Jericho will have fallen. The way will lie clear toward the promised land.

Walls which shut out threatening people, also shut in and trap people who feel threatened, and cut them off from life and service. These walls, which shut out women, shut in and trap men.

Let us realize we are engaged in a common struggle. Before entering Jerusalem, the Israeli scouts had inside help. May I pledge you in the name of Priests for Equality (Priests for Equality: a movement of deacons, priests and bishops committed to equality for women and men in civil society and the Roman Catholic Church. c/o William Callahan, S.J., 3311 Chauncery Place, Apt. 301, Mt. Rainier, Md. 20822), not only covert help but open inside work on the walls—the rough pick and shovel work of undermining—that the walls may grow receptive to your shout. We will add our own shout from within, as your cry from outside rises.

How Shall Our Story Read?

Finally, in the Old Testament story, when the walls crumbled at Jericho, the Israelites moved in and waged the slaughter that the inhabitants expected. If when these walls crumble, those outside as well as inside can manage not slaughter but reconciliation, even with those who most stoutly defended the wall, then the Good News will indeed go through the land, that Jesus has come, is alive and well, and living in the midst of our Church. A healed, sharing people will be ready to move toward a suffering but sharing Promised Land.

17

Partnership Marriage: Model of Future Priesthood

Arlene Anderson Swidler

ARLENE ANDERSON SWIDLER, M.A. taught at the University of Wisconsin, Valparaiso University, University of Maryland in Munich and Duquesne University. She has also been chairman of the National Council of Catholic Women's Committee on liturgical and ecumenical affairs. Arlene co-founded, managed and currently is education editor of the JOURNAL OF ECUMENICAL STUDIES. Her most recent work, SISTERCELEBRATIONS, is a collection of feminist liturgies (Fortress). Arlene is the author of CONCERN: WORLD RELIGIONS in the Silver-Burdett Religion Series, and WOMAN IN A MAN'S CHURCH (Paulist Press). She has translated a number of books from German, and co-translated (with Leonard Swidler) BISHOPS AND PEOPLE and WOMEN PRIESTS IN THE CATHOLIC CHURCH?

These last few years I find myself thinking and working almost full-time as a Catholic feminist—somewhat reluctantly, I should add, as I see our movement as purely a means to an end.

Feminism: Model for Ministry

What that experience has shown me—and this is more in other Christian churches than in the Catholic Church—is the feminist movement presented as a model of ministry: as a form of life and service of joyous and relaxed collaboration with fellow ministers, and collaboration with those who are ministered to; a priesthood, if you will, which is responsive to its people because it is formed by and speaks for its people.

At the same time I don't really think we women are better or

129

purer or more idealistic than men. I don't think that any model for the priesthood predicated on a relationship between unequals can be regarded as more than transiently valid. As we know, the oppressed can become the oppressors.

Marriage Imagery One-sided

I do believe we have had another model in front of us all these years, and that is the partnership marriage. I would like to present some observations on that model for your reflection.

The partnership-marriage has been both concealed and forbidden by theologians over the centuries. We women have been conned into believing that the metaphor of the married women as the People of Israel, the bride of Yahweh, or the Church, the bride of Christ, is a beautiful image; we have not realized that in accepting it we accept women as material, sinful, human, finite, and the male as divine. Lately, we have seen this imagery—when we have even thought about it—as a method by which men keep women under control. But I would like to suggest that the imagery is really very closely tied in with our idea of priesthood and ministry, and is therefore very relevant today.

Recently we've heard more and more about the way in which our ecclesiastical government reflects civil governments around it—the way, for example, in which the monarchical Church is patterned on the Roman Empire. In fact, it's on the basis of the growth of civil democracy that we have dared to hope for changes in the Church. As one theologian, Krister Stendahl, has pointed out, it is on the basis of our civil right of suffrage that we dare to claim equality in the Church.

Language, Attitude and Relationships

What we haven't examined sufficiently is the extent to which the Church sees itself as family. Holy Father the Pope, Holy Mother the Church, the bishop as spouse of his diocese, the priest as Father of his flock: this language provides the basic images of personal relationships between the various levels in the Church. But all these familial concepts are vulnerable to a shift in our understanding of the husband-wife and wife-husband-child relationship.

The basic problem in the functioning of the present Church is that old patriarchal idea that one person has to have ultimate authority, and that person is the father or father substitute. I now believe that those recurring Mass readings of "Wives, obey your husbands" are, as our poor embarrassed pastors try to tell us, not really aimed at women after all. What the Church is doing is safeguarding its own present structure. The idea that only one person makes a decision (though he ought to be benevolent—husbands, love your obedient wives) is essential to the operation of a Roman-style Church.

But if a couple can function as equal collaborators, as equal partners in decision-making, as co-ministers to one another and as collaborators with the family, the entire traditional relationship of priest to parish, of bishop to the spouse-diocese, of pope to Mother Church is threatened.

My point is not that husband-wife teams ought to be ordained together, although I do think this is extremely important; and further, I do think our already established pattern of married male deacons, with their unofficially assisting wives, can do a great deal of harm.

Partnership Marriage: Model for Ministry

My point is that if our Church is to continue reflecting upon itself in familial terms—and I am sure it will—then it is essential that we direct much more of our attention to the husband-wife relationship as the basic male-female relationship, and that we acknowledge and celebrate the partnership-marriage as a model for ministry.

In the practical order, I think we women must remember that much of our ministry ought to be directed toward helping our sisters achieve that marriage partnership. As a concrete example, although I can only applaud Sister Marie Augusta Neal's proposals, I must ask just how this Sabbatical year is going to function for women who have young families. Surely they don't dare dream of a Sabbatical year off to spend in a monastery, school, or public service. The poignant fact is that the average housewife and mother doesn't even get the Sabbath *day* off. Does anybody care?

18

Sisterhood: Model of Future Priesthood

Leonard Swidler

LEONARD SWIDLER obtained his Ph.D. in History from the University of Wisconsin and a Licentiate in Sacred Theology from the University of Tubingen (Germany). As editor and co-founder of the JOURNAL OF ECUMENICAL STUDIES his interest in ecumenism led to various memberships including the North American Academy of Ecumenists, Committee on Catholic-Jewish Relations of the Cardinal's Commission on Human Relations (Philadelphia) and Reformed Presbyterian-Roman Catholic Consultation, U.S.A. He has written extensively on renewal in the Church, including DIALOGUE FOR REUNION (Herder & Herder), THE ECUMENICAL VANGUARD (Duquesne University), and with Rabbi Marc H. Tannenbaum, JEWISH CHRISTIAN DIALOGUES, twelve entries in the NEW CATHOLIC ENCYCLOPEDIA and numerous articles. His most widely known "Jesus Was A Feminist," is only one of the many publications related to women and religion. Leonard Swidler is currently teaching in the Religion Department at Temple University.

I would like to focus on only one point, of the many, that press for analysis in this pregnant topic: future models of the priesthood. Several assumptions, however, serve as a matrix from which my remarks will flow. I would like to indicate them, though space limitations prevent me from documenting or analyzing them.

Lack of Viable Impediments

On the basis of long, thorough research, I, along with many other Catholic theologians, am completely convinced that there are no persuasive arguments—biblical, theological, traditional, or other —against ordaining qualified women Catholic priests and bishops. (I refer you to Haye van der Meer, S.J., *Women Priests In the Catholic Church*, as a most thoroughgoing study of this matter—he comes to the same conclusion.)

Reasons for Ordination

If there are no valid arguments against ordaining qualified women, it is patent to me that such women ought to be ordained as soon as possible, for several reasons.

First, it has been at least an unconscious, invincible (to use the traditional language) kind of injustice in the past to have barred women from ordination. From this time forward it will be a conscious, vincible, kind of injustice to refuse to ordain qualified women. Therefore, for the sake of justice, and for the sake of the Church's commitment to it, qualified women should be ordained.

Secondly, if the Gospel is to be fully and effectively witnessed, that is, if the Church is to carry out its mission, the talents of *all* its members must be fully utilized. Clearly this applies to the female half of the Church, including those women who have priestly and episcopal talents.

Also, if the priesthood is to be properly reformed so as to be more effective in the contemporary and future worlds, qualified women must be a part of the present priesthood so they can participate, not only from without, but also from within, in the reformation of that priestly ministry. Women must not be shoved—or step— aside until the newly formed priesthood is presented to the world. Such a reformed priesthood will automatically be mal-formed— because only male-formed.

The Church, and the world, needs as full a democratization as possible. That is, the very structures as well as the spirit of the Church must foster the fullest development of every person's potentialities in order that they may grow into mature human beings, both independent and interdependent. It is largely this goal that priestly and episcopal leadership should serve: to make every member of the Church a leader as well as a follower.

Against the background of these assumptions, I wish, as a single recommendation, to address myself to nuns. Many nuns obviously have the talent and vocation for the priestly ministry. It is also clear (from the event of the Detroit Ordination Conference) that they have the necessary organizational skills, political skills and the motivation needed to persuade the Church authorities to open the priesthood to qualified women.

Sisterhood: Urgent Need

In the carrying out of the priestly ministry, once it has been attained, and even now in working toward that goal, I urge sisters to be highly conscious that a main function of leadership ministry is to make all those they serve leaders as well. Moreover, I urge nuns to follow the example of Jesus, particularly, and to work most of all to bring to full maturity the most suppressed element of the world and of the Church: laywomen. If Jesus, a male, could identify with and champion the cause of the most oppressed of his society, women—for Jesus was indeed a feminist!—then surely nuns today can identify with and champion the cause of their sisters, laywomen.

As a nun works in a parish, school or wherever, I urge her from the beginning to seek out her lay sisters in a special, though by no means exclusive, way and to bond with them, make every effort to strive to place a laywoman alongside her in leadership, perhaps even at her head, or in her stead.

I urge that you not identify with the male clergy as over against the laity. The last thing the Church (and the world it ministers to) needs is an expanded clericalism! It will only be when our sisters, your *lay* sisters, have reached their maturity, have taken their full roles, as leaders as well as followers, in the Church and the world, that your priestly ministry will have begun to be fulfilled. Then it will be true to say, in every sense, "sisterhood is powerful!"

19
Synthesis of Ordination Conference

Mary Daniel Turner, S.N.D. de N.

SISTER MARY DANIEL TURNER is a member of the Sisters of Notre Dame de Namur (Maryland Province). Her M.A. in Philosophy is from Catholic University and her M.A. in Theology is from the University of Toronto. Having been provincial of the SNDdeN Maryland Province, she also served as Member of the Advisory Board to the American Jewish Committee's Service Center. Her experience has included teacher of theology, participant in a research project on the "Relevance of Organized Religion in the U.S." and consultant to doctoral and masters' students in research concerning Diocesan Sisters' Councils, Chapters of Congregations and women's ministries. She is currently Executive Director of the Leadership Conference of Women Religious, Washington, D.C.

We have been so long with you,
and you have not known us.

This synthesis provides an opportunity for reflection on the experience of the Detroit Ordination Conference. It provides, if you will, a moment for theologizing on the reality of those days so that we may, from that event, grow in our capacity to be Church.

At the heart of the invitation to gather for the Ordination Conference was a recognition of and respect for the empowerment that is already ours because we have been gifted by God with life and with faith. Through the happenings of the Conference days we hoped to discover how we experience ourselves as acknowledging and owning —laying claim to—this empowerment.

Through our sharings we hoped, too, to learn how we experience ourselves as women and men who live in a Church and in a society that are redeemed but not fully, in a Church and in a society that are both graced and sinful. We wanted to create a climate for facilitating our capacity to commit, or not to commit ourselves, to specific actions relative to the question of the ordained ministry.

In formulating this synthesis I have selected three issues for consideration. These issues, I believe, were central to the discussions and dialogues. While the presentations of the speakers and respondents have been used to focus the issues, the oral and written reports from the small sharing groups also reveal that the three issues were, by and large, dominant. However carefully nuanced, diversely addressed, critically examined and/or differently strategized, it seems to me that the many words spoken together were informed, directed, and enspirited by:

(1) the need for a reinterpretation of the priesthood within today's pastoral needs,

(2) a concern for bonding among women, and

(3) an emphasis on fidelity to the tradition of Church.

Rich scriptural, theological, historical, sociological and cultural analyses marked the major presentations. Some may disagree with the analyses. However, the major presentations, combined with the feedback from the respondents, evoked a desire for continuing dialogue, probing and critiquing, especially when respondents differed from and/or questioned an analysis. We heard, on the one hand, affirmation of the quality, the depth, and the scope of the research. On the other, we recognized more keenly the unfinished, multifaceted, multidimensional character of the ordination issue. Perhaps we could readily identify with Carroll Stuhlmueller's initial insight that unless the calm and incisive vision of Elizabeth Carroll and her invitation to thought and study mark our ways of addressing the issue of ordination, the apocalyptic vision of Daniel may burst upon us—possibly from within us.

The challenge Elizabeth Carroll offered (as did each of the speakers) to reinterpret the priesthood within today's pastoral needs raised a radical question: Is ordination *per se* the issue we want to address? Or is the issue the pastoral needs of people? In truth, is the question we are addressing and the one out of which we must strategize: How are the pastoral needs of the community—personal, local, national, international being served by the Church? Or to nuance the question yet more, as Marie Augusta Neal did: How does the Church—that is, you and I and all who name themselves Roman Catholic—how does the Church so minister that not only are the effects of injustice and oppression alleviated but the causes as well are eradicated?

In fine, we have been challenged by the speakers, the respondents, and ourselves to declare our posture. Will we address the question of an ordained ministry from a stance of vested interest or from the stance of the Gospel imperative that:

the poor hear the Good News;

the blind recover their sight;

the oppressed be set free;

that the Year of the Lord be proclaimed—experienced.

(Luke 4:18ff.)

The radical questions of who ministers, of how we minister, and to whom we minister place in bold relief what Richard McBrien described as "that ambiguous and often quoted text of *Lumen Gentium* (#10) that the common priesthood of the faithful differs from the ministerial or hierarchial priesthood in 'essence and not only in degree.' " Will theologians and ecclesiologists accept the challenge inherent in the ambiguity—a challenge which, responded to and clarified, will help in the creation of new models of ministry—ordained, commissioned, nonordained?

If each speaker challenged us to a reinterpretation of priesthood within today's pastoral needs, each also called us to be about this reinterpretation not in isolation but *with others*. The bonding we must be about can become, must become we are told, an alternative to domineering-subservient patterns: matriarchies are no substitute for patriarchies. We have heard unequivocally that our way of bonding must demonstrate that adult communities are characterized by the qualities of sisterhood and brotherhood. As sisters and brothers, we are gifted to be present to one another interdependently—as co-creators.

The reinterpretation of the priesthood, as Elizabeth Fiorenza reminded us, touches the apostolic and universal qualities of the Church. Our bonding and coalition building must, therefore, be universal and apostolic in character. Eleanor Kahle noted the need to know our neighbor. Among ourselves we spoke feelingly of the need to bond with women and men. Inclusiveness, not exclusiveness, is the mark of Christianity. Fear begets stereotyping and stereotyping, in turn, is a way of defining people in and out. The issue of the ordained ministry must not be permitted to be or to become, we have said, a United States, white, middle class, female, and/or nun's agenda. Only by bonding with others, only by seeing, knowing, experiencing the interrelatedness of racism, nationalism, militarism, fascism, and the other "isms" with sexism, can we bring about systemic change—and so demonstrate the apostolic and universal character of ministry.

We must bond with other peoples and nations; we must be in contact with all the so-called classes and segments of society. Nevertheless, the speakers and our own behaviors at the Detroit Ordination Conference prompt, I would say compel, us to give the bonding of women with women the highest priority in our efforts to help transform structures and to create new ministry models.

Elizabeth Fiorenza urged a praxis of sisterhood NOT based on sexual stratification. Rosemary Ruether suggested, cautiously noting the dangers inherent in her suggestion, the mobilization of women's religious orders to help effect a change in the ordained ministry. Leonard Swidler pleaded for nuns "to identify with and champion the cause of their sisters—laywomen."

Given our experiences, we must question, I believe, whether women want to identify their relationship to one another out of ecclesiastical definitions, e.g., lay-religious. Do women want to name their womanhood out of a genital sexual status—unmarried/married, celibate/noncelibate? Must women, if they want to be sisters to one another and others, not root their self-understanding in the fact that they *are women*? Is not the gift of our womanhood primary to a woman's self-definition and understanding and thus to her relationship with others and in particular to other women?

Anne Carr underlined that the task of reinterpreting the priesthood in relation to pastoral needs and of doing so bonded with others calls for fidelity to the tradition of the Church. Fidelity, as we well know and keenly experienced in Detroit, demands life-giving, critical analysis and actions. The dialectic between Christian tradition and human experience exacts discipline, reverence, creativity, courage, and risk taking.

As Margaret Farley so starkly reminded us, the question of admitting error in a Church that lays claim to infallibility requires a capacity for radical conversion. New consciousness, speakers said in many and varied ways, necessitates a change of heart, different behavior, more Gospel-inspired and directed choices. New consciousness is not an opportunity for throwing stones. "Oppression is a subjective response to a situation. . . ," George Tavard observed. And we agree. Nevertheless, an objective state of oppression does exist when examined or unexamined practices, policies, and structures are maintained and supported that define some members of Church and society as less than persons. Thus, heightened consciousness is for each of us a challenge, Leonard Swidler pointed out, to acknowledge the difference between vincible and invincible ignorance. Heightened consciousness is a call to act out the acknowledgment in our future choices. Our speakers, especially Margaret Farley, alerted us to the dangers of using myth and ideology to legitimate the status quo and to rationalize the unexamined in our behavior.

Hopefully, we will follow the advice of Richard McBrien and be about the reinterpreting of the priesthood not only in fidelity to tradition but also in the light of eternity. And I would underline that Margaret Farley offered us the question that can situate our reinterpretation of the priesthood, as well as the quality of our bonding with others and our responses to pastoral needs in the light of eternity: "What *ought* we to do?" For us to raise the moral question may become a first step in experiencing "an unconditional claim upon our action" and of bringing "eternity" to bear upon our current behavior.

To reinterpret the priesthood, to bond together for the reinterpretation and to do the task in fidelity to the Church's tradition and under a moral imperative is to enter into the death/resurrection mystery that marked the journey of Jesus—the one whom we name "brother." Dorothy Donnelly reminded us that the death of some of us is inevitable. By recalling a few of the speakers' insights we may glimpse the deaths that await us:

Can we recognize, as Emily Hewitt did,
>   that ordination is not a right but that the opportunity to test one's calling to ordination *is* a right, is, therefore, a matter of justice?

Can we take to heart Carroll Stuhlmueller's concern:
>   that the limitation of priesthood to male celibates may result in pastoral activity that is increasingly non-Eucharistic?

Will we test new models and understandings of ministry,
>   such as partnership marriage proffered by Arlene Swidler and the reconciling, celebrative models of Marie Augusta Neal?

Will we break down the symbolic walls of Jericho,

and experience in that breaking Bill Callahan's dream of reconciliation within and without the walls?
All of these activities:
>the recognizing
>>the taking to heart
>>>the testing
>>>>the breaking
>>>>>the building up
are ministries of women and men who are willing to taste death.

And to name these activities "ministries" is to bring forward
again the radical question raised during the conference: What *is* the
essence of the ordained ministry? Is the essence of the priesthood to
be defined in relation to sacraments, especially the Eucharist as
George Tavard maintains? Or are proclamation, education, service,
or the activities delineated by Margaret Farley—leadership and representation as well as sacralaty—constitutive elements of the priesthood?

The question reveals the nature and length of the journey ahead
of us. The tasks of reinterpreting the priesthood in relation to the pastoral needs of the people, of bonding among women, and of being
faithful to the tradition of the Church do not allow us, at this time, to
translate Marie Augusta Neal's sabbatical into a lived experience.
We can, nevertheless, by considering some principles of strategy and
concrete actions take steps to realize possibly Marie Augusta Neal's
and Bill Callahan's dreams of the future as well as our own.

I invite you to reflect on a Gospel parable that I believe quite ac-
curately describes who we are, how we experience ourselves, and how
we experience Church and societal structures—a parable that suggests an option constantly before us.

We are WHEAT and WEED—wheat and weed that Jesus urges
be allowed to grow together until the harvest time. But the harvest
time is NOW. Today is the day of salvation. Today is the Advent of
God.

Will we allow the wheat and weed that we are and that our structures are to be transformed by God's saving power? Will we say YES
to God's continuing irruptions among us and within us? Will we sur-
render ourselves to that death/resurrection experience that makes all
things new? In summary, will we present ourselves to each other and
to others as visible, credible expressions of the Spirit's creative, saving, transforming presence and power as we continue to address the
issue of the priesthood as it relates to the pastoral needs of people?

PART 3
LITURGICAL PRAYER

20

Lord, Teach Us
To Pray

Mary Collins, O.S.B.

MARY COLLINS, O.S.B. has exhibited leadership both in her religious community and in liturgical research. Her Ph.D. is from Catholic University, 1967, and her experience has included teaching at Benedictine College and at Kansas School of Religion, University of Kansas. Her articles on liturgical prayer and renewal have appeared in WORSHIP, CONCILIUM, LITURGY, LIVING LIGHT and other periodicals. She served on the North American Academy for Liturgy's Executive Committee, and was President of the Kansas City Society for Theological Study. While currently President of the Benedictine Sisters' Community Senate and a member of the Prioress's Council, Mary also serves as Board Member of North American Liturgical Conference, editorial committee of LITURGY, and Associate Editor for WORSHIP and RELIGION.

Liturgical planning for the Ordination Conference posed a number of challenges from the start. What would this assembly want to give ritual expression to? A full range of options was explored with the Task Force early in the planning. Should the liturgies include only women in ministerial roles? A conscious exclusion of men would put into high relief the lifelong women's experience of exclusion from liturgical service. Should the Sunday eucharistic liturgy be celebrated at all, since in the eucharistic action women feel most keenly their exclusion from sacramental ministry? Should there be simply a Word service in which women only had ministerial roles followed by a communion service at which women only ministered? Would the credibility of the group suffer through a rejection at this time of the official liturgy, since the women were asking for opportunity for ordination to sacramental ministry within the Roman Catholic Church? Finally, how could we offer a clear public ritual acknowledgment of the sense of vocation to sacramental ministry many women would be experiencing?

The Task Force objectives were clear: the conference was to bring the theological issue of the ordination of women to public discussion and prayer in the Roman Catholic Church. The mode was to be one of serious sharing of the faith perspectives of dedicated Catholic women. The apostolic delegate Archbishop Jean Jadot was to be asked not only to participate but even to preside at the final eucharist should he agree to be present during the conference.

In the light of these overall goals it became increasingly evident that this was not the event at which to deal directly with additional issues, namely the ritual forms and language of the purportedly renewed Roman Catholic Eucharist. The desired and invited ecclesiastical leadership would predictably balk, feel compromised, and withdraw from involvement in celebrating an imposed unofficial liturgy. Not only would there be a Sunday Eucharist. It would be the regular liturgy of the first Sunday of Advent. We would leave it to the sensibilities of the celebrant to attend to the most blatant sexist language.

Celebrating liturgy in an inclusive rather than an exclusive manner was our controlling norm throughout our planning. No provision would be made for presbyteral concelebration of the Eucharist. Wherever possible, ministers in both liturgies would reflect the membership of the adult community: women and men, the married and the celibate, professed religious, unmarried laity. The variety of gifts and ministries rather than sex distinctions would be celebrated in this segment of the Church trying to engender the future.

Admittedly, this thinking was not palatable to everyone present. One of the conference Task Force members told us somewhat sadly after the Saturday evening Liturgy of Blessing: "The Love Of Christ Leaves Us No Choice" that we may have offered a sense of redeemed humanity more integrated than some women participants were presently comfortable with: why were two readers men and only one a woman? why was the only vocal soloist that evening male? Had we, perhaps, done this to relegate men to current "women's roles"? In fact, we had not been that calculating.

Other judgments related to this liturgy of blessing were more conscious. It was our recommendation to the Task Force that Nadine Foley, O.P., who had presided in a ministry of service to the whole group for the previous six months in her work as chairwoman, ought to preside at the liturgical event which was the culmination of the conference. Since she maintained consistently that she had no personal sense of vocation to sacramental ministry, she was most reluctant to accept this liturgical role.

Much reflection went into determining the culminating action of the liturgy of blessing, the signing of the foreheads of those in the assembly aspiring to ordination. We knew we would be in extremely crowded, unfavorable conditions which would constrict movement. A touch gesture extended by those nearby seemed to be the available option. In the wake of the ordination of the Episcopal women priests, it seemed advisable to avoid any laying on of hands. Such a gesture could be misleading as to its intent in this context, and could easily be misinterpreted as an act of extraordinary, spontaneous, or pseudo-ordination.

The ritual gesture of the sign of the cross finally chosen condensed the meanings of the Easter mystery—new life through suffering, even death, in obedience to and for love of the transcendent God. It called forth faith and commitment from the one who offered the gesture and from the one who received it.

An unanticipated spontaneous gesture also occurred during the blessing rite. The 300 women and men who rose to receive the blessing reached out across the spaces and joined hands with friends and strangers. Carla De Sola, processional dancer during the liturgy of blessing, noted her feelings as she watched this movement: it was a strong gesture of sisterhood; it also suggested the image of galley slaves chained together in bondage.

Once the decision had been made to celebrate the Sunday Eucharist according to the Advent season, related decisions fell into place. The conference dates neared, and no member of the hierarchy had yet indicated his intention to attend. The Task Force moved to invite Boston priest John Finnegan to preside. The 1974-75 past president of the Canon Law Society of America, he had already registered as a participant on his own initiative. Task Force members recognized the leadership of the American Canon Law Society in recent years in confronting obsolescent ecclesiastical structures, and felt that his presidency at the Eucharist of the Ordination Conference would reflect his general sensitivity to the issues at stake.

Just as really, his sensitivity to the issues at stake in the conference made him concerned about respecting liturgical discipline and the jurisdiction of the local hierarchy. Pastoral responsiveness to the community of worshippers prevailed on the matter of yielding to a woman homilist.

Given our earlier decision to celebrate the official liturgy and not to impose an unofficial liturgy on any celebrant, sexist language in the eucharistic liturgy seemed inevitable. Only belatedly did this become a matter of open concern among some Task Force members and a scattered range of conference participants. What did this say about the level of conference consciousness? The pressures and the dilemma were real.

Standing by our original decision was not simply a matter of expediency. The liturgies and the conference in which they were celebrated gave honest expression to the woundedness of the historical Church and the faintest signs of new health. Sensitive readers and prayer leaders at times took the initiative to edit their own scriptural and liturgical texts. Where they did not, the very discomfort experienced in the assembly and the silent groping for new words were at the heart of the process of on-going renewal in American Catholic life and worship.

The sexist-language-in-liturgy problem is not superficial, and it cannot be treated lightly. It is intimately related to and as complex as the problem of generating new patterns of ministry for women and men. Few conference participants were calling for a simple incorporation of women into existing ecclesiastical structures. Most recognized a need for the transformation of priestly ministry itself. The liturgical situation is parallel. After the editorial pen has attended to *man* and *mankind*, *sons* and *brothers*, and the supposed generic *he*, what remains is a religious and linguistic quandry of massive proportions. How can an ancient religious literature and ritual expressing patriarchal, male-dominated community structure be rewritten to reflect a new consciousness?

As an academician combining liturgical research interests with university teaching in the area of women and religion, my considered judgment is that only strong new experiences within the Catholic faith community can genuinely reshape the tradition of public worship and legitimate its reinterpretation. Liberation theologians talk about orthopraxis—appropriate action. Until the Church is closer to this orthopraxis and lives as a Christ-redeemed humanity which has overcome alienated sex-related roles, nonsexist language may be a screen concealing reality.

Too much of Roman Catholic liturgical renewal to date has attended to words and too little to nonverbal ritual statements, as though the words were all. In recent years I have become much more interested in what people do ritually. What relationships to the Lord and to one another do they express in the unfolding movement of liturgical action? We concentrated our planning for the Detroit liturgies on ritual forms which could express the oneness of our faith in Christ, a oneness that precedes and transcends all structural distinctions. And we sought to focus on actions which suggested renewed relationships within the Church. In other words, we tried to move somewhat closer to orthopraxis.

Our options were limited by institutional reality, and the commitment of the conference leadership and participants to work within that reality at present. Yet each time some part of the Church approaches nearer to appropriate ritual action in the public worship of the baptized, the inadequacy of the male-dominated language becomes increasingly self-evident, at times ludicrous, at times offensive, at times an embarrassment.

Clearly not all aspects of the problem can be dealt with at once in a single weekend meeting. The Detroit Ordination Conference had limited goals and a controlled agenda. It was only the starting point of a process leading to the strong new experience of redemption within the Church from the demonic force of alienated sex roles. The proclamation resounded there that all the baptized share the one same Spirit of the risen Christ. The steps toward institutionalizing that redeemed future will be slow and filled with ambiguity. If the language and ritual tensions in the liturgy at the Ordination Conference embodied much of that ambiguity, it also confirmed for many participants their conviction in faith that the future could not be determined exclusively by the past.

Editor's Note:

There is greater consciousness in the U.S. and Canada than in other English-speaking countries regarding the issue of language and the liturgy. The Advisory Committee of the International Committee on English in the Liturgy addressed this in its meeting in London, passing the following resolution:

> *. . . recognize the necessity in all future translations and revisions, to avoid words which ignore the place of women in the*

Christian community altogether or which seem to relegate women to a secondary role." (8-19-75)

Rev. John Rotelle, OSA, Executive Secretary for the International Committee on English in the Liturgy, has begun a consultative group to study this further. More information can be obtained from Father Rotelle, 1330 Massachusetts Avenue, N.W., Washington, D.C. 20005.

21

A Liturgy of Invocation

Rosalie Muschal-Reinhardt

Prayer:

My sisters and brothers
Let us speak to our God.

O everliving, everloving and everunfolding God,
You have called us by name
and we have claimed our name:
We are the people of God.

We convene this Conference as an act of faith, hope and love
in you
and in the community of the people of God.

We come because we must
We have heard your good news

What you see before you was promised centuries ago by the prophet
Joel:

> In the days to come—it is the Lord who speaks—
> I will pour out my spirit on all humankind
> And your sons and daughters shall prophesy
> Your young shall see visions
> Your old shall dream dreams
> Yes, the Holy Spirit shall come upon all my servants, men and
> women alike, and they shall prophesy. (Acts 2:16-18)

We ask you now to fulfill that promise.
Embrace with your Spirit all those persons who have brought the
Conference to this moment.

Enliven with your Spirit those who will minister to this community
with a variety of gifts but one spirit

Fill with your Spirit those who are not here, but who are present with
us.

Touch each of us, enable us to speak with your will written on our
hearts and our minds, so that we may joyfully and fearlessly speak
the prophesy.

We praise you for you are a God of love and mercy.

We thank you for the gift of love and life in Jesus the Christ

We claim our power through your Holy Spirit,

One God, who lives forever in the Hearts of all people. Amen.

22

The Love of Christ
Leaves Us No Choice

Commentary: **Anne Mary Dooley, SSJ**

President: **Nadine Foley**

Dancers: **Carla De Sola**
            Sister Tria Thompson

Opening: **"Maranatha"**

Collect

Word Service

Response-Homily

Rite of Blessing

Signing of Foreheads

Dismissal and Song: **"Praise God from Whom All Blessings Flow"**

A Liturgy of Blessing

Commentary

    Tonight we anticipate the season of Advent in a celebration of the Word living in us as Church. We celebrate with silence and song, incense and dance, candles and wreath, praising God and giving thanks for what this conference has been to us as an expression of faith, a moment of hope, and as a pledge of genuine love of one another in Christ. We celebrate—because the love of Christ leaves us no choice. We celebrate as a church in process, engendering the future. We celebrate the presence in our midst of women and men with a sense of vocation to a renewed priesthood.

Advent speaks of promise and of hopes fulfilled. Our liturgy, too, looks forward to the full revelation of Emmanuel, God with us. As the holy people of God always in need of a conversion of our hearts, we join in the cry of believers in every century of the Church:

Maranatha! Come, O Christ the Lord.

Opening Collect

Yahweh, God, we ask your presence with us as we gather together on this the eve of your season of hope and promise. Ours is a new season of expectation, born of our faith in you, nourished by the personal Word we have been for one another, and ready for your inspiriting presence.

Open our hearts to hear and to cherish your Word, and confirm our belief that you will bring to completion what you have begun in us, while we lay no claim fully to understand your ways.

We pray in the name of Jesus Christ our Redeemer and of the Holy Spirit you have given us. Amen.

WORD SERVICE

Election and Mission
Eph. 1:3-6. 9-10	(New English Bible trans.)
Matt. 5:14-16	(NEB)
John 2:1-5	(NEB)

Response: "Into Your Hands, We Commend our Spirit"

Ministry in the Church
2 Cor. 6:3-6	
2 Cor. 6:7-10	(Philips)
2 Cor. 6:11-13	(NEB)

Response: Gelineau "Magnificat"

Promise and Expectation
2 Cor. 5:13-34. 17	
Acts 5:34-40a	(JB)
Luke 18:1-8	(JB)

Response

In the midst of our searching, our sharing, our planning, during this weekend of common concern, we draw apart as befits the Christian assembly, to hear again the Word. And when we do we are confronted once again with the paradox of our Christian faith. We reflect upon the Word proclaimed among us:

God has chosen each of us from all eternity—yet we dwell in the confused moment that is now.

God's hidden purposes await an appropriate time for their manifestation—yet our times are perhaps inappropriate ones.

We are alive in joy and hope and have cause for celebration—yet near us, even within us, death, in many and varied forms is ever present.

God invites us to open wide our hearts—yet we languish in awkwardness and fear.

We know the need to submit our efforts to the testing of the Spirit—yet we are impatient for our human ends.

We have certain faith that *yes*, the old order has gone and there is a new world—yet what meager measure we take of one another in this kingdom that has come.

When we bring the Word into connection with our experience, we know the meaning of the two-edged sword. We know with certain faith that what we so ardently desire, so eagerly await, has even now been already accomplished. For as Christians we live in the now and the not-yet of salvation, in historic and in mythic time.

We plod along, caught in the alien web of social relationships and sinful structures that are of our own making and that determine our human history, while we proclaim a message of peace and reconciliation and long to serve the world with the good news of the kingdom of God.

On this eve of Advent, we draw apart from our historic time symbolized by our change of space and mood, to enter into that mythic time where the central truth of our liberating redemption is both believed and experienced. This our liturgical rite allows us to do.

It is in this faith dimension of time that we share unity of belief, form the purposes of hope, and experience bonds of love.

It is here that we know our God deeply and personally—as individuals, as communities.

It is here in the inner quiet of our hearts that we know, with that experiential knowledge that cannot be denied, how God would have us be and what he would have us do.

It is here that some among us have awakened to a new realization and have said *yes* to the possibilities of a sacramental ministry for the sake of the broken world which awaits the mercy of the one who cannot and will not be contained.

Here the others of us, who have not that experience, would share your joy in this new awakening and support you for the bitterness that may be your lot.

In silence now, let us center ourselves in the presence of the Lord for a few moments and pray.

BLESSING RITE

The Word which sets us free to love is alive and active and sharper than any two-edged sword. It can slip through the place where life and spirit, joints and marrow divide. It sifts the purposes and thoughts of the heart. Everything lies naked and exposed to the eyes of the One with whom we have to reckon. (Heb 4:12ff)

So, having heard the Word together, now, in an atmosphere of quiet and reflection, we invite all of you in this assembly who aspire to ordination for sacramental ministry to stand and present yourselves openly before the community, just as you have already, within your hearts, boldly approached the gracious God to receive mercy and to find timely help.

(Pause for participants to rise. Music: antiphon of Magnificat: "The Lord has done marvels for me, holy is His name."

Having seen your prayer and the thoughts of your hearts, your sisters and brothers in Christ who wish, may rise to sign your foreheads with the sign of the cross of the Lord Jesus Christ whom you would serve. Our sign is both a blessing and a pledge of our continued prayer and support on the journey you have begun tonight.

23
Eucharistic Liturgy, First Sunday of Advent

Certain as the Dawn Is His Coming

Commentary: Joan Campbell, S.L.

President: John Finnegan

Homilist: Mary Schaefer

Entrance Song: "Wake, Awake, the Night is Dying"

First Reading: Isaiah

Response: Ps. 80

Second Reading: 1 Corinthians

Gospel Alleluia

Gospel: Mark

Eucharistic Prayer and Responses/Acclamations

Communion Meditation: "New Jerusalem"

Recessional: Sion Sing

Commentary: First Sunday of Advent

Today's Eucharist celebrates the first Sunday of Advent: it marks the first day of the dawning new age, the first day of the coming of the Christ, the beginning of the history of salvation—but not the complete victory of light over darkness. On this first Sunday of Advent, we are assembled as a church only beginning renewal, to celebrate a liturgy only beginning to be renewed. The institutionalized wounds of the Roman Catholic Church and the whole human race are embodied in the very forms we use to celebrate redemption. They

155

are embodied in our continued distinctions between women and men and in our exclusion of women in language, in liturgy and in life.

We do not deny or try to cover our woundedness in this celebration. Rather, we present ourselves for healing. As we have been roused from centuries of slumber to speak here in Detroit of new possibility, we give voice to our hope that the whole Church will awaken quickly to make ready the way of the Lord.

Opening Comment: John T. Finnegan

My sisters and brothers, I come before you to preside at your Eucharist. I come in a reality and as a symbol. I come in the reality of my brotherhood with you and my friendship and support and love for you. I come as a symbol, symbolizing that this Eucharist is still presided over by male, celibate priests. I accept that symbol. I accept its sinfulness, its inadequacy. But like each of us who have learned that in our own personal sinfulness we can find the transforming power of the grace of Christ, so we see too in this symbol that the transforming power of Christ can heal the Church; through this brokenness, a new advent promise and hope can come.

And so, may we draw within for a moment and be grateful for our inadequacy, our weakness, and yes, even our sinfulness, with repentance and faith that can renew us personally and can renew our Church.

Homily

Christ is coming. Will we the Church open the door for him? (Mark 13:33-37)

Face to face with the God of holiness, we discover that we are sinners. Will we confess our sin? (Isaiah 63:16-17; 64:1,4-8)

We have received the Spirit's gifts in order to respond to God and carry on the work of Jesus the redeemer. Are we as Church refusing God's gifts? (1 Corinthians 1:3-9)

Advent is the season for prophets: people who wait in the darkness and long for the dawn, people who hear God speak in their wilderness and stammer out that message to all who will hear. We who were lonely prophets have listened for three days to what the Spirit is saying to the Church. Advent is the season when we beg God to break through to us and dwell with us forever, shaping us into a new, responsive people. Today God's Advent word challenges this assembly and the entire Church as we renew our hope in Christ's coming, resolve to watch and wait through the dark hours, pray for perseverance until the dawn, put ourselves again in God's hands.

Advent is a time of rising expectation and deepening joy, of wonderful happiness as we cease to be rebels and welcome the Lord's redemptive presence. But we have to give up our sin, we have to make Isaiah's prayer our own. In God's presence we discover our failures. Humankind's new consciousness that relationships between women and men have been set askew by pride is a sign that God is near. But we the whole Church have still to translate this insight into practice, have still to correct the scandal of allowing human custom to inhibit the saving work of Christ.

We must be willing to abandon our sin, really willing to make Christ's coming evident in our day-to-day life. Are we disciples brave enough to open the doors for the expanding ministry of the Lord of the Church? Having experienced the claim of Jesus on our lives, can women persevere until we too share in preparing Christ's way through word and sacrament?

People need Christ's ministry, but we are powerless to provide. Behind us lies the pain of a call we may not heed, and the tears and sorrow of many women since that time when women first ministered to Jesus. Before us stretches an uncertain period of testing. Our charism to ministry will continue to be challenged, denied, ignored. How will we face the future? Today's gospel calls for *active*, not passive waiting until Christ comes. Our waiting will not be easy. It will be like the waiting of Jesus during those hidden years in Nazareth. It may be like the waiting of Christ on the cross.

Is it any more astonishing for a woman to be priest than for Saul the persecutor to become Paul the apostle? Advent prepares us for that event when God did something never done before: become incarnate. God uses powerless people, gives gifts to those who are not supposed to be chosen. We can thank God for our charism of ministry. We can live in the joyful certainty that Christ wants our heads, our hands, our hearts for his service. Let us be whatever Christ would be, do whatever Christ would do. We can be priestly women, growing more like our great high priest until the whole Church recognizes his priesthood in us. We are God's gifts to the Church; we are being prepared for the altar. Let us be confident that God is making us ready.

Let us give God the freedom to bring about Christ's priestliness in us, not grasping Jesus' ministry of word and sacrament for ourselves, not shrinking from whatever action God inspires. Our charism is God's gift, already given but waiting to be recognized. We can be sure that God will bring to completion what the Spirit has begun in our hearts. God will model us into images of Jesus the servant.

In the spirit of Paul the apostle, let us give thanks for our teachers and preachers: for the Church's spiritual leaders, whether they stand with us or against us; for all who have mediated Christ to us, especially our mothers and sisters in the faith. May our priestly brothers pray for us. We have envied them as they preach the saving word of the Gospel and break the bread of the Eucharist. We are unable to share their ministry; may they share our grief.

God is faithful. May we be faithful.

From within the heart of the Church we can pray that God will rend the heavens and come down, breaking through our human defenses, so that God's will—not man's will but God's will—be done. This is not the time to fall asleep, lose heart, silence our active witness. Christ *is* coming. Women *shall* share in preparing his way and opening the doors of the world to its savior. We don't know when the Lord will come. We must stay awake, live the Advent liturgy, wait in readiness and in growing joy.

PART 4

A LOOK AT THE ASSEMBLY

24

Greeting to the Assembly

Nadine Foley, O.P.

I greet you this afternoon in the many names by which we call our God:

—whose creating activity is continuing and all-encompassing in human history,

—whose incarnating and redeeming influence extends to a broken world through the healing ministry of a missioned people,

—whose in-spiriting and quickening life engenders reasonable hope and moves people to the unexpected and the surprising discovery of new possibilities for life.

I have asked Mary Lynch to join us on the platform as this conference opens. It was she who on December 14, one year ago, gathered together a group of interested persons and addressed to them a question:

"Is it time, in the International Women's Year, to raise the issue of the ordination of women in the Roman Catholic Church?"

Her response then was overwhelmingly affirmative; but its proportions unknown.

In the year that has intervened that response has grown to a crescendo. The 1,200 of you registered for the Conference, the 500 whose registrations were regretfully returned for lack of space, the numerous others who watch expectantly what we do, are its tangible expression.

I thought you should have the opportunity to recognize the power of one questioning woman. And that Mary should have a first-hand view of this thing which has come to pass.

In a unique way I believe that our assembling today is a special instance of the urgency of faith that catches fire on the earth and forms a people. We come together as a legitimate and authentic expression of the Church in its self-understanding as a people of God. Our leaders have called us repeatedly in our times to assume responsibility for the mission of the Church. In his letter *On the Development of Peoples*, Pope Paul appealed to the members of the Church "without waiting passively for orders and directives to take the initiative freely and to infuse a Christian spirit into the mentality, customs, laws and structures of the community in which they live" (81). The community in which we live is not only the contemporary world with its variety of political, cultural and social forms. We live also in the community called Church and we are rightly admonished to have care that a Christian spirit infuse its mentality, customs, laws, and structures.

What then brings us together from points all across our continent and abroad? I believe there is one answer only to this question. We are brought together by the urgency of the Gospel of Jesus Christ —and the love for the Church which takes that Gospel as its mission in the world. We are people immersed in the contemporary reality. We know "its joys and hopes, griefs and anxieties" (*Gaudium et Spes*, 1). Some of us—the majority of us—are women, and participants in the "true social and cultural transformation" (*Gaudium et Spes*, 4) of our times which is welling up in our experience, giving us a renewed sense of our personhood, and opening before us new possibilities for creative activity in behalf of ourselves and others. Today we have deepened motives for embracing the Gospel of one who came that all might have life and have it more abundantly. His message speaks profoundly to our emerging self-understanding. When a mentality, when laws, when customs, when structures, however, contradict our life-giving experience and stand seemingly in opposition to the liberating message of Jesus Christ, then surely we cannot wait passively, but must indeed take the initiative and find ways to infuse a Christian spirit into the Church which would be the instrument of his reconciling mission.

We come together, I believe, not to confront the Church, not to act in defiance of the Church, but to be Church. We are women and men, lay and religious, and clerical, who hold many kinds of responsibility. We are rooted in a common faith and a common baptism, and we know the magnitude of our mission in our times. Many would tell us that there are more important issues to occupy our concerns than that of the ordination of women. I believe that to be true. In a world dehumanized by hunger, disease, racism, militarism, political and economic oppression of people, our concern here may seem trivial and introspective. But I believe the evils of injustice to be interwoven, and that the unravelling can and must begin in many places.

It is also true that the Christian Church has begun to speak forcefully to the issues of social injustice in society at large, and to begin programs of action to address the problems effectively. But the official Church speaks less persuasively when it addresses the question of women and our place in its life and ministry. The Church owes women a debt of gratitude, we are told; the Church must open channels of dialogue with women, we hear; the Church must involve women in decision making, furthermore. We are grateful for the beginnings of a new consciousness that these declarations represent, and we are impatient for their implementation. But ours is another kind of consciousness. We are not a class of persons set over and against a male church which speaks consistently of itself in a masculine idiom. We *are* the Church, in coresponsible participation with all other baptized persons, and we would hasten the day when our growing self-awareness finds expression in the mentality, the customs and the laws that structure our ministerial presence in the world.

We raise here the question of the ordination of women. There are many related issues subsumed within it: the personhood of women —is it to be acknowledged fully; the effects of baptism and confirmation—are they conditioned by sexual differentiation; the possibilities of ministry—are they to be contained by an ethos from another day; the nature of theology—can the experience of women be a locus for its development; the meaning of tradition—is it only a static concept or a dynamic reality; the interpretation of the Scriptures—to what extent are they culturally conditioned; the ecumenical dialogue—can it really be impeded by existential truth; the credibility of the Church— is it genuinely the liberating embodiment of the Gospel of Jesus Christ; the powerlessness of women in the Church—are the talents and leadership of women to be denied a Church in mission?

These are weighty questions, but the answers to many of them are already available to us. We do not propose to spend our short time together in going over old ground, nor do we see our meeting as a forum for accusation and recrimination unbefitting a Christian assembly. We take the positive view that a new future in the Lord is always possible and that our efforts are needed to bring it about.

We of the task force have planned our meeting with the hope

that we can be a model of the Church in praxis—reflecting upon the presentations put before us, dialoguing in openness to and acceptance of one another, our experience and our points of view, considering the action responses that are incumbent upon us and possible for us, and sharing our faith in communal celebration. We know that there are many expectations of our meeting, that our hopes are high. It is because of them that we confidently transfer to you what leadership we have exercised in bringing this event into being. What this conference will be is yours to determine. It requires your concentration, your creativity, the focussing of your expectations. In short, it requires your work. We are confident that you can and will accept that challenge.

25

A Process Model for
Theological Reflections
and Just Actions

Nancy A. Lafferty, F.S.P.A.

NANCY A. LAFFERTY, F.S.P.A. is an Assistant Professor at St. Louis University teaching values and ethics in the School of Social Service. She has been a field education coordinator for the Corporate Ministry Program in the Department of Theological Studies and has worked with the St. Louis Theological Consortium. She holds a Doctor of Philosophy degree and a Master of Social Work degree from Washington University and a Master of Arts in Sociology from Catholic University of America. She is a member of the Franciscan Sisters of Perpetual Adoration, LaCrosse, Wisconsin. She is involved currently in creating a textbook: VALUES AND ETHICS IN PROFESSIONAL DECISION-MAKING, and has published for SISTERS TODAY and REVIEW FOR RELIGIOUS.

The purpose of the Roman Catholic Women's Ordination Conference held on November 28-30, 1975 in Detroit, Michigan was threefold. It was an open group dialogue conference initiated first, "to convene persons committed to making the talents of women fully available for ministerial service in the Roman Catholic Church; secondly, to inform the People of God about women preparing for a new expression of full priesthood, and thirdly, to provide a forum in which participants could examine the present status of the ordination issue and develop strategies for effective action."[1] The Ordination Conference Taskforce of twenty-one women hoped to raise the concern about ordained ministry for women as an issue with national visibility.

Given this focus, a process model was envisioned to implement the threefold purpose. The goal of the model was simply to initiate an open group dialogue forum in which the participants in a national conference could explore the issue: "Women In The Future Priesthood Now: A Call For Action." The major objective was to create a climate in which both theological and scriptural reflection and just actions could take place. An assumption was made early in the planning that the participants' characteristics and interests would determine the model of the conference. In oral communications and written statements on the registration blanks, the early conference registrants characterized themselves as having a great deal of professional and interdisciplinary knowledge as well as considerable ministerial experience. It became evident that the participants were interested in having theological and scriptural issues explicated by scholars as well as sharing the experiences of their own diverse ministries and expressing their hopes and plans for the future. It was decided that a reflection/action model was needed to honor the desires and characteristics of the conference participants.

The Process Model Designed

A new model of the People of God in dialogue was attempted in order to provide "education in the context of action and action informed by education," as Patricia Hughes, Conference Publicity Coordinator, later described it.[2] It was decided that the theological issues and action plans of the participants could be surfaced by randomly assigning the participants to small groups of ten members each. It was projected that one facilitator would be needed for every twenty conference participants. Three reflection/action group dialogues were planned across a three-day meeting time. The small group dialogues were alternated with presentations by nationally recognized scholars. The group dialogues were viewed as necessary and complementary to the scholarly presentations since the theological and scriptural explorations would occur in the context of concrete actions. And any action plans designed by the groups would tend to be informed by the education process taking place.

Projections were made that the conference participants would choose to re-group themselves for continuing dialogue as the process was set in motion. It was assumed that these emergent groups would arise according to the participants' theological issues, action preferences and/or common characteristics. Provisions were made so that as the participants created the realities of the conference, they could be implemented by the participants and the conference support groups as the participants so chose.

In May, 1975 several speakers were contacted and numerous professionally trained people were invited to volunteer their expertise. Among them was Marjorie Tuite, O.P., who was asked to serve as Strategist. Her first task was to meet with the Taskforce to organize the conference. She aided the Taskforce during the planning sessions and the conference itself. In the final session she offered strategies to the participants based on the issues they had raised. Another, Mary Daniel Turner, S.N.D.deN., acted as Synthesizer. She collated the theological and scriptural reflections presented by the conference speakers and the participants. Nancy Lafferty, F.S.P.A., as Process Consultant, accepted the responsibility of facilitating the small group dialogues and training the thirty facilitators that were projected as necessary for the expected 600-person conference. These three women met with the Taskforce Executive Committee, i.e. Nadine Foley, O.P., Taskforce Coordinator, Patricia Hughes, Publicity Coordinator, and Joan Campbell, S.L., Communications Coordinator, before and during the conference to deal with the issues raised by the conference support groups and the participants. By November, 1975, over 165 persons had volunteered their time and expertise to help organize and support the conference. The number of participants had mushroomed to over 1200 persons with another 500 who were turned away because of inadequate space and facilities.

On September 12-14, 1974 an Ordination Mini-Conference was organized to train thirty facilitators. The process model was explained, and the facilitators agreed to surface the conference participants' needs, their theological reflections and/or action plans. As was the case for all the conference support people, the facilitators were drawn from various parts of the country and diverse professions and occupations. For the most part they had received specialized training in group facilitation skills prior to the Adrian Mini-Conference.

One characteristic of the process model was that actions were often judged in the light of Scriptural passages that came alive for those supporting the conference as well as those participating. For the Adrian Mini-Conference facilitators the passage from Haggai 1:14-15 spoke to them of their contribution: "And Yahweh gave them a desire to rebuild the temple, so they gathered in early September . . . and volunteered their help."[3] This first training session was later supplemented by other regional meetings when it became obvious that at least thirty additional facilitators were needed to work with the expanded conference population.

At the Adrian Mini-Conference a Process Facilitation Core Group was formed to carry on the group dialogue responsibilities. This group of eight women chose to work in a collegial and consensual decision-making style. This responsibility-sharing was characteristic of the original conference planning group, the December, 1974 "thirty-one," and the January, 1975 Ordination Conference Taskforce of "twenty-one." Nancy Lafferty, F.S.P.A. as Process Consultant, coordinated the Process Facilitation Core Group. It included Ellen Zazycki as Process Facilitator, Lyn Somers as Grouping Consultant, Carol Muschal Grubb who served as Communications Coordinator for the sixty facilitators and four Core Facilitators: Meg Andrezik, O.P., Rose Colley, S.L., Ann Kelly, C.S.J., and Roberta Walsh, C.S.J. Each worked with three primary facilitators. It was decided that each primary facilitator would collate the participants' issues and action plans from five auxiliary facilitators. Thus, each of the sixty auxiliary facilitators would be with twenty conference participants—two groups of ten members each. Again, by the end of the Adrian Mini-Conference the responsibilities had been shared with another group of people willing to implement the design of the process model.

During October and November, 1975 the Process Facilitation Core Group sought out thirty additional facilitators from across the country. They identified another thirty-five persons who were qualified to work with emergent groups, train additional facilitators, act as content resource persons, content facilitators, and process observers. All these people agreed to share various responsibilities with the Synthesizer and Strategist in order to process the results of the 120 group dialogues, once the conference would get underway. By November 15th the process model was enfleshed and ready to be implemented with the conference participants of the first National Ordination Conference of Roman Catholic Women in history.

Women in the Future Priesthood Now: A Call for Action

As the participants gathered November 28, 1975 in Detroit, they began to realize that they were the focus of the conference. The Process Facilitation Core Group and the other conference support groups, including the Ordination Conference Taskforce, were there simply to enable people to deal with a question—"How can women who express a call to ordained ministry have their vocation tested?" It was one of the many questions that, as Pope Paul stated so well, "requires a discerning with wisdom—on the level of documentation and of reflection and on the level of study for the effective promotion of the dignity and responsibility of women."[4] There was a spirit of excitement and creative involvement as the participants formed into the randomly assigned groups. They readily engaged one another in forthrightly considering the difficult theological issues raised in the opening addresses. The participants quickly perceived the sixty facilitators as connectors, bridge-builders, reconcilers and resource people who could aid them in self-initiated reflections and/or just actions. And the facilitators came to understand their activities in the light of Isaiah 58:10-12:

> Your light will shine out from the darkness, and the
> darkness around you will be as bright as day.
> Yahweh will guide you continually . . . and you will be like
> a well-watered garden, like an ever-flowing spring
> Your people will rebuild the long-deserted ruins of the
> cities,
> And you will be known as "The Breach-menders"—"The
> People Who Restore Ruined Homes."

The conference participants expressed a multiplicity of ideas and diverse plans for action in the opening dialogues. The primary facilitators collated the issues late Friday night and brainstormed with the Process Facilitation Core Group, the Synthesizer and Strategist to understand the themes and plans that the participants were initiating. As the second day of the conference began, it became evident that a large number of participants were forming into emergent groups, while many others were choosing to remain with the previous day's dialogues. The process model had provided for two consultants to coordinate the activities with the projected emergent groups. By midmorning on Saturday, Sharon Stanton, O.S.F. and Donna Markham, O.P. were aiding the participants to locate other groups and individuals who had similar reflection and/or action preferences that they wished to explore together. The assumption in the process model about emergent groups proved accurate. And apparently due to the unity, equality and participation experienced by the participants, nearly fifty emergent groups became bonded together during the remainder of the conference.

The emergent groups appeared to result from the bonding experience between lay women and women religious who expressed their call to ordination, to service in the permanent deaconate and to seminary teaching and theological research. Others were concerned with theological and scriptural explorations around deeper understandings of the Triune nature of God and the use of sexist language in translations of the Scriptures. Regional and local reflection/action groups formed, such as the Women of the Northeast, the Minnesota Action Group, the Cleveland Women in Ministry, New York-New Jersey Women and the Southern California Taskforce on Women in the Catholic Church. Various groups formed out of common commitments to peace and justice issues, campus ministry and a variety of pastoral ministries among the People of God.

In the final plenary session, the participants accepted the responsibility for their own reflections and action plans. They knew there was no on-going Taskforce or organization that would implement their plans in local parishes or raise their issues for them regionally or nationally. Individuals and groups shared the results of the reflection/action dialogues and emergent groups as the spirit of unity, equality and participation increased. Some groups realized that the reflection issues and action plans were affirmed by the life-giving realities they had experienced during the conference. Others felt the need of presenting proposals and resolutions. They asked for affirmation from the conference participants as a group. But the reality of the process model was that the affirmation had already been given person-to-person and group-to-group.

Several emergent groups came together to create a national communication network with regional networks in several parts of the country. As Sunday morning ended, there were decisions on how individuals and groups would continue the reflection/action dynamic—locally, regionally and nationally. There was an exchange of addresses and phone numbers among the persons who wanted to continue contact with one another. A list of those who could engage in full-time or part-time commitment to the issue was made available for anyone who was interested along with numerous financial pledges.

One group of twelve persons was bonded together in a unique situation—they had one common characteristic. They each had come to the conference despite the fact that their registration fees had been returned to them. They were a remnant of the 500 persons who had been turned away due to lack of space and facilities. They chose to meet in Room 1416 in the Sheraton-Southfield Hotel and participate in the conference by praying together, listening to tapes of the presentations and finally worshipping with the conference participants in the Saturday evening Liturgy of Blessing and the Sunday morning Eucharistic celebration. Uniquely, they represented a cross-section of the conference population. They were one woman aspiring to ordination, five lay women, five women religious and one male priest.

One of this group's contributions to the conference was an evaluation statement reflecting on the fact that they had experienced exclusion on one dimension from a conference that was raising the issue of exclusion on another. They challenged the tactic that all participants were required to wear name tags and were requested to produce the name tags every time they entered the plenary sessions. Exclusion from the final-liturgical sessions due to the name tag reality was one of the issues the group in Room 1416 chose to resolve. They challenged the conference organizers to focus on persons and their needs and characteristics, rather than on bureaucratic procedures and pieces of paper. They chose to meet with Patricia Hughes, Publicity Coordinator, and Nancy Lafferty, F.S.P.A., Process Consultant, as the conference drew to a close. In the evaluation session the advantages and disadvantages of the process model were discussed.

Some Reflections and Understandings

The group in Room 1416 was the only small group dialogue that chose to engage in an evaluation session immediately after the conference had ended. They experienced a bonding together, and they did not allow themselves "to be divided and set up against one another, women against men, religious against lay, people against hierarchy, white middle-class against people of color,"[5] as Marquita Finley, C.J.S. later wrote as a challenge to the whole conference. They chose to experience unity, equality and participation. They refused to be led into hostility and bitterness by pressures toward polarity, feelings of subordination and desires for domination. Again their actions were informed by theological and scriptural reflections, especially on Isaiah 54:2-3. It spoke to them of the needs of the People of God in the twentieth century. They used it to make the following recommen-

dation if there was ever to be another convening of persons nationally, regionally or locally on any issue so dear to the hearts of so many
people:

> Widen the space of your tent, and stretch out your
>   hangings freely.
> Lengthen your ropes, make firm your pegs.
> For you will burst out to the right and to the left.
> Your descendants will possess the nations and the
>   peoples the abandoned cities.

One limitation of the process model was that it did not provide
for participants who would be turned away. It was limited by the
physical facilities selected for the conference, even though they had
been moved once already to accommodate the expanded population.
It was limited by the range of competency, objectivity and experience
of the facilitators. And it fell short somewhat in taking into account
the multiple expectations of the 1,200 well-educated, highly experienced and knowledgeable participants.

However, it did demonstrate one way for people to come together and explore a difficult question in quality dialogues based on
scholarly presentations. It aided people to experience some measure
of equality, unity and participation while disagreeing with one another's ideas and/or future plans. It engendered responsibility and accountability to one another among the participants. It reminded the
People of God that major religious concerns can be viewed as issues
to be faced and considered thoughtfully and prayerfully in the light of
theological and scriptural understandings. It did create, for the majority of the participants, an experience of reflection in the context of
action and action informed by reflection. It accentuated the fact that
the win/lose political model cannot be used to affirm life-giving experiences.

One major disadvantage of the process model was that it was
dependent upon the persons who chose to attend the conference. And
the majority of the participants were white middle-class women. It
did not bring together persons from two sides of various walls. And in
contrast to the Biblical tradition of Jericho,[6] it did not foster the destruction of both sides of a wall at the same time. It did bring together some lay women and women religious and some men with the
women. But it did not bring together a diversity of people and the

Roman Catholic hierarchy, white middle- and upper-class people and people of color. It illuminated one major reality as one of the few Black participants reminded the conference as it closed: "After the walls of Jericho were down, God said: 'Never will you build in this same place this SAME CITY ever again.' "

Notes

1. *Women In The Future Priesthood Now: A Call For Action*, Ordination Conference Registration flyer, August, 1975.
2. Patricia Hughes, *The Ordination Conference: A Brief History*, Chicago; Mimeographed manuscript, November 12, 1975.
3. Alexander Jones (Ed.)., *The Jerusalem Bible*, Garden City, New York: Doubleday and Company, Inc., 1966.
4. Pope Paul VI, *Speech to the Committee for the 1975 United Nations-sponsored International Women's Year*, April 18, 1975.
5. Marquita Finley, C.S.J., "Reflections", *de-liberation*, Vol. 2, no. 2, February-April, 1976.
6. Joshua 6:1-27, 7:1-26.

26
Who Are These Women?
The Answer Takes Shape

Patricia Hughes

"Just how many women in the Catholic Church want to be ordained?" The question had been asked with increasing frequency in the weeks and months prior to the Ordination Conference. That no attempt had been made to gather the data was symptomatic of the very difficulty which the Conference sought to overcome. Certainly some among the Conference participants would themselves express a sense of vocation to ordained ministry; others, both women and men, would be supportive of the possibility of these vocations being tested. Others would come with an open attitude of listening and learning and the desire to return to local groups all around the country to share their personal impressions.

In the final month before the Conference, several Task Force members sensed the potential value of information that might be obtained in a brief participant profile. While postponing until after the Conference the decision as to how, specifically, the data might be used, the Executive Committee consulted with a participant who had expressed interest in the Conference from a sociological perspective. This individual, Judith Vaughan, CSJ, offered to compile an appropriate questionnaire and collaborate in the tabulation of responses.

The accompanying statistical report indicates that many variables have yet to be tabulated. However, the extremely high return percentage for the questionnaires (76.8%), enables several conclusions to be drawn with a fair degree of accuracy.

(1) Of the 837 female respondents, 289 (34.5%) responded with an unqualified "yes" to the question "Do you wish to be ordained?"

(2) Of the 142 Roman Catholic laywomen respondents, 50 (35.2%) responded with an unqualified "yes" to the question, and of

174

the 676 Roman Catholic religious women respondents, 229 (33.9%) responded with an unqualified "yes."

(3) Therefore, even though religious women outnumbered laywomen almost 5 to 1 both in conference attendance and questionnaire responses, there was a difference of only 1.3 percentage points in the number of lay and religious women expressing a sense of vocation to ordained ministry. Approximately one-third of the total female respondents, one-third of the laywomen *and* one-third of the women religious, wish to be ordained.

(4) 38.7% of the women have, or are in the process of obtaining, graduate degrees in theology or related fields. Their pastoral experience, expressed in the registration process, was extensive and diverse.

ORDINATION CONFERENCE QUESTIONNAIRE

Recognizing the historic nature of this Conference, consultants have recommended that a profile of the participants be drawn up. Your cooperation in preparing such a profile would be greatly appreciated. Please answer the questions below and return the completed questionnaire to the marked box in the Ballroom foyer or the marked box at the Information Center. Please return the questionnaire befor the Sunday A.M. General Session.

(1) Place of residence: _____
                           (City)   (State)   (Country)

(2) Diocese _____

(3) Sex: ____ F ____ M

(4) Age ____ 11-20   ____ 21-30   ____ 31-40   ____ 41-50
           ____ 51-60   ____ 61-70   ____ 71 or older

(5) Marital Status   ____ single   ____ married   ____ separated
                           ____ divorced   ____ widowed

(6) Number of children: _____

(7) Religious Denomination: _____

(8) Designation in the Church: (Please check the applicable categories)

    ____ layman
    ____ laywoman
    ____ member of a secular institute
    ____ Protestant minister
    ____ deacon
    ____ seminarian
    ____ priest: ____ diocesan ____ religious
            ____ Episcopalian
    ____ member of a religious community:
            ____ of brothers ____ of sisters
    ____ bishop
    ____ former member of a religious community
    ____ former priest
    ____ other (Please specify): _____

(9) Type of Educational Background:

Elementary	____ parochial	____ private	____ public
High School	____ Catholic	____ private	____ public
College	____ Catholic	____ private	____ public
Graduate	____ Catholic	____ private	____ public

(10) Degrees you have received: ___ B.A./B.S. ___ M.A./M.S.
___ M. Div. ___ Ph.D. ___ D. Min. ___ S.T.D. ___ Other

(11) If you are currently working toward a degree, please indicate which one:

___

(12) If you completed a graduate degree (i.e. post B.A./B.S.) what was/were your major area/s?

(13) Parents' Educational Background:

Father ___ Elem. ___ H.S. ___ Coll. ___ Graduate
Mother ___ Elem. ___ H.S. ___ Coll. ___ Graduate

(14) Would you consider yourself a feminist? ___ Yes ___ No

(15) Since January 1, 1975 approximately how many books and/or periodical articles have you read concerning the ordination of women?

___

(16) By what year, if at all, do you predict the ordination of women in the Roman Catholic Church will occur: ___ to the permanent diaconate? ___ , to the priesthood ___?

(17) Do you favor the ordination of women? ___ Yes ___ No ___ Undecided

(18) Did you feel this way before coming to the Conference?
___ Yes ___ No

(19) How did you form your opinion concerning the ordination of women? (Check as many as applicable)

___ through reading
___ through discussion with others
___ through experience in ministry
___ other (please specify: _____)

(20) Do you wish to be ordained? ___ Yes ___ No

(21) To how many groups, with what total membership, have you been asked to report this Conference? e.g. 3 groups, memberships of 6, 50, 248

_____

(22) The conference *general sessions* were helpful in providing an opportunity for theological reflection.

___ strongly agree ___ agree ___ undecided
___ disagree ___ strongly disagree

(23) The conference general sessions were helpful in providing an opportunity for *action planning*.

___ strongly agree ___ agree ___ undecided
___ disagree ___ strongly disagree

(24) The *group dialogues* were helpful in providing an opportunity for theological reflection.

___ strongly agree ___ agree ___ undecided
___ disagree ___ strongly disagree

(25) The group dialogues were helpful in providing an opportunity for *action planning*.

___ strongly agree ___ agree ___ undecided
___ disagree ___ strongly disagree

(26) The education/action nature of the *conference* was helpful in furthering exploration of the issue of ordained ministry for women in the Roman Catholic Church.

___ strongly agree ___ agree ___ undecided
___ disagree ___ strongly disagree

COMMENTS:

ORDINATION CONFERENCE QUESTIONNAIRE REPORT

Number of participants: 1200
Number of questionnaires returned: 921
Response percentage: 76.8%

*Of the 921 questionnaires returned: 837 female
                                        84 male

*Of the 837 questionnaires returned by women:
   676 religious women
   142 laywomen
     3 members of secular institutes
    16 other (i.e. episcopal, protestant, unspecified)

An analysis of question #20 was made using the 837 questionnaires returned by women.

#20   Do you wish to be ordained?

   289 yes
     8 yes, to the permanent diaconate
    26 yes, if there are structural changes
   294 no
   115 undecided
    48 not yet
    51 no answer
     6 other

*Of the 289 unqualified "yes" responses:

   229 religious women
    50 laywomen
     3 members of secular institutes
     7 other (i.e. episcopal, protestant, unspecified)

*Of the 294 "no" responses:

   237 religious women
    51 laywomen
     6 other (i.e. episcopal, protestant)

*Of the 279 lay and religious women desiring ordination:

     4 11-20 years old
    85 21-30 years old

105 31-40 years old
 47 41-50 years old
 32 51-60 years old
  1 61-70 years old
  1 71 or older
  4 unspecified

*Of the 288 lay and religious women not desiring ordination:

  2 11-20 years old
 40 21-30 years old
106 31-40 years old
 80 41-50 years old
 52 51-60 years old
  8 61-70 years old

*Of the 279 lay and religious women desiring ordination:

  6 M. Div. (26 M. Div. degrees in progress)
172 M.A.

    29 Theology
    19 Religious Education
    16 Education
    10 Religious Studies
     8 Guidance and Counseling
     6 English
     6 Sociology
     5 Pastoral Spiritual Theology
     5 Psychology
     4 Library Science
     3 Liturgy/Church Music
     2 Pastoral Counseling
     9 Unspecified
    50 Other

 12 Ph.D. (Church History, Classical Languages and Early Christian Theology, Far East Cultural Studies, Medieval Institutions, New Testament, Philosophy (2), Psychology, Sacred Science, Scripture and Systematics, Theology)

The absence of data concerning the ministerial experience of women desiring ordination is a deficiency in this questionnaire.

Submitted by: Judith Vaughan, CSJ
M.A. in Sociology
San Diego State University

Ph.D. Candidate
The Divinity School
The University of Chicago

27

31 Women:
Ordination Conference Taskforce

ROSEMARY BEARSS, RSCJ: "My own interest in the Ordination Conference surfaced because of the needs I experienced in my ministry and the frustration I have felt about not being able to meet these needs satisfactorily." Rosemary, a Religious of the Sacred Heart, is currently an Instructor in Management at Barat College in Lake Forest, Illinois. She is an M.Div. candidate at the Jesuit School of Theology in Chicago, and a leader in the Christian Life Community Movement.

DOLORES BROOKS, OP: "The process of the ordination of women in the Roman Catholic Church will be catalytic and provide for depths of renewal in basic structures of the Church, comparable to the effect of Paul's mission to the Gentiles that initially responded to a cultural question of membership in the Christian Community." Dolores, a Sinsinawa Dominican for 25 years, is in the M.Div. program at Weston School of Theology, Cambridge, Ma. She is preparing to work in pastoral ministry that speaks to, and supports the concerns of the elderly.

MONICA BROWN, OP: "My work with this Taskforce has been an experience of Church such as I have never had. We came together from different backgrounds, and have evolved a conference. It is not neat and orderly. It is not a package. It's a process still in process—alive and therefore not predictable. For me it is Church." Monica, a Sinsinawa Dominican taught high school English for fourteen years in the Midwest and then worked at Rosary College, River Forest, Illinois, as Residence Director and Campus Minister. She has worked with Chicago Catholic Women, Illinois Catholic Committee on Urban Ministry, and is presently a pastoral associate at Our Lady of the Sacred Heart Parish, Cloquet, Minnesota.

JOAN CAMPBELL, SL: "In calling this Conference, we are asking the official church for no special favors, no special privileges. We ask that all the sacramental rights that belong to men in the Catholic Church be guaranteed to us and to our daughters forever." Joan, a Sister of Loretto, is the Communications Director for the Conference. She received her Ph.D. from the University of Iowa. She is on the Executive Board of the National Coalition of American Nuns, the Executive Board for Women's Coalition for the Third Century, is a member of the National Organization of Women, the American Association of University Professors, and is on the Steering Committee for Common Cause/Mississippi.

AVIS CLENDENEN, RSM: "The Conference is a visible witness of what is happening in the hearts of many women and men attempting to deal with a call that has no place for expression in our own Church. No one will leave this gathering of women and men alone. I think we will find encouragement to continue to speak a truth that cannot be contained simply because 'it has never been done.' I think, honestly think, God cares about this gathering." Avis entered the Sisters of Mercy in 1969 and is currently an M.Div. student at the Jesuit School of Theology in Chicago. She is also a religion teacher and retreat/liturgy coordinator at Mother McAuley High School in Chicago.

ANNE MARY DOOLEY, SSJ: "The Taskforce, with the support of many interested, dedicated, competent people, has endeavored to create a climate, framework, and process where prayerful, intelligent, and serious dialogue can take place on this issue of justice. My hope is that we shall be open to hear, to accept, and to act upon the message God will give to us." Anne Mary resides in Rochester, New York and is currently a theology teacher at Nazareth Academy. She has a Master's degree in Pastoral Studies and an M A. in Religious Studies. She was one of eight women religious who organized the National Sisters Vocation Conference and one of the Founders of the Rochester Interfaith Coalition. She joined the Taskforce while serving as Director of Continuing Education at St. Bernard's Seminary in Rochester.

MARY ANN FLANAGAN, IHM: "I hope the Conference will be an occasion when the 'listening Church' will become more aware of the real needs of the Christian Community calling forth a desired sacramental response from the women presently ministering to them in innovative and authentic ways." Mary Ann, a Sister in the congregation of the Sister Servants of the Immaculate Heart of Mary received a Ph.D. in Religious Studies: Moral Theology from the University of Louvain, Belgium, and is currently a full-time faculty member of The Institute of Active Spirituality for the Global Community, an intra-congregational renewal program for leadership in justice and peace.

NADINE FOLEY, OP: "We have found a strength, a kind of promise if you will, in our exclusion from the hierarchical ordering. But when we turn our attention outward toward the world with a sense of our co-responsibility for Gospel mission, then the issue returns with a new kind of urgency. It becomes one of the developments of ministry. For as the full and complete persons we know we are, we would be full and complete ministers of the Gospel." Nadine, a member of the General Council of the Adrian Dominican Congregation since 1974, holds a Ph.D. in Philosophy from the Catholic University of America and an S.T.M. in Scripture from Union Theological Seminary. Having taught in both secondary schools and colleges, she most recently served as a campus minister at the University of New Mexico, the University of Houston, and Drake University. Nadine holds membership in the Society of Biblical Literature, the Catholic Theological Society of America, and the Ecclesial Role of Women Committee of the Leadership Conference of Women Religious.

LOUISE HAGEMAN, OP: "I see the Ordination Conference as an historically dynamic thrust into the future. Hopefully, it will be an impetus within the Church to move from unjust structures to practicing the Christian message the Church verbally preaches." Louise, a member of the Dominicans of Great Bend, Kansas has an M.A. in Religion and Personality from Duquesne University and has lectured to various religious groups throughout the U.S.

She has written for *Envoy* and *Humanitas* magazines. Louise is presently the Chairperson of the National Sister Formation Conference and is Director of Religious Formation for the Great Bend Dominicans.

PATRICIA HUGHES: " 'Hope is what I carry in my vessel made of clay, desiring that, piñata-like, I'll break for you someday.' In working for the ordination of women, I share my hope with the Church. Where some fear possible division, I see a new wholeness made possible when we take the Incarnation seriously." Pat began her ministry as an English and religion teacher in elementary and secondary school. Then, while serving as an Associate Director of the Jesuit Retreat House in Cleveland, Ohio, she was a member of the Diocesan Spiritual Development Commission and the Taskforce for Pastoral Planning. She has written for *Liturgy*, and has been a staff member of the Ecumenical Womens' Centers in Chicago. Currently on exclaustration from the Ursuline Nuns of Cleveland, Pat is an M.Div. candidate at the Jesuit School of Theology in Chicago.

ANN KELLEY, SND: Ann was born in Beverly, Massachusetts, received an M.S. from the Catholic University of America and is currently an M.Div. candidate in theological preparation for professional team ministry at Chicago Theological Seminary. She is a Sister of Notre Dame and works as a family counselor at the Depot. Ann believes the Conference is important to her as she moves toward a ministerial orientation in her profession.

MARY B. LYNCH: "I see this Conference as the culmination of the collective effort by national organizations, religious congregations and seminaries. The hope is for a unified stance on the question of women in the ordained ministry. I see further hope that the question will be taken more seriously by the Church as a result of this Conference." Already holding a Masters of Social Work degree, Mary began work towards her M.Div. at the Catholic Seminary of Indianapolis in 1971. It was at that time that she first began to work with the *Journey*, a newsletter for U.S. women interested in the ordained ministry. She became its editor in 1972, and also participated in planning the Third National Workshop on the Permanent Diaconate. Mary is the U.S. representative of the International Movement of Women Aspiring to the Presbyteral Ministry, and convened the December 14th planning meeting that gave birth to "Women in Future Priesthood Now: A Call for Action." Mary was the founding Coordinator of the Ordination Conference Taskforce.

DONNA QUINN, OP: "The Conference is both a moment of history—a moment of truth and justice—and a global, life-giving process for the Church. Women are asked again to lead—to call for action—to renew the Church. The Spirit has moved, the Church is responding." Donna is a Sinsinawa Dominican who has an M.A. in History, an M.S. in Administrative Leadership, and is presently in Pastoral Care Education with Allied Health Professionals at Moraine Valley Community College in Chicago. She helped organize Chicago Catholic Women and continues to work with the women in Chicago for a greater part in Diocesan decision-making. She is a member of the National Assembly of Women Religious, Network, Illinois Catholic Committee in Urban Ministry, and on the Executive Board of the National Coalition of American Nuns.

ROSALIE MUSCHAL-REINHARDT: "This is a moment of herstory. The Conference is the work of the Spirit and we women are responding because we are painfully living the 'signs of the times'. We will be heard because we are exercising the purpose for which we were born—to give glory to God, and to bring peace to all people on earth." Rosalie has been married for twenty years and is the mother of four children. She has served as Consultant to Parish Religious Education Coordinators in the Diocese of Rochester, N.Y. and in Wheaton, Illinois. She organized Living Room Dialogues in Spencerport, N.Y. and worked with youth in Buenos Aires, Argentina. Rosalie is the Central Vice-president of St. Joan's International Alliance—U.S. Section, and a member of the Religion Taskforce of the DuPage Chapter of the National Organization of Women. She is presently a third year Master of Divinity candidate at the Jesuit School of Theology in Chicago.

MARY M. SCHAEFER: "This Conference marks the coming of age of Roman Catholic women and their assuming of direct responsibility for carrying out Christ's mandate to preach the Gospel to all nations." Mary writes for Canadian Catholic Conference Publications Service and is currently working on scripture commentaries for the *Canadian Sunday Mass Book*, to be published in April, 1976. In 1970 Mary petitioned Canadian Bishops for the restoration of the diaconate for women and has continued to work for Women in the Church by publishing a Newsletter with the goal of priestly ordination and by lecturing on the Role of Women in the Church. Mary has an M.A. in History of Art and an M.A. in Theology from St. John's University, Collegeville, Minnesota and worked as the Assistant Director of the Catholic Information Centre, Edmonton, Alberta.

MARY ELLEN SHEEHAN, IHM: Mary Ellen is a member of the congregation of the Sister Servants of the Immaculate Heart of Mary. After having received her M.A. in Philosophy from St. Louis University, she taught at her community's formation college, Marygrove in Monroe. Mary Ellen has just completed her S.T.D. (Dogmatic Theology) at the University of Louvain, Belgium, and will be returning to the States to resume her position as an Associate Professor of Dogmatics at St. John's Provincial Seminary, Plymouth, Michigan.

MARILYN SIEG, SFCC: "My belief is that this conference is taking place at the most opportune historical moment in both the world and Church life. Positive planning, skillful strategies, and determined, sustained effort will blend with that generative breath of the Spirit to make ordained women available for sacramental, ecclesial, service." Marilyn is a member of the Sisters for Christian Community and has an M.S. in Spanish and French. She is currently working as Coordinator of Instructional Television at WHA-TV, Channel 21, of the University of Wisconsin, PBS station and also works in Madison on a woman's team for making women more visible at the altar during liturgical worship.

KAREN STEPIEN, IHM: "In Christ there is neither male nor female. (Galatians 3:28) For this reason, I personally believe that there is no characteristic, once having been made unimportant by rebirth in Christ, which renders any person unfit to exercise the fullness of priesthood which was initiated through Baptism. I hope the Conference is one of the first steps taken to create a new situation where all persons can experience the ministry to which they are called." Karen, a Sister of the Sister Servants of the Immaculate Heart of Mary is presently Director of Research and Development for the I.H.M. Sisters. She has an M.A. in Religious Studies and is involved in giving workshops to religious communities on new forms of Chapter participation.

MARGARET URBAN, OP: "The Ordination Conference is a response to the call of the Spirit. In light of the times, it seems the moment of truth is calling us, Church, to openly surface the issue of the role of women in the coming of the Kingdom. If the Spirit is alive in and among us, He constantly calls us to new growth and awareness, and remains with us during dialogue and debate. The issue of the ordination of women is of far more import than the issue of women's rights; it has to do with the building up of Christ, and our response to His mission." Marge is an Adrian Dominican who has been in education as a teacher and administrator for eighteen years. She served for three and one-half years as Elementary Coordinator of Catholic schools in Flint, Michigan and also worked in research and development in the Spanish Speaking Catholic Commission, Lansing Michigan. Marge is a member of the Catholic Commission on Urban Ministry, the Detroit Archdiocesan Council of Religious, the Leadership Conference of Women Religious, and is currently the Director of Apostolate for the Immaculate Conception Province of the Adrian Dominicans.

GEORGENE WILSON, OSF: "I am impressed by the love for the Church and love for passionate womenhood within the Church among Taskforce members. I look to the Conference as an expression of many persons pregnant with the power of passion and compassion, willing to be Church and declare the means for proclaiming full baptismal participation in the sacramental ministries of the Roman Catholic Church." Georgene is a Wheaton Franciscan who is on the pastoral team of St. James Parish, Arlington Heights, Illinois as Sacrament Coordinator. She has an M.A. in Religious Education from Loyola University, Chicago. Georgene is on the Board of Directors of "The Well"—an Institute for Christian Ministries, and is on the Community Life and Vocation Teams of the Wheaton Franciscans.

MICHAELA M. ZAHNER, CSJ: "This Conference is a very exciting step in projecting alternative futures for the Church—futures in which women will rightfully assume complete participation in sacramental and ministerial life." Michaela, a member of the St. Louis Province of the Sisters of St. Joseph of Carondelet, is a Ph.D. Candidate at the University of Chicago. She is a member of the American Historical Association, and served as a member of the Future Secretariat of the Sisters of Saint Joseph. Michaela is currently a faculty member of St. Teresa Academy in Kansas City, Missouri.

28

The Assembly Speaks

Women Called to Ordination

We have been called to the priesthood, and we want to be ordained, not because we want to exercise power, but because we are motivated by love and a concern for our Church. Indeed, we are already functioning as ministers, but under limitations and handicaps, owing to the lack of official recognition and authorization for our ministry, especially in the sacramental area.

A major focus of the love and concern that move us is our firm conviction that we as women are indispensable to the full humanness and wholeness of the priesthood. Unquestionably, new models of priesthood are needed. We believe that women in the priesthood will inevitably produce those sorely needed new models. We call on the people of God to engage in dialogue on the nature of ministry and priesthood. We applaud and affirm the model of priesthood as presented in Hebrews 7:12, for when there is a change in the priesthood there is necessarily a change in the law as well.

We who feel called to ordination see the Eucharist as the very center of our life and our ministry. We desire to unite who we are and what we do as priests with the life-giving dynamism of the Eucharist.

Leaven, in every age—people are called to be leaven, which gives rise to new dimensions in humanness, love and service to the Church and the world. We are leaven when in our deep consciousness we recognize a call to ordained ministry and work toward that day when that call will be tested. We are leaven when we encourage one another to explore every avenue, to knock on the door of every human heart. We are leaven when we proclaim, in faith, that the Lord has done wonderful things in our lives and when we walk with confidence toward a sacramental ministry in the Church that is home for us.

ROSALIE MUSCHAL-REINHARDT
Women Called to Ordination

Epicopal Women's Statement

To our Sisters in Christ:

We Episcopal women thank you for welcoming us to this historic conference.

We affirm our common sisterhood, and the work of the Holy Spirit in the variety of ministries in which all of us are serving God by serving human needs. The Spirit, Who is leading us into truth, is enabling the Church to recognize the need for all our ministries, lay and ordained.

We have a bond as Christian women. No one shall separate us from the love of God and from each other.

ANNE C. GARRISON
Episcopal Women

Las Hermanas Statement

We talked here about bonding. We have mentioned justice. If that is what we're about here, this is for us a joyful occasion. I am grateful to be here where such words are spoken.

Part of this Conference also spoke in terms of admitting error and of being women able to be held accountable. The task before me and my sister is not very comfortable. There seems to be for us doubt —still. The doubt stems perhaps from the fact that in our sisterhood there are still areas where we both have to examine deeply. In the present ministry that we experience, in our Church—who we love and are part of—we find criteria, ideals, standards—many things which will take too much time to go into here—that have caused a lack of ministry to our people.

We claim that this is not due to the fact that God hasn't called— we know that deep within us. We simply present that in our search for the priesthood of tomorrow, we would like to be part of such a coalition that will build justice and bonding.

SISTER MARIA IGLESIAS
President, Las Hermanas
N.B. *Las Hermanas is a national group of Spanish-speaking women religious.*

Black Sister's Response

One of the other parts to the story of Joshua is that after the people took the city of Jericho, Yahweh said to them, "Never build in this place again, a city like this."

So if you go through the walls and you take the city, then don't build the same city again.

SISTER SHAWN COPELAND, O P
President, National Black Sisters Conference

Glossary

anthropology—the study of the nature of humanity and the human person.

conscientization—"consciousness-raising"; an ongoing process of learning about oneself and one's environment (especially the relationship between the social, economic and cultural dimensions of the environment) in order to join in action to eradicate injustice.

Didache—a literary source for studying the early Church. The Didache or "Teaching of the Twelve Apostles" dates back to the beginning of the second century, and offers much insight, particularly into the liturgy of that time.

ecclesiology—the theological doctrine of the Church; a reflection on the nature of the Church.

Gaudium et Spes—the Pastoral Constitution on the Church in the Modern World, from the Second Vatican Council. The Latin title comes from the opening phrase of the Preface.

glossolalia—speaking in tongues, one of the charisms or gifts of the Spirit cited in the New Testament. The forms of charism mentioned by Paul (1 Cor. 12-14) are wisdom, knowledge, miracles, discernment of spirits, gifts of government and the gift of tongues.

Lumen Gentium—The Dogmatic Constitution on the Church, from the Second Vatican Council.

magisterium—the teaching authority of the Church; e.g. official statements of Popes, bishops, Councils.

monarchical episcopate—a hierarchical ordering of the authority of bishops over priests and deacons in a geographic area.

Pacem in Terris—Pope John XXIII's encyclical Peace on Earth, April 11, 1963.

parousia—the Greek word for what is usually referred to as "Christ's Second Coming."

presbyter—a Greek word meaning "elder." One of the central New Testament ministries.

theology—human reflection on the meaning and implications of revelation and of faith.

APPENDICES

Appendix A
The Bernardin Statement

U.S.C.C. News Statement, Oct. 3, 1975

WASHINGTON—The President of the National Conference of Catholic Bishops has issued a statement affirming the Catholic Church's teaching that "women are not to be ordained to the priesthood."

Archbishop Joseph L. Bernardin of Cincinnati stated:

"It is not correct to say that no serious theological obstacle stands in the way of ordaining women to the priesthood, and that the fact that women have not been ordained up to now can be explained simply by culturally conditioned notions of male superiority.

"There is a serious theological issue. Throughout its history the Catholic Church has not called women to the priesthood. Although many of the arguments presented in times gone by on this subject may not be defensible today, there are compelling reasons for this practice."

Archbishop Bernardin was authorized to make a statement reaffirming Church teaching on the ordination of women by the Administrative Committee of the National Conference of Catholic Bishops at its meeting here September 9-10. The statement was prepared subsequently and was issued after consultation with the NCCB Executive Committee. Copies have been sent to all U.S. bishops.

Archbishop Bernardin quoted at length from a 1972 report of the NCCB Committee on Pastoral Research and Practices entitled "Theological Reflections on the Ordination of Women," which he said gave "a very powerful reason for not ordaining women."

That report states in part: "The constant tradition and practice of the Catholic Church against the ordination of women, interpreted (whenever interpreted) as of divine law, is of such a nature as to constitute a clear teaching of the Ordinary Magisterium (teaching authority) of the Church. Though not formally defined, this is Catholic doctrine."

Declaring that "a negative answer to the possible ordination of women is indicated," the 1972 report added: "The well-founded present discipline will continue to have and to hold the entire field unless and until a contrary theological development takes place, leading to a clarifying statement from the Magisterium."

Archbishop Bernardin called it a "mistake" to "reduce the question of the ordination of women to one of injustice, as is done at times."

"It would be correct to do this only if ordination were a God-given right of every individual; only if somehow one's human potential could not be fulfilled without it," he said. "In fact, however, no one, male or female, can claim a 'right' to ordination. And, since the episcopal and priestly office is basically a ministry of service, ordination in no way 'completes' one's humanity."

The NCCB President coupled his comments on ordination with a declaration that "we must . . . address ourselves seriously to the question of women in the Church."

"Women are called today to a greater leadership role in the Church; their contributions are needed in the decision-making process at the parochial, diocesan, national and universal levels," he said.

"The Church has grown more aware of the variety of ministries open to women; in a very special way they are called to collaborate with all other segments of the Church in the essential work of evangelization. The Church will suffer, indeed it will be betrayed, if women are given only a secondary place in its life and mission."

Archbishop Bernardin's Statement

The proclamation by the United Nations of 1975 as International Women's Year was welcomed by all. It has served as a catalyst for serious discussion and action on behalf of women within both the Church and society. When the Holy Father received Mrs. Helvi Sipila, General Secretary of the International Women's Year, in November of last year, he stated that the designation of International Women's Year "does not find the Church inattentive to the problem or lacking in a clear desire to solve it. On the contrary: in the contemporary effort to promote the advancement of women in society, the Church has already recognized 'a sign of the times,' and has seen in it a call of the spirit."

The Church owes women, both religious and lay, its own great debt of gratitude for their commitment and loving service. In a special way we must also be grateful to those who today manifest their loyalty and love by pressing the question of their role in the Church.

Both candor and a sense of responsibility impel me at this time to address a question which is in the minds of many people. Discussion of the possibility of ordaining women to the priesthood in the Roman Catholic Church is now a lively issue in the United States.

Such discussion can contribute to a better understanding of ministry, priesthood and the role of women in the Church. But honesty and concern for the Catholic community, including those of its members who advocate the ordination of women, also require that Church leaders not seem to encourage unreasonable hopes and expectations, even by their silence. Therefore I am obliged to restate the Church's teaching that women are not to be ordained to the priesthood.

It is not correct to say that no serious theological obstacle stands in the way of ordaining women to the priesthood, and that the fact that women have not been ordained up to now can be explained simply by culturally conditioned notions of male superiority. There is a serious theological issue. Throughout its history the Catholic Church has not called women to the priesthood. Although many of the arguments presented in times gone by on this subject may not be defensible today, there are compelling reasons for this practice. In 1972 the NCCB Committee on Pastoral Research and Practices issued a report entitled "Theological Reflection on the Ordination of Women."

This report admitted that the question was complex and that there were many aspects to it which needed further study. The report, however, gave a very powerful reason for not ordaining women:

"Revelation is made known to us from Tradition as well as from Sacred Scripture (cf. *Constitution on Divine Revelation*, #8-10). It is then necessary for theology in this question to look to the life and practice of the Spirit-guided Church. The constant practice and tradition of the Catholic Church has excluded women from the episcopal and priestly office. Theologians and canonists have been unanimous until modern times in considering this exclusion as absolute and of divine origin. Until recent times no theologian or canonist seemingly has judged this to be only of ecclesiastical law. It would be pointless to list the many authorities and the theological note that each assigns to this teaching. However, the constant tradition and practice of the Catholic Church against the ordination of women, interpreted (whenever interpreted) as of divine law, is of such a nature as to constitute a clear teaching of the Ordinary Magisterium of the Church. Though not formally defined, this is Catholic doctrine."

In commenting on this assertion, the Bishops' Committee went on to say:

"(This reason) is of ponderous theological import. Its force will not be appreciated by those who look for Revelation and theology in Scripture alone, and who do not appreciate Tradition as a source of theology. Because of (this reason) a negative answer to the possible ordination of women is indicated. The well-founded present discipline will continue to have and to hold the entire field unless and until a contrary theological development takes place, leading ultimately to a clarifying statement from the Magisterium."

It would be a mistake, I believe, to reduce the question of the ordination of women to one of injustice, as is done at times. It would be correct to do this only if ordination were a God-given right of every individual; only if somehow one's human potential could not be fulfilled without it. In fact, however, no one, male or female, can claim a "right" to ordination. And, since the episcopal and priestly office is basically a ministry of service, ordination in no way "completes" one's humanity.

It is true that the equality of women is an ideal which has yet to be fully realized in many fields, such as education, politics and employment. And it is not enough to show interest only in these areas of concern. To be faithful to the Spirit, who is at work among us, we must also address ourselves seriously to the question of women in the Church. As Pope Paul has said, "although women do not receive the call to the apostolate of the Twelve and therefore to the ordained ministries, they are none the less invited to follow Christ as disciples and co-workers." (Statement to Committee for International Women's Year, April 18, 1975; *L'Osservatore Romano*, English edition, May 1, 1975)

Through educational efforts of the Church, we must make sure that people are truly convinced of woman's dignity and equality, an equality whose essential foundation, as the Holy Father has reminded us, is found in the "dignity of the human person, man and woman, in their filial relationship with God, of whom they are the visible image."

Women are called today to a greater leadership role in the Church; their contributions are needed in the decision-making process at the parochial, diocesan, national and universal levels. The Church has grown more aware of the variety of ministries open to women; in a very special way they are called to collaborate with all other segments of the Church in the essential work of evangelization. The Church will suffer, indeed it will be betrayed, if women are given only a secondary place in its life and mission.

Fortunately progress is being made in all these fields and many others. More, however, needs to be done. While this is a task of the whole Church, bishops have a special pastoral responsibility in this regard. It is not enough to make statements; our statements must be matched by actions which will bring more women into the mainstream of the life of the local Church.

I know that many will welcome this statement. But many others will disagree with and be disturbed by what I have said with respect to the question of ordination. The important thing now is that we not engage in recriminations; that instead we approach one another with charity and mutual respect, constantly examining our own motives—not the motives of others—in order to be as certain as is humanly possible that we are indeed at all times seeking to know and do the will of Jesus Christ.

News Conference (Nov. 20, 1975)
Archbishop Bernardin's Statement

The purpose of the statement was clear: to reaffirm the teaching of the Church that "women are not to be ordained." The reason for the statement was that the ordination of women has become a topic of lively discussion within the Church. The Bishops of the Administrative Committee, who authorized me to make the statement, felt that in the light of the discussion taking place their position should be made known.

I have been asked whether the issuance of the statement means that the Bishops do not consider the matter an open one, and whether we are ruling out all discussion of the topic. In answering these questions the salient points to be remembered are as follows:

1. In our judgement, the problem *is* theological or doctrinal. The precise question is: Was the exclusion of women from the priesthood by Christ determined simply by the cultural situation which existed in His day? Or did Christ exclude women for other reasons, so that changes in culture, etc. would have no bearing on the question? Was it His will, in other words, that only men be called to the ordained ministry as a matter of principle?

2. Admittedly, this question has never been addressed by a solemn definition of the Extraordinary Magisterium. The Church, however, has consistently taught and understood that it was Christ's will that only men be called to the priesthood. This fact, in our view of the Church and how its teaching authority operates, does have a great deal of significance. When the Bishops' Committee on Pastoral Research and Practice in 1972 referred to a longstanding tradition, they were not referring simply to a custom but to a teaching that has been constant; one that has been questioned only in recent years. It is because the bishops do not see any development on the horizon which is of sufficient weight to overturn this teaching that they felt obligated to reaffirm it.

3. Does this mean that the question of the ordination of women can no longer be subjected to theological scrutiny? No. Even matters that have been solemnly defined continue to be studied so that our knowledge of them can be deepened or refined. But any study of this particular question should take place within the following framework:

   a. It must be done in accord with the accepted norms of theological research.
   b. It must take into account the fact that the Church's constant tradition has been not to ordain women and that this fact does have significance in Catholic theology.
   c. There must be a willingness ultimately to accept the judgement of the Magisterium.

Any study which is not carried on within this framework will, in my judgement, be of little value.

Appendix B
A Selected Bibliography (1965-1975)

I. BOOKS

Achtemeir, Elizabeth. *Feminine Crisis in Christian Faith*. Nashville: Abingdon, 1965.

Brunner, Peter. *Ministry and the Ministry of Women*. St. Louis: Concordia, 1971

Burns, J. Edgar. *God as Woman, Woman as God*. Paramus, N.J.: Paulist Press, 1973.

Culver, Elsie Thomas. *Woman in the World of Religion*. New York: Doubleday, 1967.

Daly, Mary. *Beyond God the Father*. Boston: Beacon Press, 1974.

_____, *The Church and the Second Sex*. New York: Harper & Row, 1968.

Doely, Sarah, ed. *Women's Liberation and the Church*. New York: Association Press, 1970.

Ermath, Margaret Sittler. *Adam's Fractured Rib*. Philadelphia: Fortress, 1970.

Fischer, Clare Benedicks; Brenneman, Betsy; and Bennet, Anne McGraw, eds. *Women in a Strange Land*. Philadelphia: Fortress, 1975.

Gibson, Elsie. *When the Minister is a Woman*. New York: Holt, Rinehart, & Winston, 1970.

Goessman, E. *Die Frau und ihr Anftrag*. Herder: Freiburg, 1965.

Goessman, Elisabeth. *Das Bild der Frau heute*. Klens-Verlag GmbH.: Düsseldorf, 1967.

Gryson, R. *Le Ministere des femmes dans l'Eglise Ancienne*. Duculot, Belgium: Gembloux, 1972.

Hageman, Alice, ed. *Sexist Religion and Women in the Church: No More Silence*. New York: Association Press, 1974.

Hamilton, Michael P. and Montgomery, Nancy S. *The Ordination of Women: Pro and Con*. New York: Morehouse-Barlow, (forthcoming)

Hannon, Sister Vincent Emmanuel. *The Question of Women in Priesthood*. London: Chapman and Hall, 1967.

Harkness, Georgia. *Women in Church and Society*. Nashville: Abingdon, 1972.

Hewitt, Emily C. and Hiatt, Suzanne. *Women Priests? Yes or No?* New York: Seabury, 1973.

Heyer, Robert, ed. *Women and Orders*. Paramus, N.J.: Paulist-Newman, 1975.

Hoeser, Wolfgang. *Wir wollen es fröhlich wagen. Aus dem Leben und Werken der Diakonissen*. Berlin: Verlagsanstalt, 1966.

Laurentin, Rene. *Bilan du Synode.* Paris: La Seuil, 1973.

Lindbeck, Violette. *Ordination of Women.* Philadelphia: Lutheran Press, 1967.

McGrath, Sister Albertus Magnus, O.P. *What a Modern Catholic Believes about Women.* Chicago: Thomas More Press, 1972.

McKenna, Sister Mary Lawrence (Margaret) *Women of the Church: Role and Renewal.* New York: Kenedy, 1967.

Maertens, Jean Thierry. *La promotion de la femme dans la Bible. Ses applications au mariage et au ministère.* Paris: Casterman, 1967.

Meer, Haye van der. *Priesterium der Frau?* (Quaestiones disputatae, 42) Fribourg-en-Brisgau, 1969.

――――. *Women Priests in the Catholic Church? A Theological-Historical Investigation.* Translated by Arlene and Leonard Swidler. Philadelphia: Temple University, 1973.

Moll, W. *The Christian Image of Woman.* Notre Dame, Indiana: Fides, 1967.

Morris, Joan. *The Lady was a Bishop.* New York: Macmillan, 1973.

Prenter, Regin. *Die Ordination der Frauen zu den uberlieferten Pfarramt der Lutherische Kirche.* Berlin-Hamburg: Lutherisches Verlagshaus, 1967.

Raming, Ida. *Exclusion of Women from the Priesthood.* Translated by Norman Adams. Metuchen, N.J.: Scarecrow, (forthcoming).

Rutler, George W. *Priest and Priestess.* Ambler, Pa.: Trinity Press, 1973.

Stendahl, Krister. *The Bible and the Role of Women.* Philadelphia: Fortress, 1966.

Swidler, Arlene. *Woman in a Man's Church.* Paramus, N.J.: Paulist-Newman, 1972.

Tavard, George H. *Woman in Christian Tradition.* Notre Dame, Indiana: University of Notre Dame, 1973.

Tiemayer, Raymond. *The Ordination of Women.* Minneapolis: Augsburg, 1970.

Turner, Rodney. *Women and the Priesthood.* Salt Lake City: Deseret Books, (n.d.)

II. ARTICLES

Albrecht, B. "Zur beruflichen Diakonie der Frau in der Gemeinde," *Signum* 39 (1967) 18-20.

Allmen, J. J. von. "Women and the Threefold Ministry," Trans. by C. D. W. Robinson. *Churchmen* 86 (Summer, 1972) 89-99.

Althouse, LaVonne. "Ordain Women?" *Woman's Pulpit* 46 (July-Sept., 1967) 4-5.

Arthur, Rose Horman. "The Diaconate for Women," *Sisters Today* 43 (April, 1972) 490-496.

Athenagoras Kokkinakas, Archbishop. "Question of Ordaining Women," *L'Osservatore Romano* (English ed.) no. 27 [379] (July 3, 1975) 9-10.

Austin, C. "Three Episcopal Women Priests Celebrate Communion Rite," *NCR* 11 (Nov. 8, 1974) 1.

Barnhouse, R. T. "Examination of the Ordination of Women to the Priesthood in Terms of the Symbolism of the Eucharist," *Anglican Theological R.* 56 (July, 1974) 279-291.

Beaton, Catherine. "Does the Church Discriminate Against Women on the Basis of Their Sex?" *Critic* 24 (June-July, 1966) 20-27.

Beckwith, R. T. and Duffield, G. E. "Towards a Better Solution," *Churchman* 86 (Summer, 1972) 100-112.

Beeson, T. "Anglican Women Priests: Has Their Time Come?" *Christian Century* 92 (May 28, 1975) 542-3.

_____ 'Unbarring the Ancient Door; General Synod of the Church of England," *Christian Century* 92 (Sept. 3, 1975) 766-768.

Begley, John and Armbruster, Carl. "Women and Office in the Church," *Am. Ecclesiastical R.* 165 (Nov., 1971) 145-157.

Bishop, B. "The Future of the Female." In *The Future of Catholic Christianity.* Edited by Michael de la Bedoyère. Philadelphia: Lippincott, 1966.

Bock, E. Wilbur. "The Female Clergy: a Case of Professional Marginality," *J. of Sociology* 72 (1967) 531-39.

Bont, W. de. "La femme du pasteur," *Supplément de la Vie Spirituelle* Nr. 83 (Novembre, 1967) 666-673.

"Born Female: Episcopal House of Bishops' Decision on Ordination of Women to the Priesthood," *Newsweek* 84 (Aug. 26, 1974) 77.

Bourgoin, M. "Signed but not Sealed," *NCR* 11 (Nov. 15, 1974) 16-17.

Boyd, M. "Who's Afraid of Women Priests? Aftermath of the Episcopalian Ordinations," *Ms.* 3 (Dec., 1974) 47.

Boyer, C. "Women and the Altar," *Unitas* 17 (Fall, 1965) 227-30

_____ . "L'Ordination des femmes," *Doc. Catholique* 47 (1965) 1101-1104.

Brand, P. "Notes sur le problème de l'acces de la femme au ministère pastoral," *Verbum Caro* 20 (1966) 46-66.

Brown, J. and others. "Order, Conscience and Sexism," *Christianity and Crisis* 34 (Dec. 9, 1974) 286-288.

Bruce, M. "Heresy, Equality and the Rights of Women," *Churchman* 85 (Winter, 1971) 274-289.

Bruegge, B. OSB. "Le diaconat de la femme," *Vie Spirituelle* 524 (1966) 184-202.

Bruening, M. "Priestertum der Frau?" *Stimmen der Zeit* 176 (1964/65) 549-552.

Buscher, W. "Falling From Faith in Christ, of the Church, and of the Lutheran Reformation; an article on the Ordination of Women," Trans. by W. Torgerson. *Springfielder* 34 (March, 1971) 280-289.

Callahan, Sidney. "No Theological Barriers to Women Priests, says Woman Author," *U.S. Catholic and Jubilee* 32 (Nov., 1969) 59.

Capon, R. F. "Ordination of Women: a Non-Book," *Anglican Theological R.*, Supplemental Series No. 2 (1973) 68-78.

Carroll, Elizabeth. "Women and Ministry," *Theological Studies* 36 (Dec., 1975)

Carroll, J. "The Philadelphia Ordination," *NCR* 10 (Aug. 16, 1974) 14.

Casey, R. "Ordination Undesirable for Anyone, Sister Says," *NCR* 9 (May 25, 1973) 3.

"Celebration of Defiance: Eucharistic Service in Manhattan's Riverside Church," *Time* 104 (Nov. 11, 1974) 120.

Chenderlin, F. "Women as Ordained Priests?" *Homiletic and Pastoral R.* 72 (May, 1972) 25-32.

"Church Tossed in Ordination Storm," *NCR* 11 (Feb. 7, 1975) 4.

Cleary, Richard Jones, OSB. "Women's Role in the Christian Community: Past Present, Future," *American Benedictine R.* 20 No. 3 (1969) 395-406.

Corrigan, D. and others. "Open Letter," *Christianity and Crisis* 34 (Sept., 1974) 185.

Cribari, S. "Theologian's Recommendations: Be Open to Women Deacons," *NCR* 7 (March 15, 1971) 1.

Cunneen, Sally. "Women and the Liturgy: The Present Paradox," *American Ecclesiastical R.* 165 (Nov., 1971) 167-74.

Cunningham, Agnes. "Ministry of Women in the Church," Cath. Theological Soc. of America. *Proceedings* 24 (June, 1969) 124-41.

―――. "Why Not Women Priests?" *U.S. Catholic* 35 (1970) 10-12.

―――. "Woman's Call to Ministry," *Sign* 54 (July-Aug., 1975) 19-22.

―――. "Women and the Diaconate," *American Ecclesiastical R.* 165 (Nov., 1971) 158-166.

―――. "Women Priests?" *The Priest* 27 (Sept., 1971).

Daly, Mary. "The Qualitative Leap Beyond Patriarchal Religion," *Quest* 1 (no. 4, Spring, 1975) 20-40.

Damian, B. "Priesthood for Women?" *Friar* 25 (Feb., 1966) 14-17.

Day, I. "Carter Heyward: She Gave Communion and Got a Scratch on the Hand: Interview of C. Heyward," *Ms.* 3 (Dec., 1974) 49.

Deedy, J. "Liturgy and Women: Case of Sister Fitzgerald," *Commonweal* 100 (April 26, 1974) 178.

Delaporte, Jacques. "Le pretre et la promotion de la femme," *Evangelisation et Paroisse* 30 (1969) 34-41.

Donnelly, D. H. "Women-Priests: Does Philadelphia Have a Message for Rome?" *Commonweal* 102 (June 20, 1975) 206-210; Discussion, 102 (Aug. 15, 1975) 323.

DuBois, Albert J. "Why I am Against the Ordination of Women," *Episcopalian* 137 (July, 1972) 22.

"Ecumenism and Women Episcopal Priests," *J. of Ecumenical Studies* 9 (Winter, 1972) 229-35.

Elliot, E. "Why I Oppose the Ordination of Women," *Christianity Today* 19 (June 6, 1975) 12-14.

"Episcopal Controversy," *Christian Century* 92 (April 2, 1975) 326-27.

Evans, G. "Ordination of Women," *Homiletic and Pastoral R.* 73 (Oct., 1972) 29-32.

Eyden, R. J. A. van. "Women Ministers in the Catholic Church?" *Sisters Today* 40 (1968) 211-226.

Federation of Organizations for Professional Women. "Order, Conscience and Sexism," *Christian Century* 34 (Dec. 9, 1974) 286-88.

Ferrari, E. "Diakonatsweihe für die Frau?" *Die Christliche Frau* 56 (1967) 106-111.

"First Things First: Episcopal Church's Issues on Ordination of Women," *Christianity Today* 19 (March 14, 1975) 61-63.

Flahiff, G. "Cardinal Flahiff on Ministry of Women," *Catholic Mind* 70 (Jan., 1972) 31-33.

Forbes, C. "When is a Priest not a Priest?" *Christianity Today* 18 (Sept. 13, 1974) 68-70.

Ford, Josephine M. "Biblical Material Relevant to the Ordination of Women," *J. of Ecumenical Studies* 10 (Fall, 1973) 669-694.

_____. "Order for the Ordination of a Deaconess," *Review for Religious* 33 (March, 1974) 308-14.

_____. "Ordination of Women?" *Continuum* 5 (Win. 1968) 738-43.

_____. "Our Lady and the Ministry of Women in the Church," *Marian Studies* 23 (1972) 79-112.

_____. "Theological Reflections on the Ordination of Women," *J. of Ecumenical Studies* 10 (Fall, 1973) 695-699.

"Form Organization for Ordination of Women: Declaration of Priests for Equality," *Our Sunday Visitor* 64 (Aug. 3, 1975) 3.

"From Sisterhood to Priesthood: First Women to be ordained as Priests in the Episcopal Church," *Newsweek* 84 (Aug. 12, 1974) 52.

Frost, J. and Morrison, L. "On the Ordination of Women," *Christianity and Crisis* 32 (Mar. 6, 1972) 49-52.

Galot, Jean. "Women and the Ministry," *L'Osservatore Romano* (English ed.) No. 49 [297] (Dec. 6, 1973) 7.

Gillen, A., Sister. "Statement on the Ordination of Women," *Catholic Mind* 71 (Nov., 1973) 2-8.

Gorres, Ida Friederike. "Women as Priests?" *Herder Correspondence* 3 (1966) 205-207.

_____. "Women in Holy Orders," *Month* 34 (1965) 84-93.

Goessman, Elisabeth. "La femme pretre?" *Concilium* 34 (1968) 103-112.

Gott, H. "Drama of Ordination: Ordination of Eleven Women," *NCR* 10 (Aug. 16, 1974) 1.

Graef, Hilda. "Theologizing Women," *Clergy Review N.S.* 54 No. 11 (1969) 877-883.

Gray, W. B. "Standing in the Way of the Spirit," *Christian Century* 90 (Sept. 12, 1973) 876-7.

Greenfield, M. "Women and the Image of God," *Newsweek* 86 (Sept. 1, 1975) 72.

Gryson, R. "L'Attitude de l'Eglise ancienne vis-a-vis du ministere feminin," *Louvain Studies* 2-3 (1969) 254-62.

_____. "L'ordination des diaconesses d'après les Constitutions apostoliques," *Mélanges de Science Religieuse* 31 (March, 1974) 41-45.

Harper, Mary-Angela. "Women's Role in the Church," *America* 115 (July 23, 1966) 91-93.

Haughton, Rosemary. "The Weaker Sex," *Clergy Review* 51 (1966) 849-862.

Hebblethwaite, P. "Britain's Anglicans say yes, no, yes yes no, to ordaining Women," *NCR* 11 (Aug. 1, 1975) 6.

Heinzelman, G. "The Priesthood and Women," *Commonweal* 81 (1965) 504-508.

Henderson, R.W. "Reflections on the Ordination of Women," *Study Encounter* 7 (No. 1, 1971).

Henning, Clara Maria. "Women in the Priesthood," *Commonweal* 99 (June 11, 1974) 360-363.

Heyward, C. "In and through the Impasse," *Christianity and Crisis* 34 (Sept. 16, 1974) 188-194.

Hodgson, L. "Theological Objections to the Ordination of Women," *Expository Times* 77 (1966) 210-213.

Holmes, V. T., III. "Priesthood and Sexuality; a Caveat Only Dimly Perceived," *Anglican Theological R.* 55 (Jan., 1973) 62-67. Reply. E. Barrett. *Supplemental Series* no. 2 (1973) 78-83.

Holstein, H. "La religieuse, suppleante ou remplacante du pretre?" *Vie Spirituelle*, Suppl. 91 (Nov., 1969) 563-572.

Hudson, E. "Women and the Diaconate," *Clergy Review* 56 (Nov., 1971) 886-890.

Hunter, D. and H. "Neither Male nor Female," *Christian Century* 82 (1965) 527-528.

Hunter, Leslie Stannard. "The Service and Status of Women in the Churches," *Scandinavian Churches*. Edited by L. S. Hunter. Minneapolis: Augsburg, 1965.

Jewett, P. K. "Why I Favor the Ordination of Women," *Christianity Today* 19 (June 6, 1975) 7-10.

Kastler, E. "Une femme pasteur," *Etudes Theol. et Relig.* 40 (1965) 109-114.

Kelley, A. and Walsh, A. "Ordination: a Questionable Goal for Women," *Ecumenist* 11 (July-Aug., 1973) 81-82.

Kelley, A. "Should Women Refuse Ordination?" *NCR* 9 (Aug. 17, 1973) 13.

Kessler, P. J. "In Sacen: Katholische Priesterinnen," *Schweizer Rundschau* 64 (1965) 365-367.

Klein, K. "Das Amt der Pastorin. Eine Thesenreihe," *Evangelische Theologie* 26 (1966) 96-109.

Lampe, G. W. H. "Church Tradition and the Ordination of Women," *Expository Times* 76 (1965) 123-125. Reply. J. Pretlove. 76 (1965) 294.

Laudien, G. "Das Amt der Pastorin in der EKD," *Kirche in der Zeit* 21 (1966) 271-274.

Lauer, R. "Women Clergy for Rome?" *Christian Century* 83 (1966) 1107-1110.

Lumen-Chenu, M. Th., van. "Feminisme chretien: jusques y compris le sacerdoce," *Revue Nouvelle* 26 (1970) 366-372.

Lyle, Jean Caffey. "Episcopal Agony over Ecclesiastical Disobedience," *Christian Century* 91 (Sept. 4-11, 1974) 812-814.

Lyons, H. "Jeanette Piccard: She Waited 50 Years," *Ms.* 3 (Dec., 1974) 50.

Madden, P. "Women and Holy Orders: an Historical Survey," *Resonance* 6 (no. 2, 1971) 9-32.

Maguire, D. B. "No More Second-Class Citizenship for Women in the Church," *U.S. Catholic* 32 (July, 1966) 18.

Maloney, G. "Women Priests and Ecumenism," *Diakonia* 9 (1974) 308-309.

Marchant, G.J.C. "Evangelicals and the Ordination of Women," *Churchman* 87 (Winter, 1973) 289-291.

Mead, M. "Women as Priests: a New Challenge," *Redbook* 145 (June, 1975) 31-32.

Meer, Haye van der. "De positie de vrouw in de Rooms-Katholieke Kerk," *Do-C* (Documentatie Centrum Concilie) paper nr. 194 (1965).

Meyer, Charles R. "Deaconess, Priestess, and Bishopess," *Catholic Digest* 30 (April, 1966) 79-83.

_____. "Ordained Women in the Early Church," *Chicago Studies 4* (1965) 285-308.

Mitchell, L. "Women Priests and the Episcopal Church," *Review for Religious* 34 (July, 1975) 511-524.

Muench, J. Th. "Katholische Priesterinnen?" *Der christliche Sonntag* 17 (1965) 325-327.

_____. "Pourquoi je veux divenir femme prêtre," *Réalitiés* nr. 264 (Juillet, 1966) 79-81.

Myers, C. K. "But the Bishop's Not Convinced," *Christianity and Crisis* 31 (Dec. 13, 1971) 275 276.

"No Theological Obstacle to Ordination of Women, states Msgr. Otto Mauer," *Tablet* 220 (Nov. 26, 1966) 1341.

Noice, E. R. "Priesthood and Women: a Lay View," *Anglican Theological R.* 55 (Jan., 1973) 53-62.

Northcott, Cecil. "Women Priests in England?" *Christian Century* 85 (1968) 101-102.

Novak, M. "Should Women Be Priests?" Reply. M. Boland. *Commonweal* 101 (Jan. 31, 1975) 375.

O'Collins, G. "Ordination of Women," *Tablet* 228 (Feb. 23, 1974) 175-176; 228 (Mar. 2, 1974) 213-215.

Ohanneson, J. "Historians Forsee Larger Role for Women in Church Ministry," *NCR* 10 (Jan. 11, 1974) 3-4.

Ollgaard, H. "Women as Clergymen in Denmark," *Lutheran Quarterly* 18 (1966) 163-167.

O'Meara, Thomas, OP. "Feminine Ministry and Clerical Culture," *Commonweal* 98 (Sept. 28, 1973) 523-526.

"On Ordaining Women Priests," *America* 131 (Aug. 24, 1974) 65.

"On the Philadelphia Ordinations," *Christianity and Crisis* 34 (Sept. 16, 1974) 187-199.

"110 Catholics Back Women as Priests," *NCR* 11 (Nov. 8, 1974) 5.

O'Rourke, John. "Women and the Reception of Orders," *Revue de l'Universite d'Ottawa* 38 (1968) 295.

Patrick, Anne E. "Conservative Case for the Ordination of Women," *New Catholic World* 218 (May-June, 1975) 108-111.

_____, "Resources," *Liturgy* (December, 1973) 29-30.

_____, "Women and Religion: a Survey of Significant Literature, 1965-1974," *Theological Studies* 36 (December, 1975).

"La Place de la femme dans le ministere des Eglises Chretiennes non-catholiques," *Concilium* 34 (1968) 145-159.

Plowman, E. E. "Women on Trial: the Wendt Case," *Christianity Today* 19 (May 23, 1975) 55-57.

Porter, H.B. and Weil, L. "Women Priests: Some Recent Literature," *Anglican Theological R.* Supplemental Series no. 2 (1973) 83-87.

Putrow, Sister M. "A Statement on Women in Ministry," *Sisters Today* 45 (Feb., 1974) 321-322.

Range, Joan A., ASC. "Legal Exclusion of Women from Church Office," *Jurist* 34 (1974) 128-142.

"Réflexions théologiques de l'épiscopat Américain sur l'ordination des femmes," *Documentation Catholique* 70 (June 3, 1973) 529-531.

Remberger, F. "Priestertum der Frau?" *Theologie der Gegenwart* 9 (1966) 130-136.

Reumann, J. H. P. "What in Scripture Speaks to the Ordination of Women?" *CTM* 44 (Jan., 1973) 5-30.

Reuther, Rosemary. "Ordination: Witness Against Evil," *NCR* 10 (Oct. 11, 1974) 7.

Roeper, A. "Weibliches Priestertum?" *Orientierung* 31 (1967) 93-94.

"Roman Catholic Statement on the Ordination of Women," *Ecumenist* 13 (Nov.-Dec., 1974) 15-16.

Rowe, K. E. "Discovery: the Ordination of Women; Round One; Anna Oliver and the General Conference of 1880," *Methodist History* 12 (April, 1974) 60-72.

"St. Joan's Alliance cites Encyclical on Ordination," *NCR* 9 (Oct. 12, 1973) 2.

Scaer, D.P. "Office of the Pastor and the Problem of Women Pastors," *Springfielder* 38 (Sept., 1974) 123-133.

Schmemann, A. D. "Concerning Women's Ordination: a Letter to an Episcopal Friend," *St. Vladimir's Theological Quarterly* 17 (1973) 239-243.

Scott, B. B. "Women Priests," *Commonweal* 101 (Nov. 1, 1974) 99-100; Reply. 101 (Dec. 6, 1974) 227.

Sheets, J. "Ordination of Women: the Issues," *Am. Ecclesiastical R.* 169 (Jan., 1975) 17-36.

Shideler, M. M. "Alison Cheek's Achievement," *Christian Century* 91 (Dec. 11, 1974) 1165-1166.

"Should Women be Ordained? Episcopalians, no; Lutherans, yes," *NCR* 7 (Nov. 6, 1970) 9.

Sinz, P. "Viragines. Ein Beitag zur Frage nach dem Weihepriestertum der Frauen," *Osterreichisches Klerus-Blatt* 101 (1968) nr. 3:36-38; nr. 4:54-55.

Sonnemans, J. "Vers l'ordination des femmes?" *Spiritus. Cahiers de Spiritualite missionnaire* nr. 29 (Decembre, 1966) 403-422.

Spencer, A. D. B. "Eve at Ephesus [Tim. 2:11-15?]" *J. of the Evangelical Theological Society* 17 (Fall, 1974) 215-222.

Stringfellow, W. "Bishops at O'Hara: Mischief and a Mighty Curse," *Christianity and Crisis* 34 (Sept. 16, 1974) 195-196.

Stuhlmueller, Carroll. "Women Priests: Today's Theology and Yesterday's Sociology," *America* 131 (Dec. 14, 1974) 385-387.

Swidler, Arlene. "An Ecumenical Question: the Status of Women (in the Church)," *J. of Ecumenical Studies* 4 (1967) 113-115.

———, "The Male Church," *Commonweal* 84 (June 24, 1966) 387-389.

Swidler, Leonard. "Jesus was a Feminist," *Catholic World* (1971) 177-183.

———, "No Penis, no Priest," *J. of Ecumenical Studies* 10 (Fall, 1973) 771-773.

Tavard, George H. "Women in the Church: a Theological Problem," *Ecumenist* 4 (Nov.-Dec., 1965) 7-10.

"Theological Reflections on the Ordination of Women," *J. of Ecumenical Studies* 10 (Fall 1973) 695-699.

"Theological Reflections on the Ordination of Women: NCCB Committee on Pastoral Research and Practices," *Review for Religious* 32 (Mar., 1973) 218-222.

Thompson, C. "High Mass," *NCR* 11 (May 9, 1975) 7-8.

Toton, Suzanne. "The Deaconess," *Word* 8 (1971) 6-8.

d'Ursel, O. "Women in the Ministry," *Pro Mundi Vita* no. 50 (1974) 20-28.

Van Beeck, F. "Invalid or Merely Irregular: Comments by a Reluctant Witness," *J. of Ecumenical Studies* 11 (Summer, 1974) 381-399.

Wallace, C. "Ordained Women: an Imperative," *Continuum* 4 (Spring, 1966).

Way, Peggy. "The Church and (Ordained) Women," *Christian Ministry* (Jan., 1970) 18-22.

Willis, E. "Women and the Priesthood," *New Blackfriars* 55 (April, 1974) 171-176.

Winiarski, Mark. "Concelebration in Wisconsin," *NCR* 12 (Nov. 7, 1975) 1.

"Women Priests," *Time* 104 (Aug. 26, 1974) 72.

"Women Priests? Church says Yes, but not Right Now," *NCR* 11 (Aug. 1, 1975) 6.

"Women Priests Offered Home Masses, One Says," *NCR* 11 (Nov. 15, 1974) 3.

"Women's Ordination Ruled Invalid," *NCR* 10 (Aug. 30, 1974) 15.

"Women's Rebellion: Ordination as Episcopal Priests," *Time* 104 (Aug. 12, 1974) 60.

Wright, J. R. "Documentation and Reflection: an Address in Favor of the Ordination of Women to the Priesthood," *Anglican Theological R.* 55 (Jan., 1973) 68-72.

Zutter, P. de. "Sister Dorothy Donnelly: Its Time for the Sacramental System to Catch up with What's Happening in Ministry," *NCR* 10 (Nov. 23, 1973) 7.

III. REPORTS

"Ministry in the Church." Report of the Theology Section of the Roman Catholic/Presbyterian Reformed Consultation, Richmond, Va., October 30, 1971. *J. of Ecumenical Studies* 9 (Summer, 1972) 589-612.

"Restoration of the Office of Deacon as a Lifetime State." Report by Members of the Catholic Theological Society of America to the U.S. Bishops at the Request of the Bishops' Committee on the Permanent Diaconate. *Worship* 65 (1971) 186-198. (paragraphs 28-34 on Women)

"The Systematic Theology of the Priesthood." A Progress Report to the National Conference of Catholic Bishops by the Committee Commissioned to Study the Priesthood, April, 1971. *NCR* 7 (April 30, 1971) 12.

"Theological Reflections on the Ordination of Women." A Report Prepared by the U.S. National Conference of Catholic Bishops' Committee on Pastoral Research and Practices, 1972. *Catholic Mind* 71 (April, 1973) 2-6.

United Presbyterian Church, U.S.A. *Report of the Special Committee on the Status of Women in Society and in the Church.* Minutes of the 181st. General Assembly, Pt. I, Journal, May 14-21, 1969. 38p.

―――― *Report of the Standing Committee on Women.* Minutes of the 183rd. General Assembly, Pt. I, Journal, May 24, 1971. 19p.

―――― *Report of the Task Force on Women and the Standing Committee on Women.* Minutes of the 182nd. General Assembly, Pt. I, Journal. 17p.

U.S. Bishops' Committee on the Permanent Diaconate. *Permanent Deacons in the U.S.: Guidelines on their Formation and Ministry.* Washington, D.C.: U.S. Catholic Conference, 1971. (paragraphs 168, 169, 179 on Women)

Women and Holy Orders. Report of a Commission Appointed by the Archbishops of Canterbury and York. London: Church Information Office, Dec. 1966.

Women in Ministry. A Study. London: Church Information Office, 1968.

"Women Priests Now?" A Report on the Episcopal General Convention, Louisville, Kentucky, Sept. 29 - Oct. 11, 1973. *Christianity and Crisis* 33 (July 23, 1973) 148-152.

IV. OTHER RESOURCES

Philadelphia Task Force on Women in Religion, P.O. Box 24003, Philadelphia, Pa. 19139. *Genesis III* published monthly.

Women's Center for Theologizing, 4051 Broadway, Kansas City, Mo. 64111. Publishes a *Worksheet* monthly.

Compiled by Donna Westley
November, 1975

Appendix C
Roster: Ordination Conference

ROSTER

ORDINATION CONFERENCE

"WOMEN IN FUTURE PRIESTHOOD NOW: A CALL FOR ACTION"

November 28-30, 1975

Detroit, Michigan

* * * * * * * * *

STATES AND FOREIGN COUNTRIES LISTED ALPHABETICALLY

ALABAMA

Sara Butler MSBT, P.O. Box 759, Mobile 36601

ALASKA

Andrea Nenzel, Holy Name School, 433 Jackson, Ketchikan 99901

ARIZONA

Marie Breitenbeck OP, Diocese of Phoenix, 400 E. Monroe St., Phoenix 85004
Ann Marie Holland, 430 N. 29th St., Phoenix 85008

ARKANSAS

Rosalie Ruesewald OSB, P.O. Box 3489, Fort Smith 72901

AUSTRALIA

Papua, New Guinea
Wendy Flannery, 5536 S. Everett Ave., Chicago 60637

BELGIUM

Odette d'Ursel, 140 Avenue de Broqueville, 1200 Brussels

CALIFORNIA

Anele Heiges OP, 19018 Bryant St. #3, Northbridge 91324
Catherine Bevanda, 39 Ocean View, Dillon Beach 94929
Diana Dale SFCC, 855 Fremont St. Apt. 3, Menlo Park 94025
M. Katherine Hammett, P.O. Box 3744, City of Industry 91744
Mary O'Neill, 3856 35th Ave., Oakland 94619
Margaret Rose Welch, 2134 E. Live Oak Dr., Los Angeles 90068
Charlene Tschirhart, 851 Tresle Glen Road, Oakland 94610
Patricia Bruno OP, Santa Catalina School, Monterey 93940
Cecilia M. Williams CSJ, 195 Brandon Road, Pleasant Hill 94523
Sally M. Brands, 1828 W. Arrow, Upland 91786
Rose Cecilia Harrington, 2957 Brighton Ave., Los Angeles 90018
Joan Henehan CSJ, 211 Third Ave., Venice 90291
Mary Riemer, 1035 9th St., Santa Monica 90403
Linda Lutz, 509 Ballard St., El Cason 92021
Dorothy Donnelly CSJ, 1765 B. LeRoy, Berkeley 94709
Elizabeth Thoman CHM, 1962 South Shenandoah St., Los Angeles 90034
Patrick L. LaBelle OP, President, St. Albert College, P.O. Box 9126, Berkeley 94709
Patricia Haire CSJ, 1775 E. 20th St., Apt. I-3, San Bernardino 92404, Diocese of San Diego

CANADA

Theresa Carmel Slavik, Holy Rosary Convent, 3975 Riverside Drive, Windsor, Ontario, N8Y 1B1
Alice Marie McDonald, Mt. St. Joseph, Box 487, Station "B", London, Ontario, N6A 4X3
Mary Ann Hinsdale IHM, 12 Howland Ave. #1, Toronto, Ontario M5R 3B3
Rosann M. Catalano, 125 Balmoral Ave., Toronto, Ontario M4V 1J5

Jeanne Evans, Victoria College, Margaret AddisonHall, Toronto, Ontario M5S 257
Mary E. Hines SND, 12 Howland Ave., Toronto, Ontario M5R 3B3
Patricia Smith RSM, 125 Balmoral Ave., Toronto, Ontario M4V IJ5
Sheila Hammond, 2000 Sherbrooke St. West, Montreal, Quebec H3H 1G4
Mary T. Malone, 783 Dufferin St., Toronto, Ontario M6H 3K8
Gloria Elliott, 64 Ursuline Ave., Chatham, Ontario
Rev. Mother Dominica, 64 Ursuline Ave., Chatham, Ontario
Gaida Iwamoto, 1908 A Davenport Rd., Toronto, Ontario M6N 1B7
Ellen Leonard, 237 Sheldrake Blvd., Toronto, Ontario M4P 2B1
Judy Atherton, 30 Dalton Rd., Toronto, Ontario M5R 2Y7
Pauline Turner, 7055 Riverside Drive E, Windsor, Ontario N8S 1C2
Michael Doyle CSSp., 53 Virginia Ave., Toronto, Ontario M4C 2S6
Joan Lenardon, 997 Waterloo St., London, Ontario N6A 3X4
Madeleine Hart, 1114 St. Anthony Rd., London, Ontario N6H 2P6
Elliott B. Allen CSB, Faculty of Theology, St. Michael's College, Toronto, Ontario M5S 1J4
Nina Glinski CND, 1117 Bronson Place, Ottawa, Ontario K1S 4H3
Nancy Hurren, 1117 Bronson Place, Ottawa, Ontario K1S 4H3
Carmel McEnroy, 12 Howland Ave., Toronto, Ontario M5R 3B3
B. Murphy, 783 Dufferin St., Toronto, Ontario M6H 3K8
Martin Helldorfer, 2629 Riverside Drive, West Windsor, Ontario N9B 1B4
Anne Johnson, 10 Montcrest Blvd., Toronto, Ontario M4K 1J7
Michael LaPierre, 3425 Bayview Ave., Toronto, Ontario M2M 3S5
Cecilia Cosgrove GNSH, 33 Hazel St., Apt. 11, Ottawa, Ontario K1S 0G1
Bernadette O'Neill, 2810 Baycrest, Ottawa, Ontario
Margaret McCarthy, 14 Ronan Ave., Toronto, Ontario M4N 2X9
Mary M. Schaefer, 1833 Riverside Drive Apt. 403, Ottawa K1G 0E8
Dorothy Konyha, 6100 Matchette, Windsor, Ontario N9 A6 J3
Marge Zounich, 489 Brunswick Ave., Toronto, Ontario M5R 2Z6
Maria Clarke Wimpenny, 150 Hillside Dr. South, Elliot Lake, Ontario P5A 1N1
Linda Spear, 157 Boullee St., London, Ontario N5Y 1T9
Katherine McKeough, St. Joseph's Hospital, 268 Grosvenor St., London, Ontario N6J 1Y2
Lloyd Robertson, President, Atlantic School of Theology, 640 Francklin St., Halifax Nova Scotia
J. Gregory Heenan, 6466 Bayers Road, Halifax Nova Scotia
Hans W. Daigeler, Canadian Catholic Conference, Ottawa, Ontario
Nuala Kenny M.D., 6484 Bayers Rd., Halifax Nova Scotia 3BL 2B1
Anne Fahey, 42 Convoy Ave., Halifax, Nova Scotia
Elizabeth Bellefontaine, Dept. of Religious Studies, Mt. St. Vincent Univ., Halifax, Nova Scotia B3M 2J6
Marion Sheridan CSH, Bethany, Antigonish Nova Scotia B0H 1B0
Therese LeBlanc CSH, Bethany, Antigonish Nova Scotia B0H 1B0

COLORADO

Helen Sanders SL, 3001 S. Federal Blvd., Box 1113, Denver 80236
Eileen Mackin SL, 4801 E. 23rd Ave., Denver. 80207
Pauline Baumgartner, 2200 Jasmine St., Denver 80207
Theresa Antista, 2633 E. 15th, Pueblo 81001
Helen Flaherty SC, 938 Bannock, Denver 80204

Sallie Watkins SFCC, 2729 Crawford St., Pueblo 81004
Mary Camilla Huber, 7860 York St., Denver 80229
Marie Catherine Pohndorf SL, 3001 S. Federal Blvd., Denver 80236
Susan M. Lamb, 9091 E. Nassau, Denver 80237
Rene Weeks OP, 622 W. 6th Ave., Denver 80204
Patricia Kennedy, 112 South Sixth, Brighton 80601
Gabe Huck, Rt. #3, Box 165A, Brighton 80601
Susan Sheeran SC, 6300 E. Asbury, Denver 80224
Marian McAvoy SL, 3001 S. Federal Blvd., Box 1113, Denver 80236
Mary Catherine Rabbitt SL, 3001 S. Federal Blvd., Box 1113, Denver 80236
Rose Ann Barmann OSB, 1980 Nelson, Lakewood 80215
Barbara Huber SC, 1661 Mesa Ave., Colorado Springs 80906
Rose Colley SL, Box 1113, 3001 S. Federal Blvd., Denver 80236
Maureen McCormack SL, 3192 W. Monmouth, Englewood 80110
Dianne Fassel SL, Box 1113, 3001 So. Federal Blvd., Denver 80236
Evelyn Houlihan, 2136 Perry, Denver 80212

CONNECTICUT

Gilmary Bauer RSH, 651 Prospect St., Box 1224, New Haven 06505
Janet Labrecque, 520 Thompson Ave., East Haven Ct. 06512
Nancy Nutting, 28 So. Highland St., West Hartford 06119
Nancy Roach CND, 223 West Mountain Road, Ridgefield 06877
Marcella Marie Tucker OP, 248 Ogden St., New Haven 06511
Claire Bonneau SSND, 345 Belden Hill Rd., Wilton 06897
Patricia Hussey, 119 Canterbury St., Hartford 06112
Maria Edward RSM, Mercy Center, Box 191, Madison 06443
GeorgeAnn Vumbaco, 200 Columbus Ave., New Haven Ct. 06519
Patricia Cook RSM, St. Joseph College, 1678 Asylum Ave., West Hartford 06117
Roberta McGrath RSM, 9 Perkins Ave., Norwich 06360
Mary Anne Foley CND, 972 W. Main St., Waterbury 06708
Eleanor Rae, 114 Rising Ridge Rd., Ridgefield 06877
Lynn L. Labrecque, 96 Providence St., Taftville 06380
Gail V. Riina, Box #154, 409 Prospect St., New Haven 06510
Anne Foley, 100 Riversville Rd., Greenwich 06830
Margaret Farley RSM, P.O. Box 1224, New Haven 06505

ENGLAND

Christina O'Neill (CSJ - English Province)
U.S. Address: Regan Hall Box 50, Catholic Univ. of America, Washington D.C. 20064
Joan Morris 27 Red Lion Street, London W.C.I.A.I.AA

FLORIDA

Mary Angela Gholston, 7911 Woodgrove Circle, Tampa 33615

GEORGIA

Lynne Nault, 2407 Kelly Lake Dr., Decatur 30032
Mary Ann Luby GNSH, 52 Peachtree Wayne, Atlanta 30305
Sheila Kelly GNSH, 52 Peachtree Wayne, Atlanta 30305
Janet Valente GNSH, 52 Peachtree Wayne, Atlanta 30305
Marcella Donahue, 636 W. Ponce de Leon Ave., Box 1549, Decatur 30030

GERMANY (Federal Republic)

Gudrun Diestel, D3 Hannover 20, Altenauer Weg 17, West Germany
U.S. Address:
Harvard Divinity School, Rockefeller.Hall, 47 Francis Ave.,
Cambridge, Mass. 02138

IDAHO

Helen Mason SP, 111 Haycraft #12, Coeur d'Alene 83814

ILLINOIS

Barbara L. Wysocki, 223 Tenth St., LaSalle 61301
Barbara Nelson IBJM, 10834 S. Perry, Chicago 60628
Jane Frances DuCharme IBVM, 10834 S. Perry, Chicago 60628
Mary Lou Weislo IBVM, 10834 S. Perry, Chicago 60628
Mary Liguori Brophy BVM, Mundelein College, Room 1004, 6363
  Sheridan Road, Chicago 60660
Francis F. Brown, 500 E. 33rd St. #210, Chicago 60616
Margaret Heinz OP, 2716 Foster Ave. Apt. H-3, Chicago 60625
Mary Carey OP, 2716 Foster Ave.,Apt. H-3, Chicago 60625
Therese Ragen RSM, 2944 South Michigan, Chicago 60616
Marion Cypser RSM, 2944 South Michigan, Chicago 60616
Mary Kanabay 108 First Street, Libertyville 60048
Jane E. Gerard CSJ, 5735 S. University, Chicago 60649
Marie W. Flood, Rosary College, 7900 W. Division St., River
  Forest 60305
Eugene A. Mainelli OP, 5427 University Apt. 3D, Chicago 60615
Ann Gillen, 1340 E. 72nd St., Chicago 60619
Maggie Fisher, 201 E. Ohio, Chicago 60611
Kathleen Keating, 211 E. Ohio St., Chicago 60611
Jacqueline Wetherholt, 2044 Newland, N. Chicago 60635
Georgene Wilson OSF, 5337 So. Justine St., Chicago 60609
Kathleen Ashe OP, 7900 W. Division, River Forest 60305
Mark Scannell OP, 5444 S. Woodlawn #3, Chicago 60615
JoAnn Brdecka OSF, St. Colette Church, 3900 S. Meadow Dr.,
  Rolling Meadows 60008
Lois McGovern OP, 1444 S. Keeler Ave., Chicago 60623
Rosemary Abramovich OP, 7914 S. Honore, Chicago 60620
Susan Weeks, 7914 S. Honore, Chicago 60620
Rosemary Bearss RSCJ, Barat College, Lake Forest 60045
Joan O'Shea, 9020 Embassy Lane, Des Plaines 60016
Lucy Edelbeck, 1410 E. Olive St., Arlington Heights 60004
Marina Hernandez, 2047 W. Fargo, Chicago 60645
Margaret M. Kopish ASC, 560 North Walnut Apt. #2, Taylorville
  62568
Therese Anne Kiefer ASC, 6211 Church Lane Centerville, E. St.
  Louis 62207
Dolores Anselment ASC, 409 E. Hull, McLeansboro 62859
Mary M. McMahon, 2047 W. Fargo, Chicago 60645
Constance Campbell, 2047 W. Fargo, Chicago 60645
Connie Huhn, 4351 W. 76th St. Apt. 204, Chicago 60652
Ethne Kennedy, 303 Barry Ave., Chicago 60657
Carlotta Oberzat RSM, 5411 S. University, Chicago 60615
William G. Guindon SJ, JSTC, 5430 University Ave., Chicago 60615
Patricia Crowley OSB, 7416-30 N. Ridge, Chicago 60645
William G. Thompson SJ, Jesuit School of Theology, 5430 University
  Ave., Chicago 60615

ILLINOIS - Continued

Loretta Kosiek, 4877 North Kenmore, Chicago 60640
Kathleen Reid, 514 N. 24th St., East St. Louis 62205
Mary Ellen McAleese OSF, P.O. Box 667, Wheaton 60187
Judy Herrhann, 1335 S. Clifton, Park Ridge 60068
Deanna M. Carr, 1307 South Wabash Ave., Chicago 60605
Virginia Dennehy RSCU, Barat College, Lake Forest 60045
Betty Boyter RSCJ, Barat College, Lake Forest 60045
Anne E. Patrick SNJM, 5430 S. University, Chicago 60615
Avis Clendenen RSM, 5415 So. University, Chicago 60615
Maryln Quinlan BVM, 5857 N. Kenmore, Chicago 60660
Anna Marie Kane BVM, 1114 So. May, Chicago 60607
Julie Neal, 429 Congress, Ottawa 61350
Mary Ann Seiler, 429 Congress, Ottawa 61350·
Charles Dahm OP, 1909 S. Ashland Ave., Chicago 60608
Carol Crepeau, 1307 S. Wabash Ave., Chicago 60605
Wendy Flannery, 5536 S. Everett Ave., Chicago 60637
A. M. McGrath, Rosary College, River Forest 60305
Anne Metzler, 430 Park Blvd., Glen Ellyn 60137
Elizabeth Rose, 4427 W. Wrightwood, Chicago 60639
M. Evangeline McSloy, 5415 Univ. Ave., Chicago 60615
Nora O'Brien OP, 8935 Kostner, Hometown 60456
Eleanor Stech OP, 8935 S. Kostner, Hometown 60456
Marguerite Cleary, Barat College, Dougherty Community, Lake
  Forest 60045
Monica Stuhlreyer, 5124 Kenwood, Chicago 60615
Patty Crowley, 175 East Delaware Place, Apt. 8804, Chicago 60611
Mary Cecile Quirke, Triton College, 2000 Fifth Ave., River Grove
  60171
Penny Dollard, 5124 S. Kenwood Apt. #3, Chicago 60615
Mary Sharon Riley, 11600 Longwood Drive, Chicago 60643
Georgianne Imberi, 8025 S. Honore, Chicago 80620
Teresa Disch OP, 5407 S. University Ave., Chicago 60615
Margaret Dewey OP, 5407 S. University #2, Chicago 60615
Susan M. Van Baalen OP, 7321 South Shore Drive, Chicago 60649
Mary Henry, Barat East Community, Barat College, Lake Forest
  60045
Clair Basar, Barat East Community, Barat College, Lake Forest
  60045
Peg Dunn, Barat East Community, Barat College, Lake Forest
  60045
Jane McKinley, Barat East Community, Barat College, Lake Forest
  60045
Aunice Callahan RSCJ, Barat College, Lake Forest 60045
Marilyn Ring, 501 S. Main, Normal 61761
Mary Ruth Broz, 9260 S. Claremont, Chicago 60620
Mary Ann Zeszutko, Illinois Benedictine College, Ondrak Lisle
  60532
Paula M. Fitzmaurice, 3017 E. 78th St., Chicago 60649
Marjorie Tuite, 400 E. 33 St., Chicago 60616
Sam Easley, c/o Tuite, 400 E. 33 St., Chicago 60616
Dorothy Bock SSSF, 5350 E. Springbrook Rd., Rockford 61111
Lenora Maier, 5350 E. Springbrook Rd., Rockford 61111
Eleanor Doidge, 5536 S. Everett Ave. #304, Chicago 60637
Kathy Bourgeois, Box 39 Barat College, Lake Forest 60045
Pat Moran, 14355 Highland, Orland Park 60462
Brenda McCarthy, 14345 Highland Ave., Orland Park 60462
Wayne L. Fehr, 5430 University Ave., Chicago 60615
Bernice McNeela, 1600 Sunset Ave., Apt. 115, Waukegan 60085

Jeanne Heidemann CSJ, 1209 W. Ogden Ave., La Grange Park 60525
Judy Maher, 1515 W. Ogden, La Grange Park 60525
Carolyn Parmer, 790 Mt. Pleasant, Winnetka 60093
Patricia F. Walter, 6108 N. Paulina, Chicago 60660
Helen Moshak, 5010 Louise S., Skokie 60076
Barbara Powers, 701 N. Division, Harvard 60033
Gilbert Ostdiek OFM, Catholic Theological Univ., 5401 S. Cornell Ave., Chicago 60615
Marilyn Sass, 1100 E. 55th St., Chicago 60615
Mary Barbara Agnew, International House, Box 729, 1414 E. 59 St., Chicago 60637
Mary Ellen Reynolds, Barat College, Lake Forest 60045
Teresa Maltby RSM, 5741 Circle Drive, Oak Lawn 60453
Donna Quinn OP, 1446 W. Berteau, Chicago 60613
Carolyn Nelson OP, 11513 Villa Court, Alsip 60658
Janet Hrubes, 1503 Rice, Melrose Park 60160
Dorothy Kramer, 1503 Rice, Melrose Park 60160
Kathryn Lawlor, 750 N. Wabash, Chicago 60611
Kathryn McHugh, 750 N. Wabash, Chicago 60611
Kathleen Sullivan, Barat College, Lake Forest 60045
Italo Scola, 11533 S. Prairie Ave., Chicago 60628
Gerry & Donald Brown, 927 Ontario, #2E, Oak Park 60301
Therese Guerin Sullivan SP, 2231 N. Major, Chicago 60639
Dorothy Gartland, 2231 N. Major, Chicago 60639
Marjorie Delaplane, 7633 South Shore Dr., Chicago 60649
Ann Heilman SFCC, 1314 Glenview Road, Glenview 60025
Gloria A. Phillips, 576 Kearsage Ave., Elmhurst 60126
Theresa Gleeson BVM, 2189 W. Bowler St., Chicago 60612
Gabriel Herbers RGS, 5536 So. Everett Ave., Chicago 60615
Judith Marie Vaughan, 649 W. 37th St., Chicago 60609
Mary Lou Halter, 11103 S. Hoyne, Chicago 60643
Josephine Sincak, 270 St. Charles Rd. Apt. G-A, Carol Stream 60187
Clare Kloeckner SSND, 9515 S. Loomis, Chicago 60643
Reid C. Mayo NFPC, 1307 S. Wabash, Chicago 60605
Nicole Goetz, 2122 W. Ainslie, Chicago 60625
Carroll Stuhlmueller OP, Catholic Theological Union, 5401 South Cornell, Chicago 60615
Anne Carr BVM, U. of Chicago Divinity School, Chicago 60637
Patricia Hughes, 7306 S. Oglesby Ave., Chicago 60649
Anne Kelley SND, 1159 E. 54th St. Apt. 1, Chicago 60615
Rosalie Muschal-Reinhardt, 6830 Fairmount Avenue, Downers Grove 60515
Toni Callahan, 1446 Berteau Ave., Chicago 60613
Anne Marie Trace, 413 Eigenmann Hall, Bloomington 47401
Rosie Kelly, 535 S. Randolph, McComb 61455
Rachael Bergschneider, 1203 W. Bradley, Peoria 61606

INDIANA

Josephine M. Peplinski SSJ, 107 S. Greenlawn Ave., South Bend 46617
Rosita Wisniewski SSJ, 107 S. Greenlawn Ave., South Bend 46617
Francis T. Zlorkowski CSC, 226 N. Hill St., South Bend 46617
Susan Kintzele CSC, 136 So. Chapin St., South Bend 46625
Barbara Balboni, Eigenmann Hall, Room 403, Indiana University, Bloomington 47401
Douglas Benbow OFM, St. Julian Frairy, 150 Doan Drive, Ft. Wayne 46816
J. Massyngberde Ford, 535 Napoleon Blvd., South Bend 46617

Continued

Jane Elyse Russell, Badin Hall, Box 402, Notre Dame 46556
Joy O'Grady CSC, St. Joseph's Hospital, P.O. Box 1935, South
Bend 46634
Judith Anne Beattie CSC, St. Joseph Hospital, P.O. Box 1935,
South Bend 46634
Mary Jo Nelson OLVM, Victory Noll-Box 109, Huntington 46750
Anselm Dennehy, Holy Cross House, Douglas Road, Notre Dame
46556
Ken Miller, Holy Cross House, Douglas Road, Notre Dame 46556
Michael McCaffery, Holy Cross House, Douglas Road, Notre Dame
46556
Susan Rosenbach, Walsh Hall, Notre Dame 46556
Dorothy Feehan BVM, Badin Hall - Box 351, Notre Dame 46556
Jane Pitz CSJ, Box 446, Notre Dame 46556
Margaret M. Healy, 251 Badin Hall, Notre Dame 46556
Eileen Stenzel, 16963 Douglas Rd., Granger 46530
John Scorzoni, Moreau Seminary, Notre Dame 46556
Liz Burger, Box 313, St. Joseph's College, Collegeville 47978
Pat McHugh OSB, Box 322, Badin Hall, Notre Dame 46556
Charles F. Caldwell, 1003 Riverside Drive, South Bend 46616
Pat Kane, 406 Peashway, South Bend 46617
Mary Kane, 406 Peashway, South Bend 46617
Natalia Vonnegut, 8800 Springmill Rd., Indianapolis 46260
John J. Egan, Univ. of Natre Dame, CCUM, Notre Dame 46556
Elizabeth Schüssler Fiorenza, Dept. of Theology, University of
Notre Dame 46556
Kathleen Hughes RSCJ, 928 Riverside Drive, South Bend 46617
Anne Marie Trace, 413 Eigenmann Hall, Bloomington 47401
Sharon Stanton OSF, C.C.U.M., P.O. Box 544, Notre Dame 46556

IOWA

Theresa Lawlor, McDonald SFCC, 14 Melrose Place, Iowa City
52240
Marlene Halpin OP, 2570 Asbury Road, Dubuque 52001
Cletus Wessels OP, Aquinas Institute, 2570 Asbury Road, Debuque
52001
Rosemary Hemesath, 440 10th St., Marion 52302
Lucille Winnike, Box 190, Hiawatha 52233
Joann Gehling, Box 190, Hiawatha 52233
Mary Ann Schmieding, 2728 Asbury, Dubuque 52001
Virginia Beattie, 1718½ White St., Dubuque 52001
Ann Knight, Box 5678, Coralville 52241
Merrill J. Meltz OP, Aquinas Institute, 2570 Asbury, Dubuque 52001
Greg Ochs OP, Aquinas Institute, 2570 Asbury St., Dubuque 52001
Ron Kreul OP, Aquinas Institute, 2570 Asbury St., Dubuque 52001
Dolores Becker, 2728 Asbury Road, Dubuque 52001
Mary Kaye Nealen OP, 2728 Asbury Rd., Dubuque 52001
Mary Ann Foy, 1951 ½ Arlington, Des Moines 50314
John F. Taylor OP, 2570 Asbury, Dubuque 52001
Joan Doyle BVM, Mount Carmel Generalate, Dubuque 52001
M. Adele Henneberry BVM, Mount Carmel Generalate, Dubuque
52001
Joanne Lucio BVM, Mount Carmel Generalate, Dubuque 52001
Mary Francis Reis BVM, Mt. Carmel Generalate, Dubuque 52001
Mary Nolan BVM, Mount Carmel Generalate, Dubuque 52001
Katherine Gray, 231 South 7th St., Council Bluffs 51501
Ann Freiburg, 2728 Asbury Rd., Dubuque 52001

KANSAS

Betty Jean Goebel, 3600 Broadway, Great Bend 67530
Rosemary Kotz, 1633 Jewell, Topeka 66604
Barbara Overman OSB, 1915 Stratford Rd., Lawrence 66044
Jolene Geier OP, P.O. Box 4089, Topeka 66604
Karen J. Smith, 138 W. 12th Apt. 7, Emporia 66801
Shirley Koritnik SCL, 817 Waverly Ave., Kansas City 66101
Diane Lickteig OSU, 3220 West 53rd St., Shawnee Mission 66205
Marie dePaul Combo, St. Mary College, Leavenworth 66048
Ellen L. Burns, St. Mary College, Leavenworth 66048
Mary Collins OSB, 1915 Stratford Road, Lawrence 66044
Louise Hageman OP, 3600 Broadway, Great Bend 67530
Michaela Zahner CSJ, 6038 Fontana Ave., Shawnee Mission 66205

KENTUCKY

Anne Margaret Cahill, St. Catherine P.O., 40061
Jan Zalla Runda, 726 Meadow Wood, Crescent Springs 41011
Jane M. Richardson SL, Koto Ba, Nerinx 40049
Lori Williams, 1115 Oak Avenue, Ashland 41101
Pat Clark SCN, 224 Inverness Ave., Louisville 40214
Betty Blandford SCN, 224 Inverness Ave., Louisville 40214
Joan Monica McGuire OP, Dominican Generalate, St. Catherine 40061
Mary Swain, Nerinx, 40049
Adrian M. Hofstetter, Center of Ecumenism, Saint Catharine 40061
Sarah M. Concannon, 1634 Windsor Place, Louisville 40204
Mary Brigio Gregory OP, 2903 Sunnyfield Rd., Louisville 40220
Renée Rust PSB, Manna-Folo, 2500 Amsterdam Rd., Covington
Susan Powers, P.O. Box 22125, [519 Lyndon Lane] Louisville 40222
Carole Kaucic SCN, 682 Atwood Ave., Louisville 40217
Marylee King SCN, 682 Atwood Ave., Louisville 40217
Joan Yelton OSB, 2500 Amsterdam Rd., Covington 41016
Nancy Finneran SL, 1634 Windsor Pl., Louisville 40204
Mary Frances Lottes SL, 1634 Windsor Pl., Louisville 40204
Dawn Dorsey SL, 1634 Windsor Pl., Louisville 40204
Rose Annette Liddell, Loretto Motherhouse, Nerinx 40049
Helen R. Dobell, Loretto Motherhouse, Nerinx 40049
M. Catherine Hunt, St. Anne Covent, Melbourne 41059
Joan Marie Boberg, St. Anne Convent, Melbourne 41059
Madonna Fitzgerald, St. Anne Convent, Melbourne 41059
Joan Campbell SL, Loretto Motherhouse, Nerinx 40049

LOUISIANA

Mary Anne Heine SSND, 5252 Maple Drive, Baton Rouge 70805
Theresa Drago O.CARM., 420 Robert E. Lee Blvd., New Orleans 70124
Albina Guillory MSC, Sacred Heart Convent, Ville Platte 70586
Fara Impastato OP, 1101 Aline St., New Orleans 70115
Mary J. Richardson, 2635 State St., New Orleans 70118
Jacqueline Toppino OSU, 2635 State St., New Orleans 70118

MAINE

Carmelle Poutré FCSCJ, 189 Main St. #2, Gorham 04038

MARYLAND

M. Charlene Walsh RSM, Mercy Provincialate, P.O. Box 10490, Baltimore 21209
Jeannine Gramick, 761 W. Hamburg St., Baltimore 21230
Doris Gottemoeller RSM, 10,000 Kentsdale Rd., Bethesda 20034
Caroline Laiso, 10,000 Kentsdale Rd., Bethesda 20034
Rosemarie B. Chase, P.O. Box 356, Leonardtown 20650
Philip S. Keane SS, St. Mary's Seminary, 5400 Roland Ave., Baltimore 21210
Sarah T. Neale SSND, 815 Hampton Lane, Baltimore 21204
Carol A. Gallagher RSM, 11332 Evans Trl. #104, Beltsville 20705
Mary Elaine Walsh MHSH, 1001 W. Joppa Rd., Baltimore 21204
Danielle Murphy MHSH, 1001 W. Joppa Rd., Baltimore 21204
Clare Walsh, 1001 W. Joppa Rd., Towson 21204
Ann Martin Gallagher, 7609 Marcy Drive, Glen Burnie 21061
Elizabeth Haley, 7609 Marcy Drive, Glen Burnie 21061
Carol E. Smith, 4606 Schenley Rd., Baltimore 21210
Dolly Pomerleau, 3311 Chauncey Pl., Mt. Rainier 20822
Irene Marshland OSF, 3725 Ellerslie Ave., Baltimore 21218
Eileen Quinn OSF, 3725 Ellerslie Ave., Baltimore 21218
William Callahan SJ, Priests for Equality, Mt. Ranier 20822
Julia A. Heaps, Archdiocese of Baltimore, 1001 W. Joppa Rd., Baltimore 21204

MASSACHUSETTS

Claire E. Lowery RSCJ, 842 Commonwealth Ave., Newton 02159
Edward Pothier, 30 Dartmouth Rd., Marblehead 01945
Margaret McDonnell RSCJ, 116 Appleton St., Boston 02116
Terri Monroe, 63 Cushing St., Cambridge 02138
Madeline T. Webster, 63 Cushing St., Cambridge 02138
Jean Ford RSCJ, 842 Commonwealth Ave., Mewton 02159
Nancy Kehde RSCJ, 116 Appleton St., Boston 02116
Bessie Chambers, 842 Commonwealth, Newton Centre 02159
Camille Noel, 10 Pelham Rd., Lexington 02173
Anne Wente RSCJ, 785 Centre, Newton 02158
Maureen Mulcrone RSM, 34 Long Ave., Allston 02134
Diane Scaro, 34 Long Ave., Allston 02134
Suzanne Hiatt, 12 Everett St., Arlington 02174
Bernadette Furin CSJ, 63 Cushing St., Cambridge 02138
Nancy M. Malone OSU, Nat'l. Institute for Campus Ministries, 885 Centre St., Newton 02159
Annette Rafferty SSJ, 6 Birch Street, Worcester 01610
Barbara Ann Thomas, 780 Boylstan St., Apt. 4D, Boston 02199
Loretta Mulvey RSM, 800 Tucker Rd., No. Dartmouth 02747
Hondra McHugh RSM, 800 Tucket Rd., No. Dartmouth 02747
Barbara Harrington, 86 Fuller St., Dorchester 02124
Georgianna Landrigan SC, 225 Walden St., Cambridge 02140
Joseph Laughlin, 52 Lithgow St., Dorechester 02124
Barbara Zanotti, 52 Lithgow St., Dorchester 02124
Mariann Ronan, 52 Lithgow St., Dorchester 02124
Maureen Kemeza, 3 St. John's Rd., Cambridge 02138
Claire McGowan OP, 86 Fuller St., Dorehester 02124
Susan L. Costa, 38 Sacramento St., Cambridge 02138
Kathryn Piccard, 60 Sacramento, Cambridge 02138
Kathleen Daly SND, P.O. Box 258, Jamaica Plain 02130
Maureen Young, Andover-Newton Theo. School, Box 265, Newton Centre 02159
Virginia Ryan, Box 214 ANTS, 210 Herrick Road, Newton Centre 02159

Frances Belmonte OP, Box 21 ANTS, 210 Herrick Rd., Newton Center 02159
Julianne Bousquet, 437 Maple St., Holyoke 01040
Julie Kelly SND, 19 Chestnut St., Peabody 01960
Laura Messier, 303 Newtonville Ave., Newton 02160
Helen Wright, 64 Chestnut St., Charlestown 02129
Roberta Marie CSJ, 339 Jerusalem Rd., Cohasset 02025
Kevin G. O'Connell SJ, Weston School of Theology, 3 Phillips Place, Cambridge 02138
Barbara Ferraro SND, 97 Great Plain Ave., Needham 02192
Kathy Riley SND, 573 Gallivan Blvd., Dorchester 02124
Marlene DeNardo SND, Harvard Divinity School, Rockefeller Hall 2A2, Cambridge 02138
Loreta Jordan, 50 W. Broadway, South Boston 02127
Nancy Simonds, 50 W. Broadway, South Boston 02127
Catherine Mooney, 47 Francis Ave., Cambridge 02138
Carol Caton, 63 Cushing St., Cambridge 02138
Leonora C. Deshond, 11 Preston Rd., Somerville 02143
Maeve McDermott, 5 Buckingham Place, Cambridge 02138
Ellen Reilly SND, 425 North St. Apt. 11, Randolph 02368
Theresa Ahern MSBT, 16 Reservoir St., Worcester 01605
Mary Matthew, 16 Reservoir St., Worcester 01605
Rita Rice, 42 Bond St., Reading 01867
Thomas Caldarola SJ, 80 Lexington Ave., Cambridge 02138
Richard Howard SJ, 20 Sumner Road, Cambridge 02138
Janet Cronin SND, Office of Religious Ed., 240 Adams St., Dorchester 02122
Peggy Comfrey, 29 Holman St., Allston 02134
Brian McDermott SJ, 3 Phillips Place, Cambridge 02138
Margaret Hutaff, 137 Oxford St., Cambridge 02140
Jeanne Andersen Allen, 99 Hancock St., Everett 02149
Michael McElhinny SM, 13 Isabella St., Boston 02116
Irene Doyle CSM, 36 Commonwealth Ave., Boston 02116
Marie Doyle, 119 Ronald Rd., Arlington 02174
Kenneth Swan SM, 13 Isabella St., Boston 02116
Elaine C. Huber OP, 58 Dunster Road, Jamaica Plain 02130
Thomas McKeown, 15 Notre Dame Ave., Cambridge 02140
Jane Redhont, c/o Williams, 163 Brighton St., Belmont 02178
Evelyn McKenna, 15 Belvoir Rd., Milton 02186
Evelyn Gladu, 201 Lake St., Arlington 02174
Dolores Brooks OP, 5 Buckingham Place, Cambridge 02138
Richard McBrien, Boston College, Institute for Study of Religious Education, Gassom 200, Chestnut Hill 02167
Marie Augusta Neal SND, Harvard University Divinity School, 70 Francis Avenue, Cambridge 02138
Emily C. Hewitt, 374 Beacon St., Somerville 02143
John T. Finnegan, Pope John XIII Seminary, Weston 02193
Jacqueline Calnan, 57 Floral Street, Newton Highlands 02161

MICHIGAN

Mary H. Smolbrook OP, 355 E. Maplehurst, Ferndale 48220
Esther Kennedy OP, 1261 E. Siena Heights, Dr., Adrian 49221
Mary Lou Putrow OP, 1261 East Siena Heights Dr., Adrian 49221
Margaret Andrezik OP, 1261 E. Siena Heights Dr., Adrian 49221
Nadine Foley OP, 1257 Siena Heights Dr., Adrian 49221
Nancy Bauer SSJ, 2875 Henry St., Port Huron 48060
Bohdan Kosicki, 1234 Washington Blvd., Detroit 48226
William G. Petron, 2236 E. Grand Blvd., Detroit 48211

MICHIGAN - Continued

Mary Alberta Bodde SC, 28801 Imperial Drive Apt. 203, Warren 48093

Noreen Ellison SC, 28801 Imperial Drive Apt. 203, Warren 48093

Helen Vrbain RSM, 17127 Stansbury, Detroit 48235

Anne Purtell RSM, 19960 Mansfield, Detroit 48235

Jane Payette OP, 9400 Courville, Detroit 48224

Pat O'Donnell, 428 N. Johnson, Pontiac 48058

Margaret Conlin SSJ, 45 Candler Ave., Highland Park 48203

Donna Hansen RSM, 17166 Stansbury, Detroit 48235

Dorothy Krolikowski SSJ, 25842 Marilyn St., Warren 48089

Joan Killoran SSJ, 25842 Marilyn St., Warren 48089

Maureen Malane RSM, 17166 Stansbury, Detroit 48235

Ramona Gerard RSM, 17166 Stansbury, Detroit 48235

Dennis Reno, 25900 Meridian, Grosse Ile 48138

Anne Karen Heath, 411 Florence St., Ypsilanti 48197

Linda Marie Werthman RSM, 29000 Eleven Mile Rd., Farmington Hills 48024

Séan Therese Halpin OP, 9400 Courville Ave. 1-W, Detroit 48224

Emily George RSM, 29000 Eleven Mile Road, Farmington Hills 48024

Mary Kay Sweeney RSM, 17127 Stansbury, Detroit 48235

Joyce DeShand SSJ, 14448 Carlisle, Detroit 48205

T. V. Breitenbeck, 578 Inkster Rd., Dearborn Hts. 48127

Theresa Blaquiere RSM, 1130 W. Centre, Portage 49081

Pauline Burger OSU, 1130 W. Centre, Portage 49081

Margaret Bosch SDS, 1130 West Centre, Portage 49081

Madeline Reno, 1261 Siena Heights Drive, Adrian 49221

Jarrett DeWyse OP, 205 Carrier NE, Grand Rapids 49505

Dixie A. McCleary, 24 Bennett St., Pontiac 48058

Josephine Gaugier OP, 10431 Crocuslawn, Detroit 48204

William J. Rademacher, St. John's Seminary, 44011 Five Mile Rd., Plymouth 48170

Carol Rittner RSM, Mercy College of Detroit, 8200 West Outer Drive, Detroit 48219

Frances Mlocek IHM, 610 W. Elm Ave., Monroe 48161

Helen Marie Burns RSM, 2214 Lake, Michigan Drive, Grand Rapids 49504

John W. Toester, 44011 Five Mile Rd., Plymouth 48170

Mary Ann Przybysz RSM, 17182 Stansbury, Detroit 48235

Virgianne SSJ, 25842 Marilyn, Warren 48089

Carol Campbell RSM, 2214 Lake Michigan Drive, Grand Rapids 49504

Mary Ellen Bennett OP, 703 N. Lapeer Rd., Lake Orion 48035

Anne Maureen Ronan OP, 205 Carrier NE, Grand Rapids 49505

Imogene Weyer SC, 22851 Lexington Ave., E. Detroit 48021

Margaret Betz, 16590 Hartwell, Detroit 48235

Janet Thill, 16590 Hartwell, Detroit 48235

Pat Heaney, 16590 Hartwell, Detroit 48235

Patricia Cooney, Marygrove College, 8425 W. McNichols Rd., Detroit 48221

Rachelle Harper RSM, 305 Michigan, Detroit 48226

Margaret Weber RSM, 29000 Eleven Mile, Farmington 48024

Mary Tardiff OP, Box 85, Orchard Lake 48034

Mary Key Nolan OP, SS. Cyril & Methodius Seminary, Box 85, Orchard Lake 48033

Joan Delaplane, SS. Cyril & Methodius Seminary, Orchard Lake 48033

Anneliese Sinnott OP, SS. Cyril & Methodius Seminary, Orchard Lake 48033
Wanda Manos, 22851 Lexington, E. Detroit 48021
Gloria Kiefer OP, 9740 McKinney 3W, Detroit 48224
Jackie Cullen IHM, 23632 Joy, St. Clair Shores 48082
Gretchen Elliott RSM, 28600 W. 11 Mile Rd., Farmington Hills 48024
Diane Kelly OP, 1220 Siena Heights Dr., Adrian 49221
Maureen Coleman OP, 1220 Siena Heights Drive, Adrian 49221
Margaret O'Neill OP, 1220 Siena Hts. Drive, Adrian 49221
Roberta Kolasa, 3119 Woodland Ct., Saginaw 48601
Marie Altesleben OP, 9400 Courville, Detroit 48224
Mary Lou Watkins, 17127 Stanbury, Detroit 48235
Linda Valli, 17127 Stansbury, Detroit 48235
Mary Hemmen OP, 29251 Bon Mar, Warren 48093
Kay Sheskaitis, 70 W. Boston Blvd., Detroit 48202
Barbara Rund OP, 29251 Bon Mar, Warren 48093
Maryetta Churches, 29251 Bon Mar, Warren 48093
Richard Peters, 3500 Three Mile Drive, Detroit 48224
Sheila Gainey IHM, 19760 Meyers, Detroit 48235
Mary Agnes Ryan, 19494 Redfern, Detroit 48219
M. Clare Nicolai, 23619 Power Road, Farmington 48024
Marcella Clancy, St. Rita Convent, 1000 E. State Fair, Detroit 48203
Luanne Yocke, 35081 Mustang Drive, Sterling Heights 48077
Sheila Flynn, 17305 Ashton St., Detroit 48219
Marie Ouellette, 17305 Ashton St., Detroit 48219
Darlene Swiderski, 17305 Ashton St., Detroit 48219
Louis Anderson, 44011 Five Mile Rd., Plymouth 48170
Elaine Gaston OP, 17173 Fairport, Detroit 48205
Irene Waldmann SSJ, Central Administration, Nazareth 49074
Jean Marie Umlor, 29000 11 Mile Rd., Farmington 48024
Bernice Nofs OP, 305 Michigan Ave., Detroit 48226
Marie Decker, 730 Rickett Road, Brighton 48116
Susan Kelly, 730 Rickett Road, Brighton 48116
Helen McAllister, 730 Rickett Rd., Brighton 48116
Gerry Sellman, 45 Candler, Highland Park 48203
Katherine R. Wachocki, 2509 Seminole, Detroit 48214
Canice Johnson RSM, 23001 Norfolk, Detroit 48219
Peggy Albert, 4835 Lincoln Ave., Detroit, 48208
Edward J. Farrell, 2701 W. Chicago Blvd., Detroit 48206
Mary Jo Walsh, 2923 Iroquois, Detroit 48214
Cecilia Begin RSM, 1151 Oakman Blvd., Detroit 48238
Fran Sulzer, 210 Pioneer Ave., Negaunee 49866
Molly Giller OP, 1257 Siena Heights Dr., Adrian 49221
Mary Frances Roberts, 356 Arden Park, Detroit 48202
Julie A. McDonnell, 6975 Lakeshore Drive, Port Huron 48060
Patricia Connors RSM, 1151 Oakman Blvd., Detroit 48238
Marcia Stroko, 1539 W. 13 Mile Rd., Royal Oak 48073
Tom Zelinski, 700 W. Boston Blvd., Detroit 48202
Mary Generose Kubesh RSM, 29000 Eleven Mile, Farmington 48024
William Hoyng, 5247 Sheridan, Detroit 48213
Blanche M. Cushing, 20175 Omira, Detroit 48203
Ann C. Joseph, 215 North Ave., Mt. Clemens 48043
Kay Tardiff, 14851 Alma, Detroit 48205
Ruth Van Oeffelen, 14851 Alma, Detroit 48205
Maureen Aggeler RSCJ, Campus Ministry U. of .D., 4001 W. McNichols, Detroit 48221
Mary Jo Maher, 610 W. Elm Ave., Monroe 48161

MICHIGAN - Continued

Barbara Sigillito, 4069 Barnaby Ct., W. Bloomfield 48033
Catherine Wagner, Justice & Peace Office, 305 Michigan Ave.,
   Detroit 48226
Stephen Krupa, 44011 Five Mile Rd., Plymouth 48170
Patricia Benson OP, 26250 Hass, Dearborn Heights 48127
Mary Pat Farnand OP, 738 W. Main, Owosso 48867
Mary Ellen Leciejewski, 15879 E. 7 Mile Road, Detroit 48205
Judy Apple OP, 1257 Siena Heights Drive, Adrian 49221
Joan Marie Weithman OP, 13231 Prest, Detroit 48227
Jean Small OP, 13231 Prest, Detroit 48227
John E. Smith, 19120 Purling-Brook Rd., Livonia 48152
Marcella Regan IHM, 18954 Wormer, Detroit 48219
Joanne Witucki IHM, 18954 Wormer, Detroit 48219
Helen LaValley, 305 Sheldon SE, Grand Rapids 49502
Margaret Babcock IHM, 2020 14th, Detroit 48216
Mary Kinney IHM, 8961 Laurence St., Allen Park 48101
Jeanne Burns OP. 1257 E. Siena Heights Dr.. Adrian 49221
Margaret Huber OP, 331 Thompson St., Ann Arbor 48108
Leo P. Broderick, St. John's Provincial Seminary, 44011 Five Mile
   Rd., Plymouth 48170
Paulette LeDuc IHM, 19500 Stratford, Detroit 48221
Theresa Koernke IHM, 19500 Stratford, Detroit 48221
Beth Hemminger, 510 N. Union St., Tecumseh 49286
Betty Kammerer CPPS, 5780 Evergreen, Detroit 48228
Betty Foster OP, 2850 17th St., Detroit 48216
Marie Cyril Delisi, 63 N. 24th, Battle Creek 49015
Patricia McCarty OP, 5273 Kenilworth, Dearborn 48126
Pat Siemen, 302 Frank, Adrian 49221
Grace Janowski OP, 925 E. Wheeler Rd., Midland 48640
Anne Cenci OP, 925 E. Wheeler Rd., Midland 48640
Kathy Morrissey OP, 925 E. Wheeler Rd., Midland 48640
Elizabeth Mills, 22426 Hillcrest Dr., Woodhave 48183
Anne Wojcicki, 8101 Locklin Dr., Union Lake 48085
Bill Hickey, 1100 E. State Fair, Detroit 48203
Loretta M. Weber RSM, 23001 Norfolk, Detroit 48219
Julienne Howell RSM, 23001 Norfolk St., Detroit 48219
Janice Brown, 4946 Leesburg Dr., Orchard Lake 48033
Janet Persyk, 666 Alter Rd., Detroit 48215
Alice Clover, 10425 Crocuslawn, Detroit 48204
Pat McCarthy, 10425 Crocuslawn, Detroit, 48204
Mary Alice MacDonald, 1030 N. River Road, Saginaw 48603
Helen Louise Slattery, 727 N. Jenison, Lansing 48915
Sandra LoPorto, 1346 Butternut, Detroit 48216
Geraldine McCullagh SMR, 17330 Quincy Ave., Detroit 48221
Celeste Schoppy, 422 W. Front St., Monroe 48161
Carmen Dominguez OP, 22851 Lexington, E. Detroit 48021
Pat Mullen SSJ, 45 Candler, Highland Park 48203
Elaine Suehar, 18572 Binder, Detroit 48234
Jan Soleau IHM, 20401 E. 8 Mile Rd., Apt. 18, St. Clair Shores
   48080
Joyce Campbell IHM, 20401 E. Eight Mile Apt. 18, St. Clair
   Shores 48080
Dorothy Bejin, 970 Woods Lane, Grosse Pointe Woods 48236
Marguerite Kowaleski, 36680 Brittany Hill, Farmington 48024
Ann Walters OP, 211 N. Otsego, Gaylord 49735
Pat Riley OP, 503 Common, Walled Lake 48088
Miriam Mullins OP, 503 Common St., Walled Lake 48088
Rosemarie Kieffer OP, 503 Common, Walled Lake 48088

Bonnie Motto OP, 1234 Inglewood, Rochester 48063
Jeanette Jabour, 1257 Siena Heights Drive, Adrian 49221
Anne Guinan OP, 1257 Siena Heights Drive, Adrian 49221
Grace Flowers OP, 1257 Siena Heights Dr., Adrian 49221
Mary Navarre, 8664 Appleton, Dearborn Heights 48127
Elizabeth Mary Burns, 29000 Eleven Mile Rd., Farmington 48024
Anne M. LaHaie, 2641 Harvard, Berkley 48072
Olga M. Bonfiglio, 703 N. Lapeer, Lake Orion 48035
Ann Chester IHM, 70 W. Boston Blvd., Detroit 48202
Pat Nagle, 70 W. Boston Blvd., Detroit 48202
Joyce Bauman, 2330 Vermont, Detroit 48216
Patricia Smith, 627 Westmoreland, Lansing 48915
Ellen Masko RSM, 17127 Stansbury, Detroit 48235
Jeannette LaCasse, 321 W. Pulaski, Flint 48505
Harriet A. Learson, 27548 Gateway Dr. E., Apt. E201, Farmington
  Hills 48024
Rose Cadaret SSJ, 1049 22nd, Detroit 48216
Pat Altermatt, 1000 E. State Fair, Detroit 48203
Adrienne R. Schaffer OP, 7798 W. Fort St., Detroit 48209
Frank J. Berge, 44011 Five Mile Rd., Plymouth 48170
Rita Marie Valade RSM, 16745 Avon, Detroit 48219
Christine Dobrowolski IHM, 529 Stewart Rd., Monroe 48161
Barbara Schlaud SSJ, Formation, Sisters of St. Joseph, Nazareth
  49074
Rita T. Schaefer OP, 1257 E. Sienna Hts.Dr., Adrian 49221
Trish Langdon, 18572 Binder St., Detroit 48232
Steve Clark, P.O. Box 87, Ann Arbor 48107
Joann DiMercurio, 14448 Carlisle, Detroit 48205
Anne C. Garrison, 136 Cowley Ave., E. Lansing 48823
Bianca R. Marguglio, Bamberwoods, 801 Oakland Drive, Mt.
  Pleasant 48858
Mary Margaret Mannard OP, 4500 Marseille, Detroit 48224
Janet Schaeffler OP, 4500 Marseilles, Detroit 48224
E. M. Brennan, 3990 Giddings Rd., Pontiac 48057
Anne M. Zimmerman, 3990 Giddings Rd., Pontiac 48057
Robert E. Majzler SJ, University of Detroit, 4001 W. McNichols,
  Detroit 48221
Kathleen McGrail OP, 14910 Vaughan, Detroit 48223
Veronica Koperski, 8925 Culver, Detroit 48213
Patricia Oliss, 8925 Culver, Detroit 48213
Judy Coyle, 150 Taylor, Coldwater 49036
Maria Lacke OSF, 107 S. Mansfield, Ironwood 49938
Alice Miller, 29105 Murray Crescent, Southfield 48076
Donna Hart, 29105 Murray Crescent, Southfield 48076
Karen Shirilla, 4160 Brown, Bridgeport 48722
Kitty Joachim IHM, 2405 Opdyke Rd., Bloomfield Hills 48013
Delores Kincaide SL, 2850 17th St., Detroit 48216
Wanda Ezop OP, 1434 Byron SE, Grand Rapids, 49506
Carol Denice Koenig OP, 411 Florence, Ypsilanti 48197
Sheila Powers OP, 411 Florence, Ypsilanti 48197
Sandra H. Boyd, 5768 Firwood Dr., Troy 48084
Vivian Hock, 13301 Ludlow, Huntington Woods 48070
Alison Giase OP, House of Studies, 1760 E. Fulton, Grand Rapids
  49503
Ann Corr IHM, 3231 West Road, Trenton 48183
Barbara Robach, 405 E. Hopson Ave., Bad Axe 48413
Frances Buschell, 405 E. Hopson, Bad Axe 48413
Chris Gellings IHM, 19500 Stratford, Detroit 48221
Janet Ryan, 1801 Palms Rd., Palms 48465
Mary Ann Feathers, 1801 Palms Rd., Palms 48465

MICHIGAN - Continued

Theresa Moran, 15031 Dexter, Detroit 48238
Lynn Marie Kriston RSM, 1151 Oakman Blvd., Detroit 48238
Dorothy Anne Lengerich OLVM, 100 New St., Mt. Clemens 48043
Ron Modras, St. John's Seminary, Plymouth 48170
Jacinta IHM, 6000 Arden, Warren 48092
Mary Therese Mackey, 6000 Arden, Warren 48092
Anne Crimmins, 6000 Arden, Warren 48092
Lois Morgan, 6000 Arden, Warren 48092
Mary James Rau OP, 2025 E. Fulton, Grand Rapids 49503
Jeannette Walter IHM, 13444 Justine, Detroit 48212
Marian Gumbleton, 2882 Adlake, Pontiac 48055
Glenn Risse, 5139 Lemay, Detroit 48213
Catherine Olds OP, 335 Elm, Wyandotte 48192
Barbara J. Walkley OP, 1600 Hudson, Essexville 48732
Sarah Cavanaugh OP, 19411 W. Chicago, Detroit 48228
Elizabeth Anderson CSJ, 45 Candler St., Highland Park 48203
Noreen Burns RSM, 326 N. Ingalls, Ann Arbor 48104
Barbara Supanich RSM, 326 N. Ingalls, Ann Arbor 48104
Anne M. Ragan, 1030 N. River Rd., Saginaw 48603
Agnes Sheehan CSJ, 420 Charles St., E. Lansing 48823
Therese Kearney IHM, D-10, 843 Whitmore Rd., Detroit 48203
Mary Margo Fitzpatrick, 6071 W. Outer Drive, Detroit 48235
Patricia Kulwicki RSM, St. Eugene Convent, 23001 Norfolk,
 Detroit 48219
Anthony R. Kosnik, SS. Cyril & Methodius Seminary, Orchard Lake
 48034
Ginny King, 14910 Vaughan, Detroit 48223
Cate Waynick, 11401 Cranston, Livonia 48150
Micheas, 7625 Westwood, Detroit 48228
Margaret B. Von Steeg, 4517 Barcroft Way, Sterling Heights 48077
Mary Martens, 1607 Robinson Road, S.E., Grand Rapids 49506
Mary Lou Owczarzak, 1030 N. River Rd., Saginaw 48603
Mary Teresa Soper, Women's Center, Northern Michigan Univ.,
 Marquette 49855
Nancy Vom Steeg, 1349 Nicolet, Detroit 48207
Margaret Basso IHM, 5549 Castleton, West Bloomfield 48033
Marie Bohn HM, 5273 Kenilworth, Dearborn 48126
Carol Crowley, 1506 River Terrace, East Lansing 48823
Sherry Dickerson, 4053 S. Lapeer Rd., Metamora 48455
Jeanette Clark, 615 W. Hancock, Detroit 48201
Sarah James Byrne SCL, 331 Thompson, Ann Arbor 48108
Mimi Lynch OP, 117 W. Liberty St., Belding 48809
Joan Hastreiter SSJ, Central Offices, Nazareth 49074
Clare Mess SSND, P.O. Box 280, 501 Fisher St., Marquette 49855
Carmela Whitton, 925 E. Wheeler Rd., Midland 48640
Edward J. Posselius (Doris), 160 Lewiston Rd., Grosse Pointe 48236
Maria Goretti Beckman, 1304 Alpine Church Rd., Comstock Park
 49321
Melanie Chateau OP, 2200 E. 12 Mile Rd., Royal Oak 48071
Margaret Brennan IHM, 610 W. Elm, Monroe 48161
Lee Farkas, 861 S. Rosedale, Grosse Pointe Woods 48236
Delphine Palkowski, 861 S. Rosedale, Grosse Pointe Woods 48236
Joanne Watko, 861 S. Rosedale, Grosse Pointe Woods 48236
David J. Funk, 700 W. Boston Blvd., Detroit 48202
Kathleen Walsh, Nazareth College, Kalamazoo 49074
Fran Knechtges, 14837 Belmont, Allen Park 48101
Margaret Hahn, 26250 Hass, Dearborn Hts., 48127
JoAnn Blundo IHM, 24855 Rensselaer, Oak Park 48237

Geraldine Cuddihy IHM, 24855 Rensselaer, Oak Park 48237
Patricia McCluskey IHM, 15379 Pinehurst, Detroit 48238
Mary B. Lynch, 17309 Quincy, Detroit 48221
Karen Stepien, IHM, 610 W. Elm, Monroe 48161
Margaret Urban OP, 19411 W. Chicago, Detroit 48228
Magoalena Ezoc OP, Sienna Heights College, 1247 E. Sienna
  Heights Drive, Adrian 49221
Brigid Johnson RSM, Mercy Center, 28600 Eleven Mile Rd.,
  Farmington 48024
Judith Kaltz, 10809 Balfour, Allen Park 48101
Michael Herman, St. Augustine's House, Oxford 48051
Eileen MacNeil IHM, 761 SCB, Wayne State Univ., Detroit 48202
Debbie Kornacki, 14560 Novara, Detroit 48205
Janice Kornacki, 14560 Novara, Detroit 48205
Eileen Karrer IHM, 70 W. Boston Blvd., Detroit 48202
Helen Gallitz CSA, 70 W. Boston Blvd., Detroit 48202
Ginny Kelling IHM, 70 W. Boston Blvd., Detroit 48202
Kathy Bruton OP, 13660 Eastwood, Detroit 48205
Carol Starrs IHM, 16843 Snowden, Detroit 48235
Brian A. Haggerty, 2849 Manning, Trenton 48183
Beverly Derbacher RSM, 70 W. Boston Blvd., Detroit 48202
Kathleen Jackson IHM, 9272 Littlefield, Detroit 48228
Peggy Schmidt IHM, 9272 Littlefield, Detroit 48228
Joan Michalik IHM, 9272 Littlefield, Detroit 48228
Pat Reno OP, 14910 Vaughan, Detroit 48223
Paul Weber SJ, 14910 Vaughan, Detroit 48223
Sue Anne Brorby, 17330 Quincy, Detroit 48221
Mary Ann Dixon, 22851 Lexington, E. Detroit 40021
Mary Ellen McClanaghan, 4500 Marseille, Detroit 48224
Donna Kustousch OP, 1261 Siena Heights Drive, Adrian 49221
Barbara Feleo, 2087 Stratford, Troy 48084
JoAnn Lucas OP, 4571 John R, Troy 48084
Donna Markham OP, 13660 Eastwood, Detroit 48205
Mary Van Gilder, 3665 Walton Blvd., Rochester 48063
Paul Larry Siroskey, 1723 N. Lafayette, Dearborn 48128
Norb Primo, 19949 Binder, Detroit 48234
Louis Escobar, St. Cyril & Methodius Seminary, Box 85,
  Orchard Lake 48033
Chris Santoro, 96 W. Ferry #17, Detroit 48202
Bob Santoro, 96 W. Ferry #17, Detroit 48202
Donna Wesley, 700 Whitmore, Detroit 48203
Stella Marie Dolan, 16570 Northlawn, Detroit 48221
Rosemary Ferguson OP, Dominican Generalate, Adrian 49221

MINNESOTA

Marilyn A. Winter OP, 551 E. 5th St., Winona 55987
Jean Breitenbucher, 5224 3rd Ave. So., Minneapolis 55419
Marietta Conroy, 606 Terry Lane, Winona 55987
Linda Kulzer, Convent of St. Benedict, St. Joseph 56374
Rita Lefevre, 427 10th Ave. E., Duluth 55805
Constance Hickok, 429 N. 10th Ave. E., Duluth 55805
Mary Ann Mueninghoff OP, 2836 33rd Avenue South, Minneapolis
  55406
Viola Kane SSND, Good Counsel Hill, Mankato 56001
Elaine Fraher, 1350 Gardena Ave. N.E., Minneapolis 55432
Iva Lang, 7950 Grafton Ave. So., Cottage Grove 55016
Regina Griffin, Bethlehem Convent, Faribault 55021
Ken Irrgang, College of St. Benedict, St. Joseph 56374
Mary Anthony Wagner, College of St. Benedict, St. Joseph 56374

Continued

William Skudlarek OSB, St. John's University, Collegeville 56321
Charlotte Ann Hesby OSF, 417 Fifth St. S.W., Rochester 55901
Loretta Klinkhammer OSF, 417 Fifth St. S.W., Rochester 55901
Margaret O'Keefe, 735 Mt. Curve Blvd., St. Paul 55116
Marquita Finley, 240 Summit Ave., St. Paul 55102
Michelle Meyers, 105½ S. 5th St., Marshall 56258
Kay O'Neil, 105½ S. 5th St., Marshall 56258
Mary Gearin, P.O. Box 334, College of St. Benedict, St. Joseph
  56374
M. Paula Young SSND, 615 E. Fourth St., Winona 55787
M. Eunice Silkey SSND, Good Counsel Hill, Mankato 56001
Mary Wagner, 2040 Laurel Ave., St. Paul 55104
Monica Brown OP, 109½ Avenue D, Cloquet 55720

MISSISSIPPI

Clara Grochowska, 1661 Lynch St., Apt. 29, Jackson 39203

MISSOURI

Carolyn Osiek RSCJ, Maryville College, 13550 Conway Rd.,
  St. Louis 63141
Martha Robbins RSCJ, Maryville College, 13550 Conway Road, St.
  Louis 63141
Genevieve Cassani SSND, 3753 West Pine Blvd., St. Louis 63108
Frances Padberg SSND, 1204 N. Grand, St. Louis 63106
Eileen Donovan SSND, 216A Newstead Ave., St. Louis 63108
Sharon Karam RSCJ, 13640 Conway Rd., St. Louis 63141
Mary Cele Breen SCL & Companion, 1817 E. 78th St., Kansas City
  64132
Mary P. Rives, 13550 Conway Road, St. Louis 63141
Judith Reed, 1817 E. 78th St., Kansas City 64132
Kathleen Kenney MMB, 918 East 9th St., Kansas City 64106
David R. Bishop SJ, Rockhurst High School, 9301 State Line Rd.,
  Kansas City 64114
Dolores Brand, The Cenacle, 900 S. Spoede, St. Louis 63131
Mary McGlone CSJ, 6800 Wydown, St. Louis 63105
Agnes Hoorman RSCJ, 13640 Conway Rd., St. Louis 63141
Gerald Rehagen, 4204 Delor, St. Louis
Marirose Donnellan, 3238 Morganford Apt. 7, St. Louis 63116
Richard E. Garcia, 2019 Schaeffer Pl., St. Louis 63139
Luanne Schinzel, 3019 Laclede, St. Louis 63103
Marie Schimelfening, 4155 Magnolia #3, St. Louis 63110
Mary Ann McGivern SL, 3700 West Pine, St. Louis 63108
Claudia Adamson SFCC, 5828 Lindenwood Ave., St. Louis 63109
Marilyn Canning RSM, 3825 West Pine Blvd., St. Louis 63108
Patricia Quinn CSJ, 3125 Chestnut St., Kansas City 64128
Nancy A. Lafferty FSPA, 3019 LaClede Ave., St. Louis 63103
Anne Kelly, 419 Couch Ave., Kirkwood 63122
Roberta Ann Walsh, 50 Hill Drive, Kirkwood 63122
Marie Francis Kenoyer SL, 5112 Tracy, Kansas City 64110
Ann White Sl, 8314 Big Bend, St. Louis 63119
Irene Skeehan, 900 Shady Drive, Kansas City 64119

MONTANA

Edla Billing PBVM, Box 160, Circle 59215
Ann Paula Loendorf SC, 600 Harrison Ave., Helene 59601
M. Catherine Dougherty SC, 600 Harrison Ave., Helene 59601
Susan Secker OP, 709 E. 3rd, Anaconda 59711

NEBRASKA

Mary Ellen Quinn RSM, 1801 S. 72 St., Omaha 68124
Maura Clark RSM, 1801 So. 72nd St., Omaha 68124
Mary Dineman, 900 North 90th St., Omaha 68114
Mary Hogan OSM, 7400 Military Ave., Omaha 68134

NETHERLANDS

U.S. Address:
Dennis van Lier SJ, Faber House, 4906 S. Greenwood Ave.
Chicago 60615

NEW JERSEY

Margaret Maureen Healy MSBT, 1026 Long Hill Rd., Sterling
07980
Kathleen Mary Henderson, 11 Joanna Place, Rahway-Colonia
07067
Patricia Aidan Lynch CSJ, St. Michael Provincial House, P.O.
Box 1053, Englewood Cliffs 07632
Suzanne Golas CSJ, 106 Chadwick Road, Teaneck 07666
Marianne Joyce SC, 80 Whippany Road, Whippany 07981
Eileen Kelly PBVM, Assoc. Vicar for Religious, P.O. Box 628,
West Patterson 07424
Ruth Whitney, 50 Fox Road Apt. 4B, Edison 08817
JoAnn Reynolds, Bayley Ellard, Madison 07940
Kathleen Flanagan, 393 Jackson Ave., Hackensack 07601
Mary McGuinness OP, Mt. St. Dominic, Caldwell 07006
Maura Campbell OP, Caldwell College, Caldwell 07006
Maura Nighland, 165 Madison Ave., Madison 07940
Althea L. Tessier, Rider College, Trenton 08602
Frank J. McNulty, Immaculate Conception Seminary, Mahwah
07430
Francis A. DeDomenico, Immaculate Conception Seminary,
Mahwah 07430
Carol Watchler, 230 W. Delaware Ave., Pennington 08534
Ann Baker, 230 W. Delaware Ave., Pennington 08534
Julie Scanlan, De Paul Convent, 1512 Alps Rd., Wayne 07470
Margaret Ann McGurn CSTB, Alphonsus House of Prayer, 87
Overlook Drive, Woodcliff Lake
Mary Lee Fitzgerald, 280 Jefferson, Princeton 08540
Carol Muschal Grubb, 553 Drexel Ave., Lawrenceville 08648

NEW HAMPSHIRE

Pat Fitzpatrick SSND, 193 Main St., Jaffrey 03452

NEW MEXICO

Catharine Stewart-Roache, 4925 Kathryn Circle SE, Albuquerque 87108
Kathryn A. Larsen, 1014 D Carlisle SE, Albuquerque 87106
Elizabeth Bumgarner, 11401 Mountain Road NE, Albuquerque 87112
Dorothy Newell, 3200 Florida NE, Albuquerque 87110

NEW YORK

Regina Bechtle SC, 3985 Saxon Ave., Bronx 10463
Jean Flannelly SC, 3985 Saxon Ave., Bronx 10463
Sharon Crist, 730 Eastwood Circle, Webster 14580
Isabel M. Passero, 75 Buell Drive Apt. #D, Rochester 14621
Charlotte Raftery, 104 Woodland Ave., New Rochelle 10805
Barbara Fox SSJ, 445 S. Plymouth Ave., Rochester 14608
Amadeus McKevitt, 323 E. 198 St., New York 10458
Evelyn A. Lamdureux, 86-44 105 St., Richmond 11418
M. Helene Mailey, 16 Breeman St., Albany 12205
Regina Kehoe OSU, 323 East 198th St., Bronx 10458
Linda Jones, 150 Laurelwood Drive, Rochester 14626
Mary Jane Mitchell, 16 Riverside St., Rochester 14613
Ursula Joyce OP, Dominican Convent, Sparkill 10976
Adele Myers OP, Dominican Convent, Sparkill 10976
Suzanne E. Elsesser, 36 Chestnut Ave., Larchmont 10538
Patricia Hartigan, Olma-Convent Road, Syosset 11791
Ann Patrick Ware SL, 475 Riverside Dr., New York 10027
Jeanne Clark OP, 85-45-159 St., Jamaica 11432
Dorothy Kane OP, John XXIII Hall, 575 Albany Ave., Amityville 11701
Kathleen McKiernan OP, St. Boniface Convent, 621 Elmont Rd., Elmont 11003
Kathleen Waters OP, John XIII Hall, 575 Albany Ave., Amityville 11701
Patricia Wolf RSM, 541 Broadway, Dobbs Ferry 10522
M. Theresa Kane RSM, Mt. Mercy-on-the-Hudson, Dobbs Ferry 10522
Kathleen Marie Faughnan RSM, Mt. Mercy-on-the-Hudson, Dobbs Ferry 10522
Letitia Brennan OSU, 39 Willow Dr., New Rochelle 10801
Helen Hofmann, 634 New Scotland Ave., Albany 12208
Patricia Jelly, 963 Scarsdale Rd., Scarsdale 10583
Kristen Wenzel OSU, 2401 East Tremont Ave., Bronx 10461
Camille D'Arienzo RSM, 455 E. 29 St., Brooklyn 11226
Eleanor Dobson RSM, 455 E. 29 St., Brooklyn 11226
Mary Boys SNJM, 535 W. 121st St., New York 10027
Elizabeth Gorvin, Holy Child Convent, 463 W. 142nd St., New York 10031
Katie Vaeth, 737 Highland Ave., Rochester 14620
Annamarie Profit, 21 W. 124th St., New York 10027
Virginia Lee OP, Corpus Christi Monastery, 1230 Lafayette St., Bronx 10474
Peter R. Riani, Wadhams Hall, Ogdensburg 13669
Marion Dellapa, 304 State St., Brooklyn 11201
Rhea Louise Bean RSM, New York Province, Mt. Mercy-on-the-Hudson, Dobbs Ferry 10522
Doris Donnelly, Old Mountain Road, Grandview 10960
Maureen McCullagh OP, 158-23 89 Avenue, Jamaica 11432
Mary Luke Tobin SL, 100 LaSalle #20 B, New York City 10027

Veronica Greeley OP, 75 Greene Ave., Brooklyn 11238
Regina Fuhrmann, 824 East 45th St., Brooklyn 11203
Patricia O'Neill, 824 East 45th St., Brooklyn 11203
Margaret Dempsey, 418 Grove St., Brooklyn 11237
Janet Wahl RSM, 1080 South Ave., Rochester 14620
Joan Sobala, 34 Monica St., Rochester 14619
Marlene J. Vigna RSM, 150 Floverton St., Rochester 14610
Barbara A. Moore, 34 Monica St., Rochester 14619
Marcella Hoesl HM, Maryknoll Sisters, Maryknoll 10545
Marie Kerwin SSJ, 82 Humboldt Pkwy., Buffalo 14214
Michele Beiter SSJ, 82 Humboldt Pkwy., Buffalo 14214
James Mang, 1107 Main St., Buffalo 14209
Frances Flanagan, 1219 Elmwood Ave., Buffalo 14222
Catherine Walsh, Mount Saint Mary, Newburgh 12550
Agnes Boyle, Mount Saint Mary, Newburgh 12550
Helene Lutz, 265 E. 162 St., Bronx 10451
Jeanne Andre Brendel, 85-45 159 St., Jamaica 11432
Barbara Powers, 600 West 122nd St., New York 10027
Ellen Burke SC, 20 Washington Square North, N.Y.C. 10011
Mary Elizabeth Earley, Sisters of Charity Center, 261st & River-
dale Ave., N.Y.C. 10471
Patricia Noone SC, Sisters of Charity Center, 261st & Riverdale
Ave., New York City 10471
Mary Anne Daly SC, Sisters of Charity Center, 261st & Riverdale
Ave., New York City 10471
Patricia Connors, 2658 Briggs Ave., Bronx 10458
Regina Murphy, 20 Washington Sq. North, New York City 10011
Mary Donagher, 20 Washington Sq. North, New York City 10011
Mary Louise Brink SC, Loretta Community, 124 Greenwich St.,
Hempstead 11550
Susan Sholinsky SC, 34-31 83 St., Jackson Hts. 11372
Margaret Collins CSJ, 1226 Lancaster, Syracuse 13210
Cecilia Moloughney, 88-19 Cross Island Pkwy., Bellerose 11426
Marie-Celine Miranda OSU, College of New Rochelle, New
Rochelle 10801
Gerry McGinn OP, 1020 Calhoun Ave., Bronx 10465
Rita Catherine Young, Msgr. Scanlon H.S., 915 Hutchinson River
Pkway., Bronx 10465
Valorie Lordi OP, 51 W. 174th St., Bronx 10453
Maryann Ventrelli OP, 51 W. 174th St., Bronx 10453
Anne Marie Fitzsimmons RSM, Box 86, Lakeview 14085
Cerness Moran RSM, Box 86, Lakeview 14085
Patricia Povlak RSM, St. Bernadette Convent, 5870 South Abbott
Road, Hamburg 14075
Rosemary Mahoney RSM, 1964 Seneca St., Buffalo 14210
Jaculyn Hanrahan CNO, 150 Corlaer Ave., Schenectady 12304
Francine Bauser CSJ, 115 Fourth St., Troy 12180
Janet Furman CSJ, 22 Greenwood Ave., Mechanicville 12118
Maureen O'Leary, 114 Grand St., Croton 10520
Paul Bernier, 184 East 76th St., New York City 10021
Louise Cutler, 52 N. Broadway, White Plains 10603
John W. Coppinger, Friars of the Atonement, Graymoor, Garrison
10524
Joseph M. Jankowiak, 2260 Lake Ave., Rochester 14612
Anne Mary Dooley SSJ, 16 Lakeview Park, Rochester 14613
Ellen Zazycki, 12 Crossbow, Rochester 14624
Carla DeSola, 309 W. 107th St., New York City 10025
Nicholas Connolly SJ, Canesius College, Buffalo 14208
Lorraine Cappellino, 134 Burlington Ave., Rochester 14619
Denise W. Mack, 32 Queensboro Rd., Rochester 14609

NEW YORK - Continued

Mary M. Angelidis, 103 Anchor Terr., Rochester 14617
Janet Wahl RSM, Mercy Motherhouse, 1437 Blossom Rd., Rochester
Barbara Moore RSM, St. Monica's Rectory, 34 Monica St., Rochester 14624
Marguerite Walsh, Apt. 4, Bldg. I, 4280 Chestnut Ridge Rd., Tonawanda 14150
Chris Parker, 4280 Chestnut Ridge Rd., Apt. 4, Bldg., I, Buffalo 14150
Elizabeth Ann LeValley, 34 Monica St., Rochester
Lyn Somers, 253 Golden Rd., Rochester 14624
Kathy Kircher, 16 Lake View Pk., Rochester 14613
Jo Carol Vedock, 170 Edgebrook Lane, Rochester 14617
Cynthia Jo Dentinger, 57 Midvale Terrace, Rochester 14619
Eleanor Celentani, 123 Braisee St., East Rochester 14445
Ada Maria Isasi-Diaz, 114 Shale Drive, Rochester 14615
Mary Jo Langie, St. Martin's Way, Rochester 14616

NORTH CAROLINA

Evelyn Mattern, 421 Hill St., Raleigh 27611
Faith Engel MHSH, 2900 Country Club Rd., Winston-Salem 27104

NORTH DAKOTA

Mary Elizabeth Mason OSB, 1321 Braman Ave.,,Bismarck 58501

OHIO

Beth Rindler, 124 Maple St., Rossford 43460
Mary Lou Knapke SC, 1756 Lincoln, Norwood 45212
Annina Morgan SC, Personnel Office, Mt. St. Joseph 45051
Gen McCloskey, 17440 Northwood Ave., Lakewood 44107
Elizabeth Kerrigan, Assoc. Vicar for Religious, 298 Tod Lane, Youngstown 44504
Laura Caldwell, 4545 Wetmore Rd., Cuyahoga Falls 44223
Geneal Kramer OP, 1641 Vine St., Cincinnati 45210
Mary Assunta Stang SC, Sisters of Charity, Mt. St. Joseph 45051
Catherine Harmer, 3622 Zumstein, Cincinnati 45208
Mary E. Middendorf, 112 E. Walnut Apt. 1, Oxford 45056
Carol English SSJ, 3430 Rocky River Drive, Cleveland 44111
Felicia Petruziello, 3430 Rocky River Drive, Cleveland 44111
Joan Wyzenbeek, 670 Avon Fields Ln., Cincinnati 45229
Joan Brosnan, Ursuline Center, St. Martin 45170
Mary Ann Andrews CSA, 5232 Broadview Rd., Richfield 44286
Michelle Teff, 4580 Colerain Ave., Cincinnati 45223
Helen Cecilia Swift SND, Apt. 306 H, Highland Greens, West Chester 45069
Margaret Telscher SND, Apt. 306H, Highland Greens, West Chester 45069
Mr. & Mrs. Michael & Margot Merz, 1532 Bryn Mawr Dr., Dayton 45406
Elizabeth M. Bowyer, 701 E. Columbia Ave., Cincinnati 45215
Mary Ann Barnhorn, 701 E. Columbia Ave., Cincinnati 45215
Libby Schaefer, 2603 Vestry Ave., Cleveland 44113
Mary Rose Burns SC, 224 Squirrel Rd., Dayton 45405
Dorothy Sadowski, 6000 Queens Hwy., Parma Hts., 44130
Marie Fillo, 6000 Queens Hwy., Parma Hts., 44130

Dolores Lintner, 870 St. Agnes Ave., Dayton 45407
Joan Pfeiffer, 870 St. Agnes Ave., Dayton 45407
Mary Ann Flanagan, 410 E. Fifth Ave., Cincinnati 45202
Barbara Westrick, 128 Rockingham St., Toledo 43610
Therese Tsuer, 435 Eastern Ave., Toledo 43609
Eileen Hageman, 435 Eastern Avè., Toledo 43609
Deacon Thomas Grilliot, 4100 Annapolis Ave., Dayton 45416
Deb Amatulli, 5150 Crispy Drive, Dayton 45440
Marie Gillich, 9407 Lake Ave., Cleveland 44102
Linda Krasienko, 9407 Lake Ave., Cleveland 44102
Kathleen Singer, 9407 Lake Ave., Cleveland 44102
Mary Jane Treichel, 9407 Lake Ave., Cleveland 44102
Christa Bauke SC, 5776 Delhi Rd., Cincinnati 45233
Virginia Quinn SSJ, 2446 Boudinot Apt. 9, Cincinnati 45238
Jane Pank HM, 3105 Franklin, Cleveland 44113
Mr. & Mrs. John G. Lucic.(Peg), 234 Fairpark Dr., Berea 44017
Eleanor Walker, Grailville, Loveland 45140
Marian Ronan, Grailville, Loveland 45140
John E. Lavelle, 20141 Detroit Rd., Rocky River 44116
Helen Walsh OP, 2345 Scottwood, Toledo 43620
Virginia A. Froehle, 3107 Epworth Ave., Cincinnati 45211
Mary Karen Powers, 3107 Epworth Ave., Cincinnati 45211
Kathleen A. Blank, 3005 Westwood-Northern Blvd., Apt. 8,
   Cincinnati 45211
Judith Girard OP, 10000 Granger Rd., Garfield Hts., 44125
Elizabeth Lavelle CSJ, 6000 Queens Hwy., Parma Hts., 44130
Donald E. Heintschel, 1933 Spielbusch Ave., Toledo 43624
Bernadine Baltrinic, 615 Moorfield Rd., Akron 44313
Rosemary Kuhns CSJ, 32020 Bainbridge Rd., Solon 44139
Renee Davis, 1423 Glendale Ave., Dayton 45406
Kathryn Cullen OSU, 2403 Collingwood, Toledo 43620
Frances Cabrini, 2403 Collingwood, Toledo 43620
Judy Barnhiser OSO, 2403 Collingwood, Toledo 43620
Katherine Andrews CSA, 5232 Broadview Rd., Richfield 44286
Marietta Starrie, Box A-6 OCMR, Oberlin 44074
Pat Kozlowski, 1211 Harrow Rd., Toledo 43615
Rita C. English, 10300 Terrace Ct., Parma 44130
Susann Shephard SNJM, Fontbonne, 5th & Broadway, Cincinnati
   45202
Margaret A. Galvin, 12031 Edgewater Drive, Lakewood 44107
Julia Ann Sheatzley, 410 E. Fifth St., Cincinnati 45202
Janet Roesener, 410 E. Fifth St., Cincinnati 45202
Molly A. Nicholson OP, 4950 Broadview Rd., Cleveland 44109
Shawn Lee SSJ, 12215 Granger Rd., Garfield Hts., 44125
Deborah A. McCadley, Plaza Apt. 230, Rt. 50E, Athens 45701
Mary Reynolds SC, 4950 Broadview, Cleveland 44109
Catherine Pinkerton, 3234 West Blvd, Cleveland 44111
Jane Cavanaugh, 3234 West Blvd., Cleveland 44111
Madeleine Laliberte RJM, 2061 Cornell Rd., Cleveland 44106
Judith Ann Mouch RSM, 1102 Clay St., Toledo 43608
Felipe de Jesus Ortega OFM, St. Leonard College, Dayton 45459
Margaret B. Morris, 376 Cornwall Rd., Rocky River 44116
Donna Marie Rego, 75 Kensington Oval, Rocky River 44116
Mary Gallagher SC, Box 323, Danville 43014
Lynda Maxwell, 3558 Madison Rd., Cincinnati 45208
Cynthia Heinrich OSU, 1339 E. McMillan St., Cincinnati 45206
Nancy Hendershot CSA, 7716 Franklin Blvd., Cleveland 44102
Catherine Walsh CSA, 7716 Franklin, Cleveland 44102
Mary Grace Betzler CSA, 7716 Franklin Blvd., Cleveland 44102
M. Elaine Becker, CONTEMPLATIVE MONASTERY, New Riegel
   44853

OHIO - Continued

Renee Krisko CSJ, 9407 Lake Ave., Cleveland 44102
Mary Kuhlman OSF, 610 S. Portland St., Bryan 43506
Mary Ann Hemenway SSJ, 410 East Fifth St., Cincinnati 45202
Rose, St. Anthony Villa, 2740 West Central, Toledo 43606
Myrtle Bailey, 2915 Eastern Ave., Cincinnati 45226
Mercedes Malloy OP, 147 Jefferson St., Youngstown 44510
Diana Culbertson OP, 147 Jefferson St., Youngstown 44510
Eileen Kazmierowicz OSF, 1312 W. Market St., Akron 44313
Maryanna Coyle SC, Mt. St. Joseph 45051
Lynn Haney, Diocesen Radio & TV, 1027 Superior Ave., Cleveland 44114
Juanita Shepley CSJ, Diocesan Radio & TV, 1027 Superior Ave., Cleveland 44114
Kim White, Box 18-A, Oberlin College, Oberlin 44074
George Tavard AA, Methodist Theological School, Delaware 43015
Eleanor Kahle, 2615 Alexis, Toledo 43613
Tria Thompson, St. Augustine Academy, 14808 Lake Avenue, Lakewood 44107
Barbara Philippart SC, Mt. St. Joseph 45051
Francis Therese SSJ, 12215 Granger Rd., Garfield Heights 44125
Mary Benedict Bodzik OSU, 3240 Fairmount Blvd., Cleveland 44118
Sheila Marie Tobbe OSU, 3240 Fairmount Blvd., Cleveland 44118

OKLAHOMA

Sylvia Schmidt SFCC, 153 N. Garnett Rd., #271, Tulsa 74116
Bridget Bamrick OP, 1420 N. 67th E. Ave., Tulsa 74115
Jane Marie Luecke OSB, 205½ South Duck St., Stillwater 74074
Judity Tate, P.O. Box 20508, Oklahoma City 73120
Betty Daughterty, Box 6127, Tulsa 74106

OREGON

Zitamarie Poelzer CSJ, 1419 Lake Drive, Eugene 97404
Mary Ann Gisler OSB, Queen of Angels Priory, Mt. Angel 97362
Jeanette Benson SP, 2327 NE 17th Ave., Portland 97212

PENNSYLVANIA

Mary Ann Dillon RSM, RSM Formation Program, Box 36, Loretto 15940
Rose Dalle Tezze RSM, 3309 5th Ave., Pittsburgh 15213
Rita Panciera, House of Prayer, 159 W. 4th St., Erie 16507
Winifred Goddard SC, Catholic Campus Ministry, Elizabethtown-York Colleges, 405 Carlisle Ave., York 17404
Maureen McCann, Sisters of Mercy, Provincial House, Dallas 18612
Margaret Berry CSJ, St. Joseph Convent, Baden 15005
Betty Sundry, 200 Ninth St., Pittsburgh 15215
Susan Stockman, The Ark & The Dove, Babcock Blvd., Gibsonia 15044
Linda Gaupin, Guys Run Road, Cheswick 15024
Ainée Ferguson RSM, Sancta Sophia, 5090 Warwick Terrace, Pittsburgh 15213
Marie Immaculée Dana, Sancta Sophia, 5090 Warwick Terrace, Pittsburgh 15213
William Brown FSC, 1213 Clover St., Philadelphia 19107
Helen Esselstyn, St. Joseph Convent, Baden 15005
Debra A. Stumpf, Egan Hall, Mercyhurst College, Erie 16501

Fran Stein RSM, Mercy Center, Dallas 18612
Maria Green RSM, 212 Dunseith St., Pittsburgh 15213
Kathi Scully, 3309 5th Ave., Pittsburgh 15213
Grace O'Donnell RSM, Our Lady of Mercy Academy, 301 College Park Drive, Monroville 15146
Bernardine Veri CSJ, 316 S. Main St., Slippery Rock 16057
Wilma Palombo CSJ, 316 S. Main St., Slippery Rock 16057
Anna Marie Gaglia CSJ, St. Joseph Convent, Baden 15005
Lillie Pang, P.O. Box 212B, Seton Hill College, Greensburg 15601
Kathleen Ryan OP, 1025 Braddock Ave., Braddock 15104
Kate Scholl, Box 198A, Seton Hill College, Greensburg 15601
Susan Jenny, Seton Hill College, Greensburg 15601
Marjorie Kelly CSJ, 35 Highland Road, Bethel Park 15102
Valerie Lesniak CSJ, 35 Highland Road, Bethel Park 15102
Judith Kubish CSJ, 35 Highland Rd., Bethel Park 15102
Irene Scaramazza CSJ, 607 Overbrook Blvd., Pittsburgh 15210
Arlene Fablan, Box 390, Ellsworth 16331
Loretta Jean Schorr CDP, 200 Ninth St., Pittsburgh 15215
Wilma Kramer OSF, 2801 Sarah St., Pittsburgh 15203
Mary Edward, 285 Bellevue Rd., Pittsburgh 15229
Elizabeth Herron RSM, 423 Sunberry St. Ext., Johnstown 15904
Pat Morgan, 435 4th St., Braddock 15104
Eleanor Desaulniers IHM, Marywood-Generalate, Scranton 18509
Anne Fulwiler IHM, Marywood-Generalate, Scranton 18509
Molly Rush, 3315 Piedmont Ave., Pittsburgh 15216
Arlene Swidler, 7501 Woodcrest, Philadelphia 19151
Leonard Swidler, 7501 Woodcrest, Philadelphia 19151
Judy Heffernan, 826 Glenview St., Philadelphia 19111

PUERTO RICO

Carmen Rosado IHM, 39 St. VV14 Bonneville Heights, Caguas 00625

RHODE ISLAND

Mary Reilly RSM, 120 Melrose St., Providence 02907
Elizabeth Morancy RSM, 120 Melrose St., Providence 02907
Claire Dugan SSJ, 87 Moore St., Providence 02905
Madonna Crawford RSM, 141 Power Road, Pawtucket 02860
Kieran Flynn RSM, 141 Power Road, Pawtucket 02860
Prudence Croke RSM, Spiritual Life Center, 141 Power Rd., Pawtucket 02860
Jeannine Maynard, 177 Lowell Ave., Providence 02909
Rae B. Condon, 27 Katama Rd., Pawtucket 02861

SOUTH DAKOTA

Sheila Schnell, 1310 S. 10th Ave., Sioux Falls 57105
Carol Grant PBVM, 1310 S. 10th Ave., Sioux Falls 57105
Joan Marie Brandner, 2000 S. 4th Ave., Sioux Falls 57105

TENNESSEE

Helen Morrison OP, 694 Hobbs Drive, Memphis 38111
Leslie Hartway OP, 694 Hobbs Drive, Memphis 38111
Mary Anne Guthrie OP, 1325 Jefferson Ave., Memphis 38104
Pat Kintz, 584 E. Trigg, Memphis 38106
Ann McKean, 4107 Franklin Rd., Nashville 37204
Jane Edward Schutz, Diocese of Memphis, 1325 Jefferson Ave., Memphis 38104

TEXAS

Cecelia M. Bennett, 9528 Ferguson #2095, Dallas 75228
Laura Gillett, 9481 Webbs Chapel #A, Dallas 75220
Frances L. Lange, P.O. Box 197, Helotes 78023
Lora A. Quinonez, P.O. Box 197, Helotes 78023
Martha Lindsey, 1404 Grand Ave., Fort Worth 76106
Martha Ann Kirk, Incarnate Word College, San Antonio 78209
Mary Elva Reyes, 4601 Calallen Drive, Corpus Christi 78410
Jacqueline Marie Merz, Route 2, Box 4, Irving 75062
M. Pauline Thames, 2937 McCart Ave., Fort Worth 76110
Linda Hajek, 4906 Bonnie View, Dallas 75241
Patricia Rioglem SSM, 4906 Bonnie View, Dallas 75241
Mary Walden, 3063 Odessa, Fort Worth 76109
Elizabeth L. Sharum OSB, 2308 9th St., Lubbock 79401
Marian Strohmeyer RSM, Route 2, Box 1680, McAllen 78501
Juline Lamb, 901 S. Madison, Dallas 75208
Diane E. Gohring, 8701 Donna Gail Drive, Austin 78758
Frances Pieters, 1500 Eden Lane, Arlington 76010
Francis Klinger CDP, 3111 Hollister, Houston 77055
Renee Ettling CCVI, 1701 Alametos, San Antonio 78201
Alice Lacey OSU, 1525 Rosenburg Ave., Galveston 77550
Sylvia Sedillo SL, Mexican American Cultural Center, P.O. Box
28185, San Antonio 78228

VERMONT

Sylvia Blaine RSM, 100 Mansfield Ave., Burlington 05401

VIRGINIA

Dorothy Canary SCMM, 709 Marshall Ave. S.W., Roanoke 24016
Mary Chupein SFCC, 3704 Shannon Rd., Portsmouth 23703
Maureen Fiedler RSM, 1719 North Troy St., Arlington 22201
Clare Guzzo, 2110 N. Kenmore St., Arlington 22201
Anne Marie Gardiner SSND, 87 Denbigh Blvd., Newport 23602
Clare McNeil SCN, 87 Denbigh Blvd., Newport News 23602
Jeanie Steele, 8405 Porter Lane, Alexandria 22308

WASHINGTON

Maureen McGlone, 1111 E. Columbia, Seattle 98122
Catherine M. LaCugna, 906 20th Ave. E., Seattle 98112
9/1/75 - 2860 Decatur Ave., #A-42, Bronx, N.Y. 10458
Joyce Stewart, 907 Terry Ave., Seattle 98104
Diana Bader OP, 907 Terry Ave., Seattle 98104
Louise DuMont, P.O. Box 248, Bellevue 98009
Margarita Acosta SP, 4510 S. W. Stevens, Seattle 98116
Katherine E. Zappone, 914 E. Jefferson, Box 116, Seattle 98122
Mary Lyn Hikel, 1717 N. 35th St., Apt. #9, Seattle 98103

WASHINGTON, D.C.

Catherine O'Connor CSJ, 1330 Massachusetts Ave. N.W., Suite 101,
20005
Robert W. Houda, The Liturgical Conference, 1330 Massachusetts
Ave. N.W., 20005
Jeannette Normandin SSA, Sister Formation Conference, 1330
Massachusetts Ave. N.W., 20005
Ruth McGoldrick SP, 1330 Massachusetts Ave. N.W., 20005

Cindi Vian, Box 537 Cardinal Station, Catholic Univ., 20064
Catherine C. DeClercq, One Scott Circle, 20036
Ann V. Bowling IHM, 1330 Massachusetts Ave., N.W. #207, 20005
Mary Kay Liston CSJ, 3700 Mass. Ave. N.W., #501, 20016
Penny Addiss, 2900 Conn. Ave. N.W., 20008
Bailey Walker OP, 487 Michigan Ave. N.E., 20017
Sandra Theunick, 9101 Rockville Pike, 20014
Susan Rakoczy IHM, 710 Lawrence St. NE, 20017
Jean Ann Gnall SNJM, 519 Varnum St. NW, 20011
Mary Beth Reissen SSND, 471 G Place NW, 20001
David Hollenbach SJ, Woodstock Theological Center, 1322 36th
St., NW. 20007
John C. Haughey SJ, 1419 35th St., NW, 20007
Edith Assaff, Public Relations Office, Trinity College, 20017
Catherine Lafferty, 801 Buchanan St., NE, 20017
Carroll Ann Kemp, 519 Varnum St. N.W., 20011
M. Gertrude Anne Otis CSC, School of Religious Studies, Catholic
Univ. of America, 20017
Mary Margaret Weber, 601 East Capitol St., 20003
William M. Shea, 4013 8th St. NE., 20017
Alice M. Talone CBS, 1224 Lawrence St. NE., 20017
Mary O'Neill, Regan Hall, Box 29, Catholic Univ. of America,
20064
Marion Carr, 1625 16th St. NW, 20009
Elizabeth Carroll RSM, Center for Concern, 3700 13th St. NE.,
20017
Rosemary R. Ruether, School of Religion, Howard University
Mary Daniel Turner SNDdeN, LCWR Secretariat, 1330 Massachusetts
Ave NW., #207, 20005
Mary O'Callaghan, 1124 McKenna Walk NW, 20001
Sonya A. Quitslund, George Washington Univ., 2106 G Street NW.,
20052
Brian McDermott SJ, 3700 Massachusetts Ave., NW., Apt. 501,
Alban Towers, 20016
Donald P. Skwor SDS, Assoc. Sec. CMSM, 1330 Massachusetts Ave.,
NW, 20005
Nancy L. Kearney, Box 6 - Regan Hall, Catholic Univ. of America,
20064

WEST VIRGINIA

Gretchen Shaffer, 161 Edgington Lane, Wheeling 26003
John Eudes Duffy, Box 6862, Wheeling 26003

WISCONSIN

Terry McGinniss, 509 N. Lake St. #309, Madison 53703
Elaine Smurawa SSJ, 1300 Maria Drive, Stevens Point 54481
Francis Borgia Rothluebber, 1501 South Layton Blvd., Milwaukee 532099
Kate Raterink, 4059 N. 25th, Milwaukee 53209
Margaret Michaud, Priory Road, P.O. Box 66, Eau Claire 54701
Mary Irene Deger, 1022 N. 9 St., Milwaukee 53233
Diane Schmidt, 4059 North 25th St., Milwaukee 53209
Hope Koski, 417 Clemons Ave., Madison 53704
Thomas Allen, Box 66, Green Bay 54305
Pat Elliott, Box 66, Green Bay 54305
Claire Marie Wick OSF, Sacred Heart Hospital, Room 336, Eau
Claire 54701
Agnes Marie Henkel, 4031 West Morgan Ave., Milwaukee 53221
Marian Schreiner, 4031 W. Morgan, Milwaukee 53221

WISCONSIN - Continued

Joanne Meyer, 3673 E. Plankinton, Milwaukee 53110
Fran Ferder FSPA, 1321 Main St., LaCrosse 54601
Celine Goessl, Holy Cross Convent, Merrill 54452
Judith Smits, Box 139 R #2, Hilbert 54129
Charlotte Smits, Box 139 R#2, Hilbert 54129
Rose Marie Dischler, 117 N. Wisconsin, Jamesville 53545
Mary Ann IHM, SSSF, 6516 5th Ave., Kenosha 53140
Noreen McNamara, 503 Wisconsin Ave., Sheboygan 53081
Patricia Gallagher, Dominican Generalate, Sinsinawa 53824
Mary Paynter, Dominican Generalate, Sinsinawa 53824
Judith Jon Ziemann, 4405 Elizabeth Waters Hall, Madison 53706
Linda Kaminski, 6919 W. Van Norman Ave., Greenfield 53220
Edna Redder FSPA, 1416 Cummings Ave., Superior 54880
Eileen Brewer, Dominican Novitiate, Sinsinawa 53824
Mary Iannucilli, Dominican Novitiate, Sinsinawa 53824
Deb Rodoe, Dominican Education Ctr., Sinsinawa 53824
Nancy McCabe, Dominican Education Ctr., Sinsinawa 53824
Michelle Olley, 1109 Douglas Ave., Racine 53402
Barbara Kukla, 1109 Douglas Ave., Racine 53402
Ruth Berra FSPA, 1233 Sherman Ave., Madison 53703
Mary Ann Peters OSF, 1233 Sherman Ave., Madison 53703
Ann Sipko OP, 914 Lake Ave., Racine 53403
Carol Stilwell, 1223 Hammond Ave., Superior 54880
Jane Eschweiler, 1238 No. 28th St., Milwaukee 53208
Sandra Setterlund, 1300 Maria Drive, Stevens Point 54481
Marilyn Sieg SFCC, 4725 Sheboygan Avenue, Madison 53705
M. Eileen Matthews, 4715 Sheboygan, Madison 53705
Kathy Power, Dominican Novitiate, Sinsinawa 53824
Marie Therese Brown, Justice & Peace Center, 3900 N. 3rd.,
Milwaukee 53207

ADDENDUM (Non-Geographical)

Chris Bennett SSS, 5890 Birch Ct., Oakland, California 94618
Frank Hillebrand SJ, Univ. of Detroit High School, 8400 Cambridge
Detroit 48221
Jane Kappus CSJ, 6400 Minnesota Ave., St. Louis, Missouri 63111
Robert Hayer, Editor, Paulist Press, 1865 Broadway, New York City,
N.Y. 10023
Dorothy Stoner OSB, 330 E. Tenth St., Erie, Penn. 16503
James L. Tahaney, Drtr. of Permanent Diaconate, The Chancery, 75
Greene Ave., Brooklyn, N.Y. 11238
Eleanor Craig SL, 5112 Tracy, Kansas City, Missouri 64111
Melissa Waters OP, Provincial, Dominican Motherhouse, Sinsinawa,
Wisconsin 53824
Joseph A. Tetlow SJ, President, Jesuit School of Thology, 1735 LeRoy,
Berkeley, California 94709
Judith Ann Heffernan, 826 Glenview St., Philadelphia, Pa. 19111
Carol Fleming OP, Dominican Motherhouse, Adrian, Mich. 49221
Jan Kappus CSJ, 6400 Minnesota Ave., St. Louis Missouri
63111
William J. Davis SJ, Jesuit Office of Social Ministries, 1717
Massachusetts Ave. NW., Washington D.C. 20036
Sylvia Blaine RSM, Mount Saint Mary, Burlington Vermont 05401
Paul Besanceney SJ, CMSM Representative, Jesuit Provincial
Office, 602 Boulevard Center Bldg., Detroit, Mich. 48202

Leah Henkes, Box 190, Hiawatha, Iowa 52233
Robert Ferguson OMI, Dean, Oblate College of the Southwest,
 285 Oblate Drive, San Antonio, Texas 78216
Janet Kalven, Grailville, Loveland, Ohio 45140
Barbara Ann Foos, Nazareth College, 4245 East Avenue,
 Rochester, N.Y. 14610

Appendix D
Public Endorsement of the Conference

Sister M. Francine Zeller OSF
Past President
Leadership Conference of Women
   Religious
520 Plainfield Avenue
Joliet, Illinois 60435

Sister M. Daniel Turner SNDdeN
Executive Director
Leadership Conference of Women
   Religious
Washington, D.C.

National Assembly of Women
   Religious

Franciscan Sisters of Perpetual
   Adoration
Central Province
Hiawatha, Iowa

Sister Mary Ellen Quinn
Provincial Administration
Sisters of Mercy
Omaha Province

Sister Elizabeth Michaels SND
Boston Province
Sisters of Notre Dame de Namur
328 Dartmouth Street
Boston, Massachusetts 02116

Sister Margaret Dowling, President
Sisters of Charity of St. Vincent de
   Paul of New York
Mount St. Vincent-on-Hudson
Bronx, New York 10471

Sister Mary Daly RSM
West Hartford, Connecticut

Sister Helen Hafman
634 New Scotland Avenue
Albany, New York

Sister Betty Jean Goebel OP
3600 Broadway
Great Bend, Kansas 67530

Sisters of Saint Joseph
Cleveland, Ohio

Sister Mary Assunta Stang SC
President
Sisters of Charity of Cincinnati

Sister Lenora Maier, Provincial
   and
Executive Team, Mt. St. Francis
   Province
School Sisters of St. Francis
Rockford, Illinois

The General Council
Adrian Dominican Sisters
Adrian, Michigan

Sister M. Victoria Andreoli RGS
Provincial Convent of the Good
   Shepherd
Mount St. Florence
Peekskill, New York 10567

Eugene A. Mainelli OP
Center for Studies in Religious
Education
5427 S. University, Apt. 3D
Chicago, Illinois 60615

Sisters of St. Joseph
1412 East Second Street
Superior, Wisconsin 54880

Religious of Christian Education
36 Hillcrest Road
Belmont, Massachusetts 02178

Sister Elaine Smurawa
Sisters of St. Joseph, Third Order of
St. Francis
1300 Maria Drive
Stevens Point, Wisconsin 54481

Sister Gail Lambers, President
Community of the Holy Spirit
San Diego, California

School Sisters of St. Francis
Omaha Province
900 North 90th Street
Omaha, Nebraska 68114

Sister Elizabeth A. Conyers FMM
Provincial Superior, U.S. Province
Franciscan Missionaries of Mary
225 East 45th Street
New York, New York 10017

Sister Louise Dempsey
Sisters of St. Joseph of Peace
1330 Massachusetts Avenue NW
Washington, D.C. 20005

Sisters of Loretto
Nerinx, Kentucky 40049

Gregory Baum
St. Michael's College
University of Toronto

Sister M. Theresa Kane RSM
Provincial Administrator
Sisters of Mercy Provincialate
541 Broadway
Dobbs Ferry, New York 10522

St. Joan's International Alliance
U.S. Section
P.O. Box 856
Waukegan, Illinois 60085

Brother Philip L. Dougherty CFX
Provincial, Xaverian Brothers
American Central Province
10516 Summit Avenue
Kensington, Maryland 20795

Brother James Hutchinson OSB
Glastonbury Abbey
16 Hull Street
Hingham, Massachusetts 02043

Dominican Province of St. Albert the
Great
Chicago, Illinois
Fr. Gerard B. Cleator OP, Provincial

Sister Ellen Louise Burns SCL
Pastoral Leadership Development
Rockhurst College
Kansas City, Missouri 64110

Sister Nicole Goetz
2122 W. Ainslie
Chicago, Illinois

Thomas Michel SJ
Lecturer in Islam
Northwestern University - Evanston
5525 S. Woodlawn
Chicago, Illinois 60615

Sister Mary Lou Putrow OP, Director
Office of Mission and Ministry
Dominican Station
Adrian, Michigan 59221

Sister Angelita Myerscough ASC
Executive Director
St. Louis Theological Consortium
3825 West Pine
St. Louis, Missouri

Terri Monroe
Weston School of Theology
34 Long Avenue
Allston, MA 02134

Anne E. Patrick SNJM, Chairperson
Committee on Women in Church &
    Society
National Assembly of Women
    Religious
5430 S. University
Chicago, Illinois 60615

Rev. Roland Calvert OSFS,
    Chairman
Peace and Justice Committee for the
    Oblates of St. Francis de Sales
1512 W. Washington Street
Jackson, Michigan 49203

Barbara Nauer
WOMAN Research Center
P.O. Box 206
St. Louis, Missouri 63166

Reverend Grace Moore
Women Committed to Women
817 West 34th Street
Los Angeles, California 90007

William G. Thompson SJ
Professor of New Testament
Jesuit School of Theology
5430 University Avenue
Chicago, Illinois 60615

Sister Josephine Marie Peplinski,
    Pres.
Sisters of St. Joseph, Third Order of
    St. Francis
107 S. Greenlawn Avenue
South Bend, Indiana 46617

Cletus Wessels OP, President
Aquinas Institute of Theology
2570 Asbury Road
Dubuque, Iowa 52001

George Hinger
3201 Churchill Drive
Madison, Wisconsin 53713

Superior General
    and
Members of the General Council
Loretto Abbey
101 Mason Boulevard
Toronto 20, Ontario

International Association of Women
    Ministers
Rev. Susan W. N. Ruach, President
Mrs. M. Pauline Thames, Official
    Delegate

Eleanor Walker
National Staff
The Grail
Grailville
Loveland, Ohio 45140

Sister Mary Bryan SHCJ, Provincial
Sisters of the Holy Child Jesus
Westchester Avenue
Rye, New York 10580

Northern Virginia Catholic Women's
    Alliance
Annandale, Virginia 22003

Appendix E

Theological Questions on the Ordination of Women

Joseph A. Komonchak

One of the conclusions of the meeting at Detroit was to have similar meetings around the country. The following essay was one of the talks from the New York Conference in March, 1976. The editor agrees that it is so pertinent as to merit inclusion in these proceedings. REV. JOSEPH A. KOMONCHAK, S.T.L. studied at the Gregorian University and is presently a Th.D candidate at Union Theological Seminary. Father Komonchak is Professor of Dogmatic Theology, St. Joseph's Seminary, Dunwoodie, N.Y.

When I was asked to deliver this lecture, I was given the task of reviewing and evaluating the theological issues involved in the question of the ordination of women. Presuming that an exhaustive list was not required—since the issues which someone or other believes involved are many and range from the sublime to the ridiculous—I have decided to deal with the matter by addressing the short paper issued in 1973 by the Committee on Pastoral Research and Planning of the National Conference of Catholic Bishops.[1] Entitled "Theological Reflections on the Ordination of Women," the paper was offered as "a contribution to the continuing dialogue on a subject of great importance," and, as the bishops said, "to encourage further study and discussion while making honest efforts to identify the major questions which must be examined in depth before conclusive answers can be given." The paper is most successful in gathering under seven general headings most of the major objections against women's ordination. If, I think, it is less successful in its theological evaluation, at least it has the merit of involving the "official teachers" of the Church in the process by which the issue will eventually be resolved; and that represents a better model of theological development than commonly is visible. My purpose is not principally to criticize the

241

statement—though that will be done—but to use its list of arguments as a convenient collection of the issues and then to offer some theological comments on them.

1. *The Example of the Old Testament*

The bishops refer first to the practice under the Old Covenant, in which "authentic priesthood was limited to males." But, they add, this custom, which was "in keeping with the strongly patriarchal Hebrew society," while it represented God's will for the Old Testament, has no "direct bearing" on the issue of priesthood in the New Covenant.

The description itself is accurate enough: women did not play active roles in either the political or religious life of Israel. The interpretation and evaluation of this fact, however, is perhaps more complicated than the bishops indicate. Woman's exclusion from a role in official worship may have been part of a reaction against the presence of women as sacred prostitutes in ancient Canaanite cults. There can be little doubt that the many ritual impurities that women could contract also influenced the legislation. Finally, the "patriarchal" presuppositions of Israelite society were also re-inforced by certain theological explanations of the "submission" of women to men.

Now, while we may have moved from Old Covenant to New, and, presumably, out of immediate fear of infection by ancient fertility-cults, the latter two considerations did not lose their force under Christianity. The society in which Christianity was born and into which it quickly spread was also "strongly patriarchal" and would not have encouraged assigning important social, public roles to women. And the Levitical legislation about OT priesthood in time came to play an important role in patristic reflection upon Christian ministry.

Christian ministers were not commonly called "priests" until the latter part of the third century. The ascription of this title to them is often related to two other developments—the clarification of the sacrificial nature of the Eucharist and the tendency to draw parallels between the institutions of the Old and the New Covenants. As the one who presided over the sacrifice of the Eucharist came to be called a "priest," so also the NT "priesthood" came to be surrounded by ideas, practices, symbols, laws which reflect the sacral nature of Old Testament priesthood. Among these was the notion of sacral purity or cleanliness which it was believed was compromised or lost by engaging in certain activities, especially any that involve the sexual powers. This is the chief basis for the development of the church's legislation about clerical continence, and it could also have served to prevent the idea of a woman-priest from even being raised seriously, since women were considered to be subject to more such impurities than were men. The idea of ritual purity has been used by church-leaders right up into the twentieth century to defend clerical celibacy;[2] and van der Meer believes that it would "not be entirely off the track to see in this sexual taboo the principal reason in the psychological area why the idea that a woman can also be a priest has never pre-vailed."[3]

I bring this up, not to revive the idea or to suggest it to new minds, but because I think it is part of the Old Testament heritage that affects our discussion. The bishops are right to label the OT argument as the weakest; but they do not mention that the early Church drew more than the name "priest" from the Old Testament. And, of course, the fact that an argument cannot be defended intelligently does not mean that it will not function on levels where intelligence and reason do not lead.

2. *Women as "Deacons"*

The bishops next take note of the ministry of women as "deacons" or "deaconesses" in the NT and in the early church. While acknowledging that this "tradition" can be "helpful" to the discussion, they caution against using it to construct a case "for or against the sacramental ordination of women" because of the "fragmentary and indefinite" nature of the information. They mean by this that it is often difficult to determine what the title means or to whom it refers and to evaluate the significance of the rite by which women were "ordained" to the "diaconate."

It is true that all the data on women-deacons are not clear, but, among Roman Catholics, Gryson and Congar have both concluded that women-deacons did at least in some churches exercise a genuine "order" for several centuries and that they were admitted to this "order" by an "ordination" which was formally indistinguishable from that of their male colleagues.[4] Both scholars, however, also argue that the women's diaconal ministry was much less extensive than that of the men, being largely confined to ministries which it was considered indecorous for men to perform. If this ministry were to be revived, they go on, it would, to be meaningful, have to be given a different office or function.

The real pertinence of this discussion, of course, is its implication for the ordination of women to the presbyterate. And when this is introduced, then it is not quite true to say that about women-deacons "theology has not the least misgivings";[5] —or, if that technically is true, it remains that there are "theologians" who have some misgivings, and the American bishops seem to share them. For in their conclusions they remark that "it is possible to draw distinctions between the diaconate and the episcopal-priestly order, and within the diaconate itself." It is clear that the distinction they have in mind would in effect consider a female diaconate *not* to be a part of the Sacrament of Orders; it would rather be "a diaconate of service, non-sacramental and non-liturgical, which would be conferred on women."

The reason for this distinction is not far to seek: to say that women may receive the sacramental diaconate is to say that they are capable of receiving the Sacrament of Orders, and, if they can receive it on one level, why may they not receive it on the others? The argument here is rather simple: The Code of Canon Law states that only a man can validly receive the sacrament in any one of its three "orders." This principle would be undone if it were established that in the early church women did validly receive the "order" of diaconate or if they were to receive it today. The sacrament is a unity, so that if one may validly receive it in one order, one may validly receive it in any. This logic controls, it seems, the bishops' discussion of the issue and suggests that an effort will be made to offer women a "diaconal" ministry, perhaps even through some formal liturgical rite, which will nevertheless not be the same diaconate which men receive.

It is important, I think, to understand the reasoning behind this view. It rests upon the development in the theology of orders which took place in the West during the Middle Ages. In the patristic period, ordination was generally considered to be the rite by which a person was admitted into an "order" or group (class) of ministers— one did not "receive" "Orders," one *was received* into an "order." The orders were distinct, and to have been received into one was to have no claim on the others. The diaconate, presbyterate, and episcopate were related organically. The churches which ordained women to the order of deacons, then, could quite consistently refuse, as they did, to ordain them to the other two orders.

But gradually, and especially in the West, the theology of orders began to focus on the "priesthood" as the central role of ministry. The lower "orders" were considered to be steps towards the priesthood, and, theoretically, all the other orders (including even the episcopate) were conceived in function of the Eucharistic powers residing in the "priesthood." The Sacrament was thus conceived in a unitary and hierarchical fashion, and it became obvious that a person who could not be ordained to one order—the priesthood—could not be ordained to any order.

There results a very paradoxical situation. To appeal to the primitive tradition of women-deacons has relevance to the question of women-priests only on a theory which the primitive church did not share. On the other hand, to work with the later theory is to face embarrassment before the primitive tradition (which may be why some theologians and bishops question the sacramental character of its women-deacons) and to require alternate, "non sacramental and non-liturgical," forms of ministry for women today.

This is not a simple exercise in pedantry. The question of the ordination of women is only one of many issues confronting the theology of ministry and orders today. The classical theology of orders with which most theologians work was elaborated as a reflection on the church's practice. We are in the course today of major changes in that practice, and many of them do not seem to fit within the classical theory. Without an ordination, no one in the early church, man or woman, would have been entrusted with the tasks that many laymen and laywomen exercise in the church today. Women today are engaged in many more ministries than even women-deacons would have exercised in the ancient church. Where the "unordained" regularly do what once only the "ordained" could regularly do, what is the point of ordination? In the Roman Catholic Church today, women share in pastoral authority, teach, preach, baptize, distribute Communion. A good number of people in the Roman Catholic—and Anglican and Orthodox—Church would be quite content to "ordain" women to such ministries. As I understand it, the movement for the ordination of women is a movement towards the exercise of the chief sacramental ministry of the Church, the celebration of the Eucharist. If that is so, then it is no service to the movement to link it with efforts to "de-sacramentalize" the ministry—a "de-sacramentalized" ministry is precisely what many think women should be content to exercise.

3. The New Testament and the Subordination of Women

In their third paragraph, the bishops discuss the NT texts that require "women [to] hold to a subordinate position in the Church, keep silence in the Church, keep their heads covered, tend the home and family, etc." Their discussion of these texts, however, is astonishingly brisk. They remark, first, that "these texts are of Pauline authority alone," an observation they do not clarify. Further, they maintain that recent developments in the Church's teaching on woman and the admission of women to the role of lector and commentator "demonstrate that these Pauline texts should not be cited as arguing against the ordination of women."

From a methodological standpoint, both remarks are extraordinary. What does it mean that these texts are of "Pauline authority alone?"—that they may be disregarded? that they are of no theological or practical import? that they are not binding on the Church? That the latter is intended seems to be implied in the reference to the teaching and practice of the recent Church which directly contradicts the Pauline injunctions. If this is the case, a good number of our ecumenical partners-in-dialogue would have some questions to ask, and there will be some interest in the Church, no doubt, in exploring what other "merely Pauline" teachings or practices might not be questioned and jettisoned.

I do not raise this question because I think the Pauline description of woman's role should be resurrected, but to draw your—and even the bishops'—attention to the paradox that what Paul directly counselled or forbade is contravened by the Church today, while what he did not directly address—the ordination of women—is held to be sacred.

For the bishops' dismissal of these texts, in the light of the history of the question—is astoundingly casual: "these Pauline texts should not be cited as arguing against the ordination of women." In fact, throughout the tradition, they were constantly cited; and one may question whether theologians and canonists would have considered the exclusion of women from orders to be *de iure divino* without them. Moreover, they continue to be cited. In 1970, Pope Paul VI quoted 1 Cor 14:34—"Women should keep silence in the church"—as meaning "that woman is not meant to have hierarchical functions of teaching and ministering in the Church."[6] Finally, the literature on the question is filled with attempts to explain the Trinitarian, Christological, ecclesiological, or other theological bases for what many people do not believe can simply be reduced to socially or culturally conditioned injunctions.

My problem is not with the bishops' conclusion: I do not believe these arguments should be cited against the ordination of women. But the point is that this is a *conclusion*, and it is extremely important for the discussion to know how it was arrived at, on what assumptions, on what principles of NT interpretation, by what argument. I think a theologically respectable case can be made for the recent Church's abandonment of the Pauline instructions, but I wonder whether it would leave any NT basis for continuing the ban on women's ordination.

4. *The "Order of Creation"*

That is the question addressed directly in the bishops' fourth consideration, where they take up "the New Testament [though it too is of "Pauline authority alone"] doctrine on 'headship' as reflected in the order of creation." The texts cited here are 1 Cor 11:3-12 and 1 Tim 2:8-15 (on what principle 1 Cor 14:34-5 and Eph 5:21-33 are omitted is not at all clear). The same reasoning which grounds the NT "leadership of men and the subordination of women in the Church," the bishops note, "is advanced to explain the ordination to the priesthood of men but not of women." The bishops in fact are singling out one of the many attempts to provide a theological basis for the traditional discipline.

The argument proceeds more or less as follows: According to Paul, it was part of the divine order of creation that woman be subordinate to man. In 1 Cor 14:3-12, the ground is the fact that "man was not made from woman, but woman from man. Neither was man created for woman, but woman for man." This founds in nature the order of mediation and subordination: "The head of every man is Christ, the head of a woman is her husband, and the head of Christ is God." A man, then, is "the image and glory of God, but woman is the glory of man."

Now it seems to me that the relevance of this text for our question is considerably weakened when one notes that this whole argument serves the single purpose of explaining why woman may not pray or prophesy with her head unveiled. It does not prohibit her from public prayer and prophecy, but proscribes only a practice which few people today would describe as either very important or very evil. The problem is, of course, that this text has in the tradition been linked with 1 Cor 14:34-36, where women are forbidden to speak in the church, and that today an easy passage is made from 1 Cor 11 to Eph 5 and 1 Tim 2 and out of the three an argument against the ordination of women is constructed.

Neither step seems justified. One might argue that Paul's teaching about headship and subordination underlies 1 Cor 14, if this latter text did not in fact contradict what Paul himself says in 1 Cor 11. A consensus is growing that 1 Cor 14:34-5 should be regarded as a later interpolation into Paul's letter. If this is so, then in 1 Cor Paul did not draw any consequences from the order of creation against public worship-roles for women. And one may ask the point of retaining the argument when the practical point it was designed to press—the veiling of women—has been discarded.

This leaves the texts in 1 Tim 2 and Eph 5. The first of these begins with an injunction that "the men" (*andres*) of the congregation should pray peacefully and that "women should adorn themselves modestly and sensibly in seemly apparel, not with braided hair or gold or pearls or costly attire, but by good deeds, as befits women who profess religion." And then the author goes on:

> Let a woman learn in silence with all submissiveness. I permit no woman to teach or to have authority over men; she is to keep silent. For Adam was formed first, then Eve; and Adam was not deceived, but the woman was deceived and became a transgressor. Yet woman will be saved through bearing children, if she continues in faith and love and holiness, with modesty (1 Tim 2:8-15).

This is the strongest NT text that is brought against the ordination of women. It builds first upon the priority of man in creation: what was created first is considered to have been created superior. But another point is also introduced, that it was the woman who was first deceived and not the man, with perhaps the implication that the man would not have fallen if she had not been seduced and then seduced him. The logic behind the first argument is not entirely clear, and it is doubtful whether anyone would wish to employ it today. Besides taking the account of the Fall rather more literally than most would today, the second assigns to Eve the role which Rom 5 reserves for Adam and also suggests a greater susceptibility to sin on woman's part, which cannot be seriously defended either.

We are left, then, with the practical injunctions. We should note, first of all, that there are several of them: only the men are to pray in the assembly, women keeping silent; women are not to wear the hairstyles or jewelry of the fashionable; women are not to teach or to have authority over men. Of this mixed bag, the first is regularly disregarded in our liturgical assemblies, which would be considerably quieter if only men could pray aloud. Church-leaders are not regularly required to pass judgment on hair-styles and jewelry. Women regularly teach both in church and in society; and in society—and even in the church—women have had authority over men. The church, then, has felt able to exercise considerable freedom in interpreting these practical injunctions. One is left wondering how this text can continue to be cited, when the practical injunctions have been put aside and the arguments by which they were urged have been called into question also.

There remains Eph 5. but, since this text is usually brought forward in the same fashion as the bishops' fifth argument, I would prefer to discuss it under that heading.

5. *The Priest as Representative of Christ*

The fifth consideration is the "divine plan" that "the Word of God took on flesh and was made man—as a male." From this it is argued by some "that this divine plan is expressed in the priesthood, because the ordained priest must act officially in the person of Christ (cf. *Decree on the Ministry and Life of Priests*, #2). It is argued that a male priest is required to act in the person of the male Christ."

This argument from the representational character of the priestly ministry takes many forms. A first begins with the representative role of Christ himself. As the incarnation of God's redemptive word and grace, Christ is the representation of God. Now the Scriptures chiefly portray God as Father, the term which Jesus himself used in his most intimate prayer to him and which he taught his disciples to pray. The Fatherhood of God, it is argued, could not have been represented by a woman. That the Incarnation took place in a male, then, is not simply a concession to the male-dominated society into which Jesus was born, but reflects itself the initiating and generative mercy for which the Scriptures commonly use male images. Christ's maleness was intrinsic to his redemptive role; a woman could not have said, "He who sees me, sees the Father."

Further, in the ministry and especially in the Eucharistic ministry, the priest is the representative of Christ. He stands over-and-against the community, speaking Christ's word and sacramentally mediating his grace. As the Second Vatican Council puts it, the priest acts *in persona Christi*;[7] he is in his ministry a "personation," a body-ing-forth, of Christ. As a woman, so the argument goes, could not have represented the Father's love, so a woman cannot represent the redemptive role of the male Christ.

In a second form, this argument builds upon the doctrine of Ephesians that Christ stands to the Church as a husband to his wife. The order of creation—discussed in the previous section—supplies the created symbol of the authority and the life-giving Headship of Christ over his Church. Conversely, in this mystery is revealed the genuine meaning of both man and woman, whose relationship is not simply a matter of sexual differentiation for the sake of procreation, but is an "ontological" difference-in-unity whose final theological purpose is to mirror forth the relationship between Christ and the Church.

Now the priest represents this spousal relationship of Christ to the Church. In certain traditions, the priesthood is even considered to be the sacrament through which Christ continues to be present to his Church as Head to Body, as Husband to Wife. This sacramental presence of Christ to the church it is impossible for a woman to embody.

What may we make of these arguments? First, I think they should be taken seriously, for a few reasons. For one thing, they are regarded as the theological heart of the matter by many of the opponents of women's ordination. For another, they argue from symbols that are central to our whole religious tradition and which speak to and from deep personal and interpersonal human experiences. C.S. Lewis is correct, I think, in warning against treating fundamental religious and personal symbols lightly.[8] If the ordination of women were to prevent us from addressing God as Father or from conceiving of Christ as Bridegroom of the Church, we would be in danger of cutting ourselves off from our biblical and traditional roots. The question, of course, is whether ordaining women should be considered to have such implications.

As for the first argument, it may be noted that the NT does not seem to have any theological interest whatever in the maleness of Christ. I have found only three texts in which the word *aner* is used of Christ (Lk 24:19; Jn 1:30; Acts 2:22), and none of them exploits Christ's "maleness." It is interesting that in Rom 5, where Christ is presented as the "one man" through whose obedience the disobedience of the "one man," Adam, was undone, the word for both figures is *anthropos*, not *aner* The point, obviously, is not to question

Christ's maleness nor to suggest that one's relationship to him is not affected by it, but simply to show that theological emphasis on the maleness of Christ's humanity is foreign to the NT. Preliminary inquiries suggest that the same thing is true of the Fathers.

Secondly, while it is true that the great majority of Scriptural symbols and images of God are male, there is no lack of female imagery as well. If the Lord is the Father of his people, his tenderness is that of a mother for her child (Is 49:14-16). And if the Lord's cries as he goes out to redeem his people are like those of a "man of war," they are also like those of "a woman in labor," gasping and panting (Is 42:19). We may note with what ease the Scriptures can move from one fierce or gentle image to the other, without embarrassment and without fear of betraying the religious relationship.

If, then, the masculine images of God are to be pressed, this must not be done in such fashion as to violate the laws of analogical predication of God or to prevent our using the full range of biblical images. It is precisely because God infinitely transcends our images and ideas that the great number of symbols is needed. For the symbols are concrete and anyone of them, if it is not to be distorted in its interpretation, needs the others. At one moment in our religious experience it is important to know that God is our rock and our stronghold, at another that he is the spring of living water. If sometimes we need to know that he is our light and our salvation, at others it is good to be able to take refuge in the shadow of his wings. Similarly, if we must approach him as Father or as Bridegroom, we also know moments when we may be with God "like a weaned child on its mother's lap" (Ps 131:2), "not like an infant crying loudly for his mother's breast, but like a weaned child that quietly rests by his mother's side, happy in being with her."[9]

Moreover, Christ did not hesitate to use feminine and maternal images to describe his work. The love he shows in eating and drinking with sinners is that of the male shepherd foolishly off in search of the one lost sheep; it is that of the father indecorously running down the road to welcome his penitent son; but it is also that of the woman who turns the house upside-down in search of an insignificant coin (Lk 15). Christ has come to gather Jerusalem's children to himself as a mother-bird's wings surround, protect and warm her brood (Mt 23:37). And his death and resurrection are the birth-pangs of the Messiah (Jn 16:21; see Rev 12; Mk 13:8).

Finally, the feminine images are continued in the description of

Christian ministers. Paul called himself a father, but he also did not hesitate to call himself a "nurse taking care of her children" (1 Thess 2:7) or to compare himself to a woman suffering birth-pangs until Christ be formed in his people (Gal 4:19).[10]

Now the point of these references is not to pretend that male images do not predominate, but to suggest that there are dimensions of God's love for man, of Christ's redemptive role, and of official Christian ministry which only feminine images can communicate. Christ represented these to the world, although he was a male; Paul represented them to the church, although he was a male. If a male could represent such feminine dimensions of the divine love, it is difficult to see why a woman cannot, in turn, represent to the Church dimensions of God's love in Christ for which masculine images are used. Reasonably intelligent people understand how all these symbols function and do not press them beyond their intent. The argument against a woman's representing Christ often works with rather rigid norms of symbolization which do not always escape the "prose-fallacy."

It is the assumptions of this argument that most need clarification. Is it assumed that, while a man can represent both the masculine and the feminine, a woman can represent only the feminine? Are God's initiative and free grace more masculine than feminine? Is a wife's subordination to her husband the only reason why Christ may be considered the Church's Bridegroom? What assumptions and predispositions—theological, cultural, psychological, and otherwise—lie behind the description of certain attitudes and ministries as "masculine" and others as "feminine"?[11] May women have a say in the matter, or is this already a violation of "the eternal feminine"?

A last comment: it seems to me that the Christian tradition might be explored for help on these ideas of sexual symbolism for God and for the ministry. Margaret Farley has outlined some interesting thoughts on the feminine within the Trinity.[12] Eleanor McLaughlin has uncovered three considerations from the Middle Ages, including Juliana of Norwich's well-known habit of addressing Christ as "Mother."[13] Aelred Squire has noted how abbots were frequently called "handmaids of the Lord" and said to exercise maternal roles,[14] and similar images were also used of bishops in medieval commentaries on the Song of Songs. Finally, there is a beautiful prayer of St. Anselm to St. Paul, which wholly turns on the maternal images the NT uses for Christ and the Apostle.

Paul, my mother, Christ bore you also;
so place your dead son at the feet of Christ, your mother,
    because he also is Christ's son.
Rather, throw him into the heart of Christ's goodness,
    for Christ is even more his mother.
Pray that he will give life to a dead son,
    who is not so much yours as his.
St Paul, pray for your son, because you are his mother,
    that the Lord, who is his mother too,
        may give life to his son.
Do, mother of my soul,
    what the mother of my flesh would do. . . .

    And you, my soul; dead in yourself,
run under the wings of Jesus your mother
and lament your griefs under his feathers. . . .

    Christ my mother,
you gather your chickens under your wings;
this dead chicken of yours puts himself under those wings.
For by your gentleness the badly frightened are comforted,
    by your sweet smell the despairing are revived,
    your warmth gives life to the dead,
    your touch justifies sinners.
Mother, know again your dead son,
both by the sign of your cross and the voice of his
    confession.
Warm your chicken, give life to your dead man,
    justify your sinner.[15]

If I do not expect that prayer to be introduced into our liturgies tomorrow, it surely may be taken as some evidence that "maleness" is not an exhaustive representation of the love of Christ for his Church or of a minister's relationship to his people.

6. *The Example of Christ and the Early Church*

The sixth consideration brought forward by the bishops is "the selectivity of Christ and the early Church." If Jesus, who did not hesitate to break with other social and religious customs, nevertheless did not call any women to be apostles (the bishops add, incorrectly, "disciples"!), and if the Apostles did not include women among the possible successors to Judas (although they too filled the requirements) or among the possible assistants chosen in Acts 6—then the limitation of ministry to men "goes beyond sociological conditions of that day and points to a divine choice."

This argument, too, is a serious one, if for no other reason than that it convinces so many people. Pope Paul VI made use of it recently in his famous dependent clause: "If women do not receive the same call to the apostolate that was given to the Twelve and thereby to ordained ministers. . . ."[16] And Professor John Meyendorff, from an Orthodox standpoint, recently argued that the decision not to include women belongs to those aspects of NT Christianity which are normative for all ages of the Church.[17]

We have here perhaps another one of the paradoxes that seem to surface in this discussion. For this argument seems to take its force from what some people like to call Jesus' "feminism." If, in fact, Jesus did break with social and religious restrictions about contact with women, then is there not some significance in his not choosing them as apostles? This is perhaps the place to remark, then, that one should be somewhat cautious about our ability to know Jesus' "feminism." Besides the anachronism of the term, we should keep in mind that in an age in which NT scholars have taught us to be rather cautious in our statements about the messianic consciousness of Jesus, we cannot expect to know much about Jesus' attitude towards women. The Gospels are first of all witnesses to the churches of their respective writers and not to the deeds much less the words of the "historical Jesus."[18]

To some degree this particular argument finds both sides assuring the other that they have the burden of proof. The opponents of women's ordination place that burden on those who would contradict the practice of Jesus and of the primitive church. The proponents, on the other hand, want the others to bear the burden of showing that there was something more than cultural or social accommodation at work here. One consideration at least to introduce here is the fact that the argument too easily passes from the word "apostle" to the word "priest," particularly when the content of this word especially concerns the Eucharist. The NT has no direct indications about who might preside over the Eucharist. Now, while one might reasonably presume that the Twelve and other "apostles" fulfilled this office, one cannot without begging the question assume that other ministries, including those which women are said to have performed, did not include a Eucharistic presidency. The NT data, in other words, do not require a restriction of presidency over the Eucharist to "apostleship," while, on the other hand, Paul (especially in Rom 16) did speak of women's ministries in terms similar to those used for his own and others' missionary and "apostolic" work. The diversity of ministries within the NT churches requires that the discussion be undertaken with considerably more nuance than is usual, and especially that statements and conclusions about what Jesus did or did nor order about the ministry reflect the caution which contemporary NT scholarship recommends.

7. *The Argument from Tradition*

The last objection the bishops propose is the one they take most seriously: that "the life and practice of the Spirit-guided Church," consistently excluding women from the priestly ministry, constitutes "a clear teaching of the Ordinary Magisterium of the Church. Though not formally defined, this is Catholic doctrine." Though they began their reflections with the statement that "there is no explicit authoritative teaching concerning the ordination of women that settles the issue," they conclude them with the comment that this last argument "indicates" a negative answer.

This argument, too, must be taken very seriously and for a number of reasons. For one thing, the Church is an historical community and for it to disregard its traditions is to flirt with amnesia. For another, the argument carries great weight with a good number of our fellow-Christians, both in and outside the Roman Catholic Church.

An approach to tradition must move between two extremes. The one is represented by passionate outbursts that the issue should not even be raised, that it represents "Western" deformations of the creed and ministry, that it is a *casus irrealis* simply because the tradition has not addressed it.[19] The other extreme is represented by Simone Weil's comment that "history . . . is nothing but a compilation of the depositions made by assassins with respect to their victims and themselves."[20] The middle ground is perhaps best expressed by a word of Cyprian: *Consuetudo sine veritate vetustas erroris est*—A custom without truth is simply the antiquity of error.[21] That dictum argues the need for the twofold hermeneutic which Paul Ricoeur has described: a "hermeneutic of restoration," which attempts to bring the power of ancient symbols to bear upon the present, and a "hermeneutic of suspicion," which brings a critical and emancipatory mind to the works of the past.[22]

Thomas Hopko, an Orthodox theologian, puts the issue well and applies it to our discussion:

> Is there some theological and spiritual reason why the Church has ordained only certain of her male members to the sacramental offices of bishop and presbyter? Or is this merely a fact without reason, or perhaps with many reasons that are not theologically and spiritually justified and are no longer socially and culturally acceptable.[23]

Methodologically and ecumenically, it is very important to find an Orthodox theologian admitting at least the possibility of the tradition's being "a fact without reason," for it requires the question to be addressed with Ricoeur's two-pronged interpretative intention. If there is a "theological and spiritual reason," the hermeneutics of restoration will discover it and mediate its transmission; if none can be found, then the hermeneutics of suspicion will uncover the *consuetudo sine veritate*.

In other words, the tradition is not simply "there"; it has to be understood, judged and evaluated. What were the conditions in which the question was raised in this century or in that? What were the concrete implications of the issue? Who was deciding it? On what assumptions and principles? By what logic? With what notion of scriptural interpretation? Under the influence of what explicit or implicit view of woman and of ministry and of priesthood?

When such questions are answered, there are questions for a critical evaluation: Do these conditions remain? Are those implications truly involved? What motives guided those who decided the issue? Are the assumptions, the principles, the logic, the hermeneutics defensible? Do we mean the same thing today when we ask about "ordaining" "women" to the "priestly" "ministry"?

Van der Meer has asked many of these questions, and he is of the view that none of the arguments brought forward in the tradition grounds a conclusive answer against ordaining women. If one accepts his conclusion, then one may say to the argument from tradition, that if the reasons advanced against ordaining women are not valid, what authority does the mere custom have? If the assumptions, logic and argument are seriously flawed, with what confidence can it be said that the conclusion against women priests was valid?

In this context, it is worth noting that many of the reasons brought against the ordination of women today are not to be found, at least not explicitly, in the tradition itself. This is true both of some of the sillier arguments and also of such serious speculations as those in Thomas Hopko's recent essay on the Trinity. The Fathers and medieval theologians and canonists simply referred to the OT example, to the example of Jesus, to the words of St. Paul, to settle the issue. Those who attempt the new justifications do so out of a sense that the tradition has an "instinct" for the truth even independent of the reasons any one generation might be able to articulate. One can respect that view while insisting that the new arguments are not themselves the tradition and must also be brought under critical examination to determine their "theological and spiritual" value.

The defenders of the tradition, in other words, must *defend* it; it is not enough to repeat it, nor is it reasonable to require an unthinking deference to it. In a day when many other practices of the Church have been examined and evaluated, and long-standing traditions and customs reversed or permitted to disappear, it is difficult to see on what grounds this tradition must be considered more "sacred" than others. It is our conviction that tradition can be a great bearer of the truth that makes us something more than mere "traditionalists." If truth is not what is borne to us and tradition is promoted for its own sake, then the existential history of the Church risks being merely the "dead hand of the past."

Conclusion

In these pages I have tried to present a serious and respectful evaluation of the more frequent and more important arguments brought against the ordination of women to the priesthood. I do not myself find any one of them—nor all of them together—a convincing defense of the traditional discipline. I would be happy if my remarks have enabled you to focus on the basic and central issues and contributed at least modestly to their clarification and evaluation.

Notes

1. *Theological Reflections on the Ordination of Women* (Washington: United States Catholic Conference, [1973]); the text is also reproduced in the *Journal of Ecumenical Studies*, 10 (1973), 695-99.

2. See Bernard Verkamp, "Cultic Purity and the Law of Celibacy," *Review for Religious*, 30 (1971), 199-217.

3. Haye van der Meer, *Women Priests in the Catholic Church? A Theological-Historical Investigation*, trans. Arlene and Leonard Swidler (Philadelphia: Temple University Press, 1973), p. 128.

4. R. Gryson, *Le ministère des femmes dans l'Église ancienne* (Duculot: Gembloux, 1972); Yves Congar, "Regarding the Diaconate of Women," an unpublished paper made available to me in English translation; see also Peter Hünermann, "Conclusions regarding the Female Diaconate," *Theological Studies*, 36 (1975), 325-33.

5. Hünermann, p. 332.

6. *The Pope Speaks*, 15 (1970), 221, in a talk reflecting on his naming St. Teresa of Avila a "Doctor of the Church."

7. Vatican II, *Presbyterorum Ordinis*, 2. The interpretation of this phrase is still a matter of discussion among theologians; for a brief review of its history, see B.-D. Marliangeas, " 'In persona Christi', 'In persona Ecclesiae'. Note sur les origines et le développement de l'usage de ces expressions dans la théologie latine," in J.-P. Jossua and Y. Congar (eds.) *La liturgie après Vatican II: Bilans, Études, Prospective* (Unam Sanctam, 66; Paris: du Cerf, 1967), pp. 283-88. According to H.-M. Legrand, it has nothing to do with the "being" and "person" of the priest himself; see "Bulletin d'Ecclésiologie: Recherches sur le presbytérat et l'épiscopat," *Revue de Sciences Philosophiques et Théologiques*, 59 (1975), 687, 689, 695.

8. See his remarks as quoted in E.L. Mascall, *Women Priests?* (Westminster: Church Literature Association, 1972), pp. 14-17.

9. Artur Weiser, *The Psalms: A Commentary*, trans. Herbert Hartwell (London: SCM Press, 1962), p. 777. Weiser restricts the force of the image by continuing: "Here his heart has found rest; he knows himself to be safe with God and to be sheltered in the love of his heavenly *Father*" (my emphasis).

10. The easy transition from masculine to feminine images both of God and of a minister is illustrated at Qumran in 1 QH VII, 19-22 and IX, 35-36; see Michel Saillard, "C'est moi qui, par l'Évangile, vous ai enfantés dans le Christ Jésus (1 Co 4, 15)," *Recherches de Science Religieuse*, 56 (1968), 5-40, at p. 14-15. A parallel study of Gal 4:19 might have something to contribute to the discussion of women-ministers.

11. The most outrageous example of this line of argument is the view reported by Leonard Swidler, *Journal of Ecumenical Studies*, 10 (1973), 771-73, namely, that to celebrate the Eucharist is a "phallic act." The nearest thing in the tradition to this curiosity is an objection against a woman's baptizing that St. Thomas considered: that the waters of baptism represent a mother's womb, so that the minister must be male in order to represent a father's role. St. Thomas refutes the objection on the ground that it is Christ who baptizes and that, therefore, the sex of the minister is irrelevant (*Summa theologica*, III, q. 67, a. 3, ad 3m).

12. Margaret A. Farley, "New Patterns of Relationship: Beginnings of a Moral Revolution," *Theological Studies*, 36 (1975), 627-46, esp. p. 640-43.

13. Eleanor L. McLaughlin, "The Christian Past: Does it Hold a Future for Women?" *Anglican Theological Review*, 57 (1975), 36-56.

14. Aelred Squire, *Aelred of Rievaulx: A Study* (London: S.P.C.K., 1973), p. 129-30, 150-51.

15. *The Prayers and Meditations of St Anselm*, trans. and introd. Sister Benedicta Ward (Harmondsworth: Penguin Books, 1973), p. 155-56.

16. *The Pope Speaks*, 20 (1975), 39; the sentence concludes, "they are nonetheless invited to follow Christ as disciples and co-workers." The following paragraph hints at the pope's conclusion from this fact: "We cannot change either our Lord's actions or his call to women. Our duty is rather to acknowledge and help develop the role of women in the mission of evangelization and in the life of the Christian community. To do so will not be to introduce novelty into the Church, for we find traces of such participation, in various forms, even in the original communities and, later on, in many a page of Christian history."

17. John Meyendorff, "The Orthodox Churches," in *The Ordination of Women: Pro and Con*, ed. Michael P. Hamilton and Nancy S. Montgomery (New York: Morehouse-Barlow, [1975]), pp. 129-30.

18. This is the merit of Raymond Brown's study, "The Meaning of Modern New Testament Studies for the Possibility of Ordaining Women to the Priesthood," in *Biblical Reflections on Crises Facing the Church* (New York: Paulist Press, 1975), pp. 45-62.

19. For an example, see Alexander Schmemann, "Concerning Women's Ordination: Letter to an Episcopalian Friend," in *Sexuality—Theology—Priesthood: Reflections on the Ordination of Women to the Priesthood*, comp. and ed. H. Karl Lutge (San Gabriel, Calif.: Concerned Fellow Episcopalians, n.d.), pp. 11-15.

20. Simone Weil, *The Need for Roots* (New York, 1971), p. 225, as quoted by Elisabeth Schüssler Fiorenza, "Feminist Theology as a Critical Theology of Liberation," *Theological Studies*, 36 (1975), 611.

21. Cyprian, *Epist.* 74:9. The African church also bequeathed to later generations of reformers the other pithy saying, "The Lord said in the Gospel, 'I am the truth;' he did not say, 'I am custom;' " see Gerhart B. Ladner, *The Idea of Reform: Its Impact on Christian Thought and Action in the Age of the Fathers* (New York: Harper Torchbooks, 1967), pp. 136-39; and, for the use of the axiom during the Gregorian Reform, Glenn Olsen, "The Idea of the *Ecclesia Primitiva* in the Writings of the Twelfth-century Canonists," *Traditio*, 25 (1969), 61-86, esp. p. 61-65.

22. See Paul Ricoeur, *Freud and Philosophy: An Essay on Interpretation* (New Haven: Yale University Press, 1970), pp. 20-36.

23. Thomas Hopko, "On the Male Character of Christian Priesthood," *St. Vladimir's Theological Quarterly*, 19 (1975), 147.

274